THIRD EDITION

CAMELOT

A Role Playing Simulation for Political Decision Making

JAMES R. WOODWORTH

Miami University

W. ROBERT GUMP

Miami University

Wadsworth Publishing Company
Belmont, California
A Division of Wadsworth, Inc.

To those who brought Camelot to our lives
as we sought to create Camelot for others:
Marilyn, Deborah, and Victoria
Patricia, David, Laurie, and Timothy

And to the memory of Virginia Roper Woodworth

Political Science Editor: Brian Gore
Editorial Assistant: Jennifer Dunning
Production Services Coordinator: Debby Kramer
Production: Scratchgravel Publishing Services
Print Buyer: Karen Hunt
Permissions Editor: Jeanne Bosschart
Copy Editor: Chris Bernard
Cover: Christy Butterfield
Interior Illustrations: Greg Draus, Scratchgravel Publishing Services
Compositor: Scratchgravel Publishing Services
Printer: Malloy Lithographing, Inc.

This book is printed on
acid-free recycled paper.

International Thomson Publishing
The trademark ITP is used under license.

Printed in the United States of America

2 3 4 5 6 7 8 9 10—98 97 96 95 94

Library of Congress Cataloging-in-Publication Data
Woodworth, James R.
    Camelot, a role playing simulation for political decision making /
James R. Woodworth, W. Robert Gump. — 3rd ed.
        p.   cm.
    Includes bibliographical references and index.
    ISBN 0-534-23040-7
    1. Municipal government—United States—Decision making-
-Simulation methods.   2. Political science—Decision making-
-Simulation methods.   I. Gump, W. Robert.   II. Title.
JS335.W76   1993
352'.0004725'0973—dc20   93-23463

Preface

Camelot was created as a response to student concerns that our urban politics course readings provided theory and background understanding but gave the students little feel for how politics really work. In natural science courses, students use laboratories to test theory. Simulations provide the laboratories for political science. *Camelot* is a *role playing* simulation of political decision making in a medium-sized city that uses the council-manager form of government. As one reviewer commented recently, *Camelot* is unique; there is nothing else like it on the market today.

CAMELOT'S OBJECTIVES

Students too often look upon the outcomes of political decision making as predictable or predetermined, perhaps even rigged in some cases. *Camelot* introduces them to a world of contending and sometimes contentious groups and people, whose values and goals range from extreme liberal to extreme conservative. That world includes a rich diversity of viewpoints—on feminism, right to life, social moralism, affirmative action, defense of freedom of expression, defense of property rights, gay rights, and more. Students learn quickly that it is this competition among interests, with their varying degrees of organization and cohesiveness, which makes political decision making so complex and time consuming.

A second assumption widely held (at least implicitly) among students is that most urban problems could be solved easily if only they were in charge or if someone in charge would listen to them. That is where a simulation is most instructive, for it is a controlled reality that creates situations like those encountered in the real world. Students discover that their viewpoints and their solutions may not be widely shared, that other citizen-students (playing their roles) may disagree vigorously with them. In order to make any decision, some degree of agreement must be obtained, and in order to gain agreement broad enough to include a majority, some compromise usually is necessary. Yet if decision makers compromise their principles in order to gain majority support, some of the citizens who elected them may feel betrayed and angry. Because *Camelot* includes an election, lessons learned often involve the pain of defeat.

For both the students and the instructor, a simulation provides a change of pace. From its inception some 20 years ago *Camelot* has been a popular experience for students. Again and again, student evaluations have praised it as a great learning experience. It is *not* just a game. Because it is a role playing simulation, with 17 different issues from which the instructor can choose those that will reinforce the objectives of the course, students can become totally involved. Though it may seem hyperbole to someone reading this preface, in years of experience we have found that, *if students play their roles,* then Camelot becomes a real city to them. The debriefing and critique session (discussed in detail below), which is scheduled at the end of the simulation, gives the instructor an opportunity to make sure that the lessons of the simulation are brought home to the students.

CAMELOT'S FEATURES

The Roles

While *Camelot* can be, and has been, run with as few as 15 students, a total of 73 roles are provided. The students are expected to play particular roles as realistically as possible. Each key role is provided with a rather detailed description of who the individual is and what his or her values are. The following is only a *sampling* of the roles:

The Decision Makers
City Council, including a Mayor chosen by Council from among its
    members
Planning Commission
City Manager

The Organized Interests

Developers

Entrepreneurs (for example, a massage parlor operator, a beauty salon owner, and owners of small and large businesses)

Media (a reporter and the editor of *The Camelot Daily News,* a newscaster)

Religious groups (for example, representatives of main-line and minority churches and fundamentalism)

Moral conservatives (proponents of right to life, antiobscenity, and so on)

Moral liberals (for example, proponents of freedom of choice and freedom of expression)

Institutional groups (for example, police and public health officials)

Others

Clerk of Council

Attorneys (three)

ACLU representative

NAACP, head of local chapter

Retired professional football player

High school teacher

President, League of Women Voters

Student Body Vice President, Camelot State University

(These are just some of the roles.)

The Issues

The instructor may choose from 17 different issues in *Camelot* that involve budgets, revenues (including possible tax increases), moral questions, zoning, affirmative action, and more. Following are some examples:

Budget

Resources are always scarce. Students must choose whether to provide funds for the police (SWAT Team, drug enforcement), health protection programs (gynecologic programs, Planned Parenthood), and revitalization of decaying areas in order to provide jobs and increased revenues. In order to pay for any or all of these, taxes must be increased, which in turn may incur citizen anger and cause defeat at the next election.

Moral Issues

Shall Council continue to fund a publicly supported art museum that displays photographs viewed by some critics as obscene?

Shall there be a ban of upper-body nudity in public places, specifically, a topless bar?

Shall zoning laws be revised to prevent the establishment of additional abortion clinics?

Regulatory Issues

What decibel levels should be permitted for automobile stereos, or for noise from residential properties? How should the restraints be enforced, and what should the penalties be?

What growth rate should the City of Camelot aim for?

What controls, if any, should be placed on handguns?

Zoning Issues

Should the maximum height section of the zoning laws be changed to permit the construction of a downtown hotel? The hotel and its plaza would revitalize one square block of a decaying downtown, would cost the city nothing, would provide jobs and increased revenues. It would also require that a historic church and cemetery be moved and the sacrifice of one-third of the only park in downtown Camelot.

Should an exception be made to permit a beauty salon to operate in a residential area?

Should developers be permitted to build a strip mall in an area of single-family dwellings on land zoned for senior citizen housing?

(This is only a sample of the issues.)

The Election

Camelot provides all the information that students need to carry out the election. A nomination petition is included in the book, as is a sample ballot. All the instructor should have to do is remind the Clerk of Council to prepare the ballot(s) in advance of election day.

CAMELOT'S ORGANIZATION

Part One

Part One provides students with the necessary background information for them to participate in the simulation. Because some instructors have adopted *Camelot* for the local government portion of the American National Government survey course, we have expanded almost every chapter in this edition.

Chapter 1 explores the several meanings of the word *community,* focusing particularly on the separation of community from what we call "government."

Chapter 2 emphasizes the relationship between political resources and political influence. It also calls attention to the writings of Paul Peterson and Clarence Stone who, despite significant areas of disagreement, emphasize the convergence of interests of entrepreneurs with those of elected officials, the former for profits, the latter for tax revenues to pay for citizen demands for city services.

Chapters 3 and 4 deal, respectively, with the legal authority of cities in policy-making endeavors and with constraints imposed by the types and amounts of revenue available to local government. In this third edition, Chapter 3 has added some discussion of more recent uses of eminent domain. On the topic of revenues, Chapter 4 calls attention to some newer revenue sources for cities, especially riverboat gambling.

Chapters 5, 6, 7, and 8 focus on organizing and operating local government decision making, including such topics as the involvement of organized interests (Chapter 5), how policy and recruitment choices are made (Chapter 6), local governmental and electoral forms and procedures (Chapter 7), and land-use planning (Chapter 8).

Part Two: The Simulation

Chapter 9 is an introduction to simulation for the student. It reviews the purpose of a simulation and instructs students on what to look for during the simulation.

Chapter 10 explains how to start the simulation and how to use the materials. A sample role request form is provided. So that everyone knows what has happened recently, students can (and should) read "Yesterday's Edition" of *The Camelot Daily News.*

Other helpful materials included in Chapter 9 are:

- Council proceedings: a sample meeting
- Rank order of commonly used motions (a parliamentary procedure guide)
- Agendas for the first two council sessions
- Agendas for the first two planning commission meetings

Chapter 11 provides descriptions of the 17 issues. Each of these issues has been classroom tested many times, and additional supporting information has been provided in the third edition for some issues. Three of the issues are new for this edition: the Strip Mall Issue, the Affirmative Action Issue, and the "Obscene Photographs" Issue. Many of the other issues have been revised to bring them up to date.

Chapter 12 includes a collection of helpful (and in a few cases, essential) reference materials:

- A very brief description of the City of Camelot.
- A description of each of the neighborhoods of Camelot.
- The Charter of the City of Camelot. This is based on a real charter, modified slightly to fit the needs of the simulation. Although many of the students will not read most of the charter, it can be a very useful tool for the more alert and energetic students who choose to explore its provisions. Two of its features can be important: those relating to restrictions on the behavior of members of council (for example, attendance) and those that explain the procedure for initiative, referendum, and recall.
- Zoning Regulations. Students often discover that it is necessary for them to refer to these regulations. They are based on an actual zoning code but are presented in a compact outline form.
- A description of the "sunshine law." This includes the standard wording that requires all meetings of public bodies to be open to the public (with exceptions listed). More often than not, this law comes as a surprise to students.

Chapter 13 takes students and the instructor through an election. The election is one of the highlights of the simulation and becomes a rich source for discussion during the debriefing and critique session. (See the discussion below on the debriefing and critique session.)

Chapter 14 provides descriptions of the roles. How detailed the description of the person is correlates directly to the importance of the role within the simulation. The more crucial roles are more fully described. Instructors will see that the importance of a role in real life is not always reflected in the simulation. For example, the university president has, at most, only modest involvement in a few issues, but a beautician has a central role in a zoning issue.

Inside the front and back covers of *Camelot* is a map of the city of Camelot. It shows the locations of the various neighborhoods and the zoning of each one.

SUPPLEMENTARY MATERIALS:
THE INSTRUCTOR'S MANUAL

Note: *If you are interested in adopting Camelot for your course, the publisher will be pleased to provide a copy of the Instructor's Manual. We consider the manual an indispensable tool.*

The Instructor's Manual has been designed to take the instructor step by step through the entire simulation, one day at a time, including preparation and debriefing discussions. The authors know from personal experience how useful it is to keep the manual handy as a reminder of details that are easy to forget. Following is a list of features of the Instructor's Manual:

Chapter 1 offers a brief introduction to simulation, its goal and objectives.

Chapter 2 prepares the instructor for the simulation. It explains:

- Things to keep in mind when making role assignments
- What roles to be sure to include for different sizes of classes, from fewer than 15 students to the maximum size of 73 or more students
- How to inform students of the value, indeed the necessity, of working with other students and learning to form coalitions and alliances

Chapter 3 walks the instructor through each of the sessions, offering guidance in:

- What to do before the simulation begins
- What to bring to class
- What is possible and what is probable during each class
- What to watch for

Chapter 4 covers all the issues from the instructor's viewpoint. Various alerts and cautions are offered, as well as suggested topics for discussion of each issue.

Chapter 5, The Debriefing and Critique, may well be the most important part of the simulation. Typically, it is the high point of the simulation for the students in terms of its popularity. From a pedagogical point of view, it serves well the purpose of helping the students understand what they have learned. To assist the instructor, three pages of suggested questions and topics for class discussion are presented.

Chapter 6 presents two flowcharts of issues for the simulation—one for six sessions of more than 60 minutes each, and one for eight session of less than 60 minutes each.

A FINAL NOTE

There is a student evaluation sheet at the end of *Camelot*, located just before the Topical Bibliographies. We ask students to fill in this sheet each time *Camelot* is used. We urge you to do the same. Not only has it been gratifying to read how most students enjoyed the experience, but it is equally reassuring to discover what they believe they learned.

We would like to extend our appreciation to the manuscript reviewers: Dr. Michael Carey, Seton Hill College; Dr. Nancy S. Lind, Illinois State University; and Dr. John Whitney, Lincoln Land Community College.

We are especially appreciative of the assistance provided by several of our colleagues at Miami University and by interested friends outside the university. Professor Clyde Brown, Political Science, provided an updating of the chapter on organized interests; Sherin Shumavon, consultant to mental health groups, and Professor Douglas Shumavon, Political Science, were especially helpful in ensuring accuracy in "The Home for the Mentally Ill Issue"; and Professors Susan Kay, Political Science, and Marilyn Throne, English, offered thoughtful suggestions on the manuscript in general and on the role descriptions in particular.

Contents

List of Figures

PART ONE

Understanding Political Decision Making

INTRODUCTION

Camelot was created with a reasonably uncomplicated objective in mind: to simulate for students what they might expect to experience as a member of a city council or planning commission, or as a citizen dealing with those bodies. It was believed that you, the student, would find these simulated council and planning commission sessions both enlightening and just plain fun. Twenty years of "living" in and with our imaginary city has justified these hopes. Yet somewhere along the way, *Camelot* changed—not so much in what it did or what its player-citizens did, but rather in what it conveyed to students, what they learned. *Camelot,* it seems, is more than it appears to be.

What *Camelot* does, without ever emphasizing the point, is to introduce you to decision making, and by extension, to the policy process. To reword that sentence in nonjargon terms, the simulation reveals that the adoption of a city ordinance (whether it be a budget, a zoning land-use issue, or a value-laden issue such as gay rights) is not a simple matter. You will discover that other people may or may not agree with you on many of the issues encountered by planning commissions and city councils—that there is such a thing as conflict over values. As with many truisms, these are truths which everyone accepts in the abstract and as not worth discussion. Yet simple abstract truths frequently are discovered to yield painful experiences when one has to deal with them.

What is more, you will come to realize that there are many stages to decision making: from the earliest beginnings of an idea or proposal, to its inclusion on some public body's agenda, to its adoption, and finally, to its implementation. This is what is meant by the term *the policy process.*

As soon as one views *Camelot* as an example of the complexities of decision making in the policy process, it then becomes apparent that some interesting parallels exist. Urban politics, at least when decision making is involved, is in some ways not unlike national politics. Our attention all too frequently focuses on the uniqueness of each of the levels of politics, and we fail to see the similarities because the names and titles of the actors are different and the scale of the activity is different.

Invariably, the process involves a struggle among conflicting values and groups; inevitably, the conflict widens as coalitions form; frequently, the values are so deeply felt that resolution is impossible and deadlock occurs; yet, fortunately, on most issues, the hard bargaining leads to compromise and resolution. You will find, perhaps to your surprise, that the underlying lessons of *Camelot* are applicable to all levels of the policy process.

Although the primary objective of *Camelot* is to give you a "hands on" experience in the form of a simulation, it is equally important that the simulation experience be viewed within a social science context, specifically to introduce you to problems of human choice and interaction.

The stark facts of historical change are clear. For hundreds of thousands of years, our remote ancestors lived as hunters and gatherers of food, a way of life that under most circumstances restricted the size of a group to perhaps 15 to 20 or so persons. Today over half of all Americans live in metropolitan areas having more than a million residents! Extraordinary changes have occurred in the pattern of human existence over the past ten to twenty thousand years—at first exclusively hunters and gatherers, humans later became principally farmers and herdsmen; then, the past two centuries alone have seen the emergence of factory workers, railroaders, truck drivers, auto mechanics and television technicians. Most recently, we have witnessed the rapid development of the service sector of our economy, driven especially by the many companies that help furnish communication services and information processing to this nation and others. We remind ourselves that 95% of this nation's labor force was engaged in tilling the soil and raising livestock when the U.S. Constitution was adopted, and the major cities of the land—New York, Philadelphia, and Boston—had populations hardly sufficient to constitute a medium-size suburb today.

Perhaps we can recognize in our prehistoric ancestors clustered in small groups the rudimentary form of what today we call a *community*. Later, over time, the smaller groups (troops, tribes, clans, and so on) grew to ever larger groupings, each of which may be termed a community. But the term *community* does not have the meaning today that it had as recently as several centuries ago. Beginning in the next section of this chapter, and continuing to its end, we will examine the way the meaning of "community" has altered in the past century.

Another term warranting consideration is *government*. Most of us take for granted the existence of some form of government, even though the hunters and gatherers described above had nothing recognizable today as a government unless the concept is stretched beyond what we would acknowledge.

Nevertheless, the word *government* has been with us for many centuries, though its meaning has varied from time to time and place to place. More often than not the term has referred to a command system headed by an authoritarian ruler or ruling clique. But at other times, as in the Athens of Socrates and Plato, or in the United States and certain other industrial democracies during the past century or so, the structure and processes of government have been called *democratic*.

Chapter 1 of this book considers the difference between government and community. Chapter 2 then turns to the questions, "What is meant by democracy? How can a government (more particularly, a city government) be made democratic or kept democratic? Is it important to know *who* governs?"

Subsequent chapters pursue the theme of local democracy by examining legal and fiscal constraints on the citizenry's capacity for self-determination in U.S. cities (Chapters 3 and 4), by discussing the relationship between democracy and the local activities of organized interests (Chapter 5), by examining the implementation of mechanisms and procedures that sustain democracy (Chapter 6), and by surveying the structures (or forms) of local government, differentiated according to the relationship between the chief executive officer and the council (Chapter 7).

We turn now to an examination of the meaning (or meanings) of the term *community*.

1

Local Government: Why Study It?

GOVERNMENTS AND COMMUNITIES

Today, if we wish to have a good understanding of cities, it is not enough to speak and write first of the state or the nation and then regard the city simply as a component of that larger government, the nation-state. Cities are in part governments, but often they are referred to as communities as well. Government is only one facet of that complex entity we call "city." A city may be viewed as a community, or perhaps a cluster of communities, and so we turn now to an examination of the term *community* so that we may have a better foundation for understanding Camelot.

TWO MEANINGS OF COMMUNITY[1]

Probably nobody knows the total number of definitions of the term *community*. A sociologist friend of the authors quit counting after collecting sixty-five. This section of *Camelot* will limit its attention to only two meanings of community, but those two meanings offer us a pair of very important and contrasting definitions that, taken together, substantially increase our understanding of urban processes and change.

---

[1]The following discussion relies heavily on the very thoughtful discussion by Scott Greer in *The Emerging City,* 1962, New York: Free Press of Glencoe.

The first way of understanding the meaning of *community* is to define it in terms of the perceptions of its members. In this view, community is defined as a group of persons having a sense of shared (or common) destiny. The members of the community have an awareness that they are all "in the same lifeboat together." Defined in this fashion, the members of a community usually share a geographic location as well as a destiny. It is the awareness of shared destiny that distinguishes this definition of community from such phrases as "community of scholars" or the "Italian-American community in New Haven." In the latter two instances, the notions of shared *values* and shared *interests* are emphasized, but the notion of shared *destiny* becomes less prominent, perhaps diminishing to insignificance. And it is the sense of shared destiny that is critical to our discussion here. Awareness of shared destiny, rather than the more limited awareness of shared values or interests, furnishes the basis for common endeavors in village, town, or city.

Five hundred years ago, the people of an English village or town could be expected to have a strong sense of common destiny. Their lands were part of the fiefdom of the local baron, to whom they owed allegiance that included payment of taxes and specified labor on the roads each year. In return, the baron owed them justice and protection against predations by outsiders. They shared the risks of such hazards as drought, storm, crop failure, plague, epidemic, pestilence, and the danger of being caught in the middle of a conflict between rival lords. Today, the hazards are different, but the geographic scope of our personal notion of community still is relatively small. We may live in the Chicago metropolitan area, but identification of our community is likely to be more specific—such as Wilmette, or Bensenville, or Homewood. We may live in the Dallas–Fort Worth metropolitan area, but if we live in one of the suburbs—such as Arlington, Irvine, or Plano—our community identification is almost certain to be with that suburb.

The second way to understand the meaning of *community* begins again with an examination of life in that English village or town of five centuries ago. Each person needed food, clothing, and shelter. Since humans are social beings, each person also needed some companionship, usually including a spouse in adulthood. Each villager or town resident also needed to pay or exchange something for the necessities of life. That something might be labor, or an item of handicraft, or agricultural produce, or an animal. (Only the well-to-do were likely to have many coins to use as a medium of exchange.) To phrase the matter more analytically, the *functions* of providing food, shelter, clothing, companionship, and so on were performed by the population of the town and the surrounding farms and forests. Commodities, services, friendships, kinship, entertainment, the consolations of religion—all these were available (if at all) in the town or its immediate vicinity. If a need or want could not be satisfied within a radius of, say, ten miles (a half-day journey, one way), people did without it. Thus, when we define that English community in terms of its *performance of functions* for the population, we find that the geographic extent of the community was about the same as the geographic extent of the community previously defined by a sense of shared destiny.

We can illustrate this point by imagining that you, the reader, lived in that town five centuries ago. Imagine yourself living at some point, call it *X,* within the town (see Figure 1-1). Now imagine a map of the town and the countryside that locates your home, point *X.* Imagine further that the map locates suppliers important to you, such as the shoemaker, the butcher, the baker, and so on. Imagine still further that the map also locates those persons who supply your suppliers. Thus, the shoemaker receives cured hides from the tanner, the tanner receives the uncured hides from the slaughterhouse which is operated by the butcher, the butcher receives the cattle and hogs for slaughter from the farmers. Another example is the baker, who receives flour from the miller, who receives wheat and oats from the farmers in the area. Place on the map all these connecting lines (and the many others that also will occur to you), and you have sketched the approximate geographic extent of the *community* by these lines that show the *interdependence* of the people on one another for performing the *functions* that meet our needs, wants, and desires in life. These *lines of functional interdependence* can be used to outline the boundaries and define the community in one way just as the awareness of a shared destiny can be used to outline the boundaries and define the community in another way.

Five centuries ago, the community defined by these lines of functional interdependence had approximately the same geographic boundaries as did the community defined by a sense of shared destiny. Each type of community reinforced the other, for their boundaries coincided. But what has happened today? The two communities have been wrenched apart by technological change. Not only have the

FIGURE 1-1   The Community

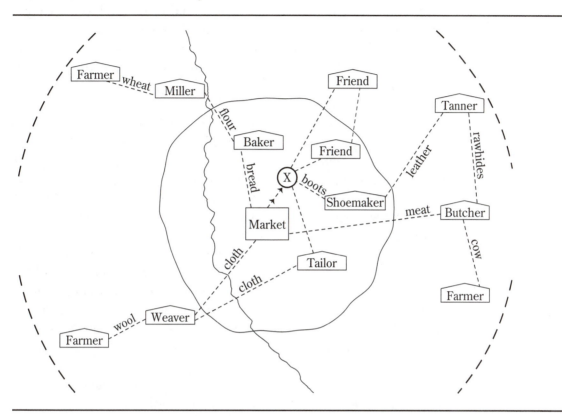

connecting lines lengthened dramatically in many instances, but those lines no longer stop at the same outer boundary. Some connecting lines extend across the ocean—witness the introduction of the Beatles to the United States in the 1960s, or American rock groups to Japan today, or the internationalization of classical music via compact discs which bring orchestras and soloists from all the industrialized nations together in an international record market. Automobiles, electronic appliances, clothing, toys, computer games, computers, medical discoveries, fashions for both men and women—the list goes on and on. Think for a moment of the examples that come to mind. And let us not overlook the communication of information. The social impact of television camera and broadcast station linked together by a satellite 22,000 miles above the earth's surface almost beggars description. Some needs still are obtained relatively close to one's home. Bricks for a new house have low value and substantial weight, a combination not conducive to marketing across a large region or nation, let alone overseas. Potato chips and deli salads also tend to be produced locally—chips because they do not hold up well in shipping, salads because they are easily subject to spoilage. (Proctor and Gamble's development of Pringles, which are uniform in size and shape, is an attempt to use technology to solve the shipping problem of potato chips and thus eliminate the need to produce them locally.)

Social relationships present a more complicated picture. While on the one hand they are no longer confined to the small locality of five centuries ago—many or most of us have friends in other communities, other states, and perhaps other nations—still, the majority of those social relationships are located within an area that seems relatively small by today's standards, even if relatively large by the standards of earlier centuries.

To summarize, the two communities that once reinforced each other have been wrenched apart by change, and the boundary of the community defined by functional interdependence has become blurred and impossible to discern at its edges for two reasons. First, the impact of tremendous increases in the *speed* with which goods, people, and information are transported today has permitted the development of regional, national, and now international trade on a vast scale. Second, extraordinary decreases in the *costs* of transportation have made economically feasible these extensions of markets. This, then, is the setting in which U.S. cities must be understood today. Cities are psychologically less significant to their citizens than were their predecessors; while they remain functionally significant in *some* very important respects, it also is true that they are functionally important in *somewhat fewer* respects than were their predecessors. But the crucial change has been in the reality of the concept of a community defined by functional interdependencies, for the changes described above have caused such a community to disappear. It has been replaced by what is now called *the organized local community,* most of which is governmental, and includes neighborhoods, villages, suburbs, and cities.

THE ORGANIZED LOCAL COMMUNITY

Perhaps the most significant aspect of the title of this section is the necessity to put modifiers in front of the word *community.* It is no longer accurate to use the word *community* by itself. We live in a world of *communities,* meaning that we create, make use of, work with, play with, or do many other things with many different groups of people who as collectives perform particular functions, whether for social, business, governmental, or other purposes. When the word *community* is used, it requires some modifier to fully define the term; thus the choice of words for the title of this section.

It has been noted that the community of functional interdependencies has disappeared. One consequence is the increase in the number of choices for the individual at the local level. Two hundred years ago, the local community defined the choices for the individual; now the reverse is more often the rule. Nevertheless, in some local situations today, the need for collective action precludes individual choice on some topics. One of the writers of this text recalls visiting his grandfather's farm many years ago. Water was supplied by the well or the spring, the privy and a dry well eliminated the need for a waste collection system, a good part of the food was produced on the farm, and a collie dog and shotgun provided the police protection. It is a rare person today who can provide any of these functions by himself or herself. Most people recognize immediately the need for collective action to provide a safe water supply, adequate police and fire protection, and a waste and trash collection service.

Regulatory functions are a second example of where collective action is required, and they are a consequence of the growth of ever larger populated areas. While the focus of *Camelot* is to provide an experience of how medium-size cities operate, the urban reality is one of geographically huge centers of population made up of dozens, perhaps hundreds, of cities and suburbs. Some of the problems created by these masses of population require regional, or even national, regulation to protect the health and/or safety of the population. Thus pollution controls are ineffective if limited to one municipal corporation, and the creation and disposal of hazardous waste is of immediate concern to a large population.

Another problem where collective action is needed is that of public convenience, an example of which is the engineering required for highway construction, or even traffic control mechanisms. The creation of left-turn lanes, center turn lanes, and left- and right-turn highway arrows are all examples of public support for collective action, in this case regulatory functions involving highways.

The preceding paragraphs suggest that though communities may exist at the local level, they are highly fractionalized, and often issue specific, and may lack the ability to sustain public support over time.

If one type of policy choice involves collective action to obtain services, create regulations, and generate finances for publicly perceived conveniences, then another type of choice might be categorized as *lifestyle*. The term *lifestyle* has come to be equated in popular language with such topics as sexual behavior, sexual preferences, or family size and living arrangements. Yet long before these particular subjects dominated public agendas and discussion, many other examples existed of what may be called lifestyle preferences, some of which were established by governmental action, others by nongovernmental action. For example, the public may have wished to regulate how land was used in a particular local community, or there may have been a desire to preserve historic structures, or property owners may have wished to require that grass and weeds be cut on all land at certain times each year. Zoning, historic preservation, and weed control require collective action by a local government in order to be effective. These objectives may or may not be essential, but they quite clearly are actions that reflect public lifestyle preferences as opposed to public needs.

Other lifestyle topics do not require governmental action, but they too reflect local public preferences. Local service clubs may decide to support sports programs or flower gardens. One of the latest examples is the "adopt a highway" program, in which various service organizations (Boy Scouts, college fraternities or sororities, or other private organizations) agree to clean up the litter along a specified section of a public highway. Groups of individuals will at times organize a neighborhood effort to discourage the sale of drugs, or clean up trash, or perform crime-watch services. Noisy teenagers, abortion clinics, or porno shops have experienced organized nongovernmental efforts to enforce community expectations that go beyond governmental regulation.

In summary, this chapter began with a question: Why study local government? The discussion then described briefly the changes that have occurred in the meaning of the word *community*. At one time it was assumed that *community* and *village,* or *community* and *town,* had similar meanings. The residents of a place shared the same values, interests, and sense of goals or destiny. No longer do we assume that the city in which we live is our "community," a place of shared values, interests, and destiny.

A second change occurred as a result of the changes in what is referred to as functional interdependence, meaning the extent to which the services and the goods we need or want are provided by our local community. The essentials of modern living—whether fuel, electricity, food, water, fire and police protection, food safety, and so on—are delivered locally but originate in distant places. If one adds information to this list, the concept of a functionally interdependent community is stretched beyond recognition. For example, anyone today with a home computer and a modem, can, by means of Internet, access the library in Berlin, Germany, to see if their holdings include a needed document or book title.

Thus the word *community* today requires a modifier. We speak of religious communities, educational communities, or (to choose the example of particular interest to Camelot's citizens) "the organized local community." These are the functions where local governments attempt to develop some collective action, whether it be a zoning restriction, the preservation of a historic landmark, or an attempt to get everyone to cut their grass (or pull their weeds), or to enforce a particular code of morality. Local government touches our lives every day in a very direct way, which is one of the main reasons we study it. And it is on this aspect of local government that *Camelot* focuses.

2

Who Governs, and
to What Ends?

POLITICS, GOVERNMENT, AND DEMOCRACY

Chapter 1 examined the term *community* and described the increasing separation between two of that term's important meanings. The first meaning of community was defined by the awareness of citizens that their individual destinies are to some degree tied to the destiny of the community—the members of a community have a sense of shared destiny—and the second meaning of community was defined by the lengthening radii of functional interdependence. Chapter 2 will examine the community's politics and government, focusing especially on the question of whether democracy can be found there and, if so, under what circumstances.

First, it will be useful to clarify several terms: politics, government, and democracy. David Easton's definition of *politics* as the authoritative allocation of values for a society, perhaps the most widely used of all definitions in political science, is the starting point. The values belong to the citizens, both individually and collectively, and the chief instrument for allocating those values authoritatively is government (the city government for our purposes in *Camelot*). *Government* is an instrument, or tool, used by the community to help in making the decisions of politics.

Candidates for local office often invoke the concept of democracy and talk about their vision of how their community can become more democratic. This has appeal, for the words *community* and *democratic* suggest something desirable and valuable. Each of these words tends to evoke a warm feeling, a favorable response, in the listener. But on reflection, it appears that democracy is a trait or characteristic of government rather than a trait of a community. Thus, we correctly may describe a city government as democratic, undemocratic, or somewhat democratic, as the case may be; and we correctly may say that a community has a democratic government; but it would be misleading to attribute the quality of being "democratic" to a community itself rather than to the government of the community.

Definitions and descriptions of democracy abound. A general description used by the authors of *Camelot* is that *democracy is a way of choosing who shall rule and, broadly, to what ends.* That description, while accurate as far as it goes, does not give an adequate basis for differentiating democratic from nondemocratic, nor does it distinguish more democratic from less democratic. To do that, one must specify criteria, or elements, by which democracy can be identified. The two elements of democracy used by *Camelot*'s authors are as follows:

1. A pattern of accountability of the rulers to the ruled, usually sought via competitive elections and supplemented by such techniques as interest-group activity, court challenges to officials (in the U.S.), and the spotlight of discussion and publicity played on issues and on actions of officials, both elected and appointed, during the intervals between elections.
2. The free play of ideas in the formation of public policy (that is, freedom of expression).

Thus, the working definition of democracy used in *Camelot* is that *democracy is a way of choosing who shall rule and, broadly, to what ends, by pursuing accountability of the rulers to the ruled through competitive elections and freedom of expression.*

The difficulty with definitions is that, while they can tell you what to look for, they don't tell you what you will find when you look. If you examine the governmental structure and processes of your home town, will you find a democracy? Until you or someone you trust has made such an examination, the answer may be unclear. You may hope to find a democracy but find instead a city dominated by a crime syndicate. You may look for the "democratically elected representatives of the people" and find instead a "political machine." Often, political machines have been associated with corruption at the ballot box, in hiring and firing employees, and in contracting for public works, but does such corruption indicate that democracy is not present? Or may democracy sometimes coexist with corruption? Does more democracy necessarily produce better government and wiser public policy outcomes?

Consider the following: Some mayors have earned enviable reputations as policy entrepreneurs who set forth an agenda of progress and economic development for their cities. Tom Johnson in Cleveland in the early 1900s, Richard Lee in New Haven during the 1950s, Ivan Allen in Atlanta during the 1960s, and William H. Hudnut in Indianapolis in the 1980s come to mind as examples. But some other mayors have chosen the role of ideological demagogue until removed from office by disappointed and angry voters. In the past two decades, Dennis Kucinich in Cleveland and Frank Rizzo in Philadelphia manifested this type of divisive approach to mayoral leadership, and most commentators judged it counterproductive. Are only the first four officials illustrative of democracy, or are all six consistent with local level democracy? The election of a demagogue, followed by his removal by voters at another election, may well be evidence that democracy is alive and well. No one claims that voters always make the best choices, but it is essential to the maintenance of a democracy that voters be allowed to make such choices, whether wise or unwise.

The question is made more complicated by frequent references to a *community power structure* when Americans discuss an action, or perhaps inaction, by their city government. Such references suggest a belief that an economic elite, possessing wealth and social status, shapes decisions within the city. Such references tend to tarnish the public's image of local government's decision making, but are the references accurate? Is there in many (or most) U.S. cities a set of persons who control governmental decisions, or who at least bring to bear considerable influence on governmental decisions? If the answer is affirmative, how do we incorporate that into our understanding of the prospects for local-level democracy? How important is the question of who actually sits at the levers of control in our city governments? Clearly, the popular references to community power structures reflect the belief that if we know *who,* we also will know much about *what, why,* and *for whom*.

Although a huge amount of scholarly research into patterns of decision making and influence within cities was undertaken by social scientists, primarily sociologists and political scientists, in the past half century or so, the findings have been far from conclusive. The research generated much disagreement among scholars in each field and even more disagreement between the fields. Intense debate flared during the late 1950s and much of the 1960s. More recently, the intensity of debate has diminished as numerous areas of agreement have emerged, and the findings of that research will be examined in the later pages of this chapter. But first, the meaning of several terms used in the phrase *community power structure* should be clarified.

Power or Resources?

Since Chapter 1 already has provided discussion of the meaning of "community," attention now may be directed toward the second term in the phrase *community power structure.* The word *power,* for all of its popularity in ordinary conversation, seems to defy an accurate definition that would easily provide a basis for research by scholars. For example, most writers using the term *power* have chosen to speak of types or classifications of power in order to develop their analyses, but few authors seem to agree on which classification scheme to use. Thus categories such as positive power, veto power, and filter power were used by M. Kent Jennings, while Nobel Laureate Kenneth Boulding used the categories of "threat power, economic, and integrative power."[1]

As a consequence of the difficulty of obtaining agreement on analytic categories, some scholars have abandoned the term altogether and have thought and written about "resources" instead. While the authors of *Camelot* do not endorse all of the conclusions of this group of scholars, the authors believe that students probably can understand their own communities more easily and accurately by thinking in terms of resources rather than of power.

Use of the term *resources* permits us to see that the components of power—in other words, its resources—are both numerous and varied. It also enables us to see that power has limits, for resources can be used up. Another benefit of using the concept of resources is that it becomes easier to see that some people use a particular resource with

---

[1] M. Kent Jennings, *Community Influentials: The Elites of Atlanta.* New York: The Free Press of Glencoe, 1964; Kenneth E. Boulding, *Three Faces of Power.* Newbury Park, Calif.: Sage Publications, 1990.

skill while others may use that same type of resource unskillfully or even wastefully. We employ the notion of resources in this discussion to take advantage of the greater accuracy and flexibility achievable with that concept.

What Is the Degree of Structuring in Community Decision Making?

Turning now to the word *structure* in the phrase *community power structure,* we will see that this term, too, must be used cautiously. Whether there really is such a "structure" in a particular community, and if there is, how strong and durable it is, and what its pattern or configuration is, are empirical questions. They are questions to be investigated by the collection of information. The answers are not to be assumed or accepted uncritically without evidence. Indeed, there are numerous communities (including perhaps your own) where one must wonder whether any person or group of persons is capable of making effective decisions. But that answer may depend in part on the subject matter of the decisions. Different topics are likely to require different resources. Thus one sees that the possibility of difference or variation from one policy topic to the next adds another wrinkle of complexity to our understanding of community decision making.

EVOLUTION OF COMMUNITY POWER PATTERNS

It was stated earlier that, despite frequent and often intense disagreement among scholars with respect to many aspects of the study of community power, numerous areas of agreement have emerged. The first area of agreement concerns change over time. Scholars today are in virtually unanimous agreement on the proposition that patterns of influence—that is, the structure of influence—differed in the United States in the nineteenth century from what we observe today. Though we must be ever mindful that there was then, as now, substantial variation from one community to another, when one traces the influence pattern (or structure) through a period of time in a single U.S. community, one usually finds that in the nineteenth century and the earlier decades of the twentieth century, the community displayed a higher degree of structuring than is seen at present. Prior to the turn of this century, in a given community there appears to have been a greater concentration, in the hands of a smaller number of persons, of resources having political significance. Thus it is accurate to say that more influence was concentrated in the hands of fewer persons than is true today.[2]

In the past, resources tended to accumulate, rather like kernels of popcorn being stuck onto a popcorn ball. An owner-manager of a prosperous business also was likely to hold local offices such as mayor or council member during the course of a lifetime. Moreover, the social structure of the community was likely to reinforce the patterns found in the workplace and in politics. Thus, those individuals who were more successful in terms of wealth and social status also tended to be more influential in community decision making. Even in towns or cities where there was little evidence of corruption or bossism, voters tended to believe that wealth and social prestige were correlated with wisdom in political affairs. This "popcorn ball" effect was reinforced by the fact that geographic mobility of people was less than it is today, which in turn meant that the social structure of a community was more stable, slower to change, than today.

Today's transfers of executives and managers from office to office and city to city as they climb the corporate ladder have been chronicled often and widely. And despite the development of efforts and practices to speed the assimilation of new arrivals, in most communities the level of commitment to the community and to civic affairs seems to be dwindling. Resources are scattered, rather than concentrated as in the past. Education seems to loom larger as a resource, in part because of the snowballing importance of expertise in technical fields and in part because of the divorce of ownership from professional management in the nation's large and medium-size business enterprises. Professional managers who report to superiors at a company's headquarters in a distant location are less likely to become involved in community controversy. They are more likely to limit their civic participation to matters for which a community consensus already exists, for many corporations are more concerned about their corporate image than about contributions to community life that their branch managers could make.

In today's world, it has become more difficult to find persons that we might describe as generally influential across a broad range of issues. The scattered distribution of resources, the great variety of

[2] For a thorough discussion of the concept of cumulative versus dispersed resources, see Robert A. Dahl, *Who Governs, Democracy and Power in an American City* (New Haven, Conn.: Yale University Press, 1961), pp. 85–86.)

resources, and limited commitment all combine to produce specialization of influence. There are few, if any, general power wielders. Different issues or topics are likely to be influenced by different persons with different resources available to them. As a consequence, the "richest man in town" no longer seems to carry the political weight of former years. Influence seems to be organized around more narrow specialties, and a winning coalition must be more broadly based. It must include more persons, along with their resources, than in the past. Looking at the matter from the other direction, in most American cities it is much more difficult to initiate, gain approval for, and implement a community decision today than in yesteryear. The reason is that the pattern of resource distribution is less concentrated today than in the earlier part of this century and in the nineteenth century. There seem to be more "popcorn balls" of influence today, but each popcorn ball appears to be somewhat smaller than in the past. In particular, "power generalists" believed to have influence across a broad range of issues are less numerous today.

Another point of agreement is that public officials have larger roles in decision making and are more influential than in the past. There are several reasons for this, but only two need detain us here. First, the growth of governmental bureaucracies has increased the number of officials with stakes in the implementation of governmental policies, and it has coincided with a trend toward greater professionalization of those officials, as may be seen in the rising educational standards and the lengthening job tenure within many municipal administrations. Second, the development of greater emphasis on democratic accountability has increased the significance of such tools of direct democracy as the Initiative and the Referendum. This has given a larger role to those persons who have the resources (skill, position, knowledge, and so on) to offer political leadership. Increasingly, these persons are public officials—persons with past experience in successful mobilization of voters. Votes can be an important resource for influencing some types of community decision.

Often one hears an argument that goes something like this: There must be a power structure in this community because the government officials so often take the actions requested by highly visible citizens such as land developers, factory owners, bankers, and publishers. The difficulty with this argument is that it fails to suggest evidence of a causal link. It begs the question; it *assumes* that developers, industrialists, bankers, and publishers are influential rather than *offering proof* that they are. That is to say, if A and B agree on a public issue, what basis is there for assuming that A is accepting orders from B? Why not the reverse? Should it always be assumed that the more wealthy person is giving orders to the less wealthy person? Might not A and B share a common perception of a common goal?

A thoughtful and challenging analysis has been suggested by Clarence Stone in an article describing "systemic power."[3] Stone agrees that the old debates about *who* has power seem profitless today. The more important question, as James Q. Wilson pointed out more than two decades ago, is, what difference does it make?[4] Stone argues that there are certain tendencies and directions built into the operations of communities. Communities are, after all, work sites. Jobs are of vital importance, and in a society whose population is growing, it is essential that new jobs be formed to match the population increase. So it is, too, with communities. However, growth in jobs (economic development) almost always involves some changes in land use; new sites must be found for light manufacturing, for shopping facilities, for schools to accommodate workers' children, and so on. But neither the capitalist-entrepreneur nor the government official can achieve such economic development without assistance from the other. This means that the interests of the two—capitalist developer and government official—converge to a significant degree. Though they may quarrel over design details such as who shall pay for the costs of traffic engineering changes to accommodate the development, they have a common stake in its success. Thus casual observers may draw the mistaken inference of collusion between developer and official even though the better explanation is that their coinciding desires to see the development task completed produce the apparent convergence of goals. The developer reaps profit while the official reaps political credit for promoting jobs that have the incidental effect of augmenting the tax revenues of the treasury. These augmented revenues, in turn, will give added flexibility to next year's budget—a point that is never lost on a public officer.

[3] Clarence Stone, "Systemic Power in Community Decision Making: A Restatement of Stratification Theory," *American Political Science Review 74* (December 1980) pp. 978–990. Though Stone's more recent work develops a more complex scenario for such a situation, the greater complexity does not diminish the points made in this discussion. Interested readers may wish to investigate Clarence Stone, *Regime Politics: Governing Atlanta 1946–1988*, University of Kansas Press, Lawrence, Kans., 1989.

[4] "Book Review," *American Political Science Review 64* (March 1970), p. 198.

WHO GOVERNS IN CITIES TODAY?

The preceding section described some changes that appear to have occurred over a span of many decades of American life. Resources that have political and governmental policy significance have become more varied, as can be seen by anyone who watches election returns on television. In addition, the emergence of a greater variety of resources that have policy-shaping potential seems to have been accompanied by wider distribution of control of those resources. However, this identification of changes and trends does not provide an answer to the question of whether democracy is to be found at the local government level. That question now claims attention.

The briefest answer to the question, "Who governs?" is that it depends. The obvious follow-up then becomes, "On what does it depend?" The answer is offered below as a list of nine factors that have been found to affect patterns of decision making in American cities. Additional factors may occur to you, but this list will show the variety and complexity of the answer.

1. The size of a city's population is a factor. The larger the city's population, the more varied and complex will be the values and interests of the citizens. As the variety of values and interests increases, there will be more chances for conflicts to be spawned by clashes of values or interests. In addition, where there is more variety of values and interests, there are likely to be more varied resources that have some potential for use in political conflict. Divergence, rather than convergence, of interests is the likely pattern as population size increases, and divergence of interests between holders of resources often leads to conflict, which in turn may reduce or constrain the influence of any of those holders of resources. The chances for conflict, then, increase when population size increases, for that usually produces greater social diversity.

2. The nature of a city's economic base is a factor. Here, too, diversity is a crucially important consideration. The greater concentrations of economic resources, and also the greater opportunities for wielding influence within a city, have been found most often where a single employer dominates an area's job market. Relatively few such examples survive today, though the copper mines of Butte, Montana, or the U.S. Steel plant in Gary, Indiana, might be cited. More frequently encountered is a concentration in a metropolitan area of several large firms

belonging to a single industry. The dominance of packing houses in Kansas City, of automobiles in Detroit, of moviemaking in Hollywood, and of steel in Youngstown, Ohio, provides examples of such concentration recent enough to be meaningful, even though they are less significant now than four decades ago.

As the variety of manufacturing and commercial enterprises within a city increases, patterns of influence may be affected. Conflict between employees and managers is common and well understood, but it is less well understood that the diversity of enterprises within a city increases the chance that the interests of a company and its personnel will diverge from, and perhaps conflict with, the interests of another company and its personnel. The familiar conflicts of capital, management, and labor within an organization may be overlaid by the varied needs and objectives of different types of enterprises. Just as we discussed in the preceding paragraph, fragmented and varied interests increase the chances of conflict and inhibit the concentration of resources required for the appearance of a pattern of influence in which influence is concentrated in the hands of a few general power wielders.

3. The ethnic composition of a city's population is a significant factor. In the last half of the nineteenth century and early twentieth century a pattern of ethnic dominance existed in some cities. It developed when a large ethnic group discovered that votes could be used to influence others in ways advantageous to the group, and the era of "machine politics" grew out of this discovery. Today, the varied and sometimes competing traditions of major ethnic groups may reduce the likelihood that a resource such as votes can be used effectively against the economic resources available to merchants or managers.

4. The character of a city's labor forces is a significant factor as well. Especially important during the past fifty years has been the proportion of union membership within the labor force of the city. Though the proportion of workers who belong to a union is smaller today than three decades ago, unionization still has political significance. The skills possessed by and the educational level of the labor force are resources that may sometimes have political significance.

5. History is a factor, too. Chance, or historical accident, may produce different patterns in communities that in many other ways are similar. And should anyone be surprised if an older city shows different behavior and character from those of a newer city? Cities that

experienced rapid growth only after the development of automobiles may differ significantly from cities based on earlier growth. Boston differs from San Diego, as does Minneapolis from Las Vegas, and the differences are in part historical, not simply geographic.

6. The degree of interparty competition in a city can be a factor of significance in some cities. For more than a hundred years, political parties have helped recruit and mobilize members of the American electorate, urging them to support the party's candidates on election day. In doing this they have created an additional cleavage across which competing social and economic groups, holding conflicting views about which governmental policies to pursue, face one another. The growth of nonpartisan elections in cities has considerably diminished the influence of political parties. Even so, there are examples of nonpartisan cities where parties function effectively behind the scene, especially in the role of candidate recruitment.

7. Many cities use types of ballots that tend to inhibit and discourage the operation of parties in local elections. Chapter 6 will examine the impact of nonpartisan ballots and the at-large method of election in more detail.

8. Since the end of World War II, the urban areas of the United States have experienced a movement of people toward the suburban areas of cities, and this fact is widely recognized. Not so well understood is the fact that many jobs have either moved to the suburbs or been newly established in suburban areas. The result is that the percentage of workers who must cross a municipal boundary line (that is, travel from one municipality to another) in going from home to work has increased dramatically. Since persons having more years of formal education tend to have higher incomes than persons having fewer years, that in turn permits the better educated and more affluent persons to follow their preference for suburban living. And since educational attainment correlates significantly with various leadership skills and resources, the central cities of the U.S. have experienced a net decline in the number of persons within the central city who possess many of the resources useful for leadership. Those leadership resources include, but are not limited to, past leadership experience, flexible work schedules, secretarial support in some instances, a network of acquaintances to tap for information and counsel in confronting new problems,

and practice in the persuasive expression of their judgments and preferences.

9. The type of issue being addressed is the final item on this list of factors that help answer the question of who governs. The type of issue is important because resources that are quite useful in addressing today's issue may not be the type of resources that would be helpful in addressing tomorrow's. If, for example, today's issue pertains to more effective enforcement of traffic laws, the alignment of interested persons likely will differ from the alignment on tomorrow's issue, which may pertain to storm-water flooding in some recently built residential areas. Complaints about traffic enforcement may come from any sector of the city. But in the discussion of tomorrow's issue, irate homeowners from the affected neighborhoods may appear in the council chamber to confront officials. A developer who wishes to sell more houses (and who thinks the problem is due to the inadequacy of city trunk sewers rather than to the storm sewers he installed in his own subdivision) may urge officials to order an engineering survey as the first step toward correction of the problem. On yet another issue, a petition of voters throughout the city may be useful. On the day after that, immediately available funds may be the most important resource when legal talent must be hired by citizens to file a lawsuit challenging the city's authority to invest public funds in the development of an industrial park as a joint venture with certain private investors.

WHAT CAN WE CONCLUDE?

1. The first conclusion to be drawn from the preceding discussion is that decision patterns vary greatly: they vary by decade, and they also vary by locale; city-to-city variation is common. In addition, decision patterns vary according to the type of issue, for the resources useful for one issue may be not at all appropriate for the next.

2. The second conclusion to be drawn from the chapter's discussion is that the popular notion of a community power structure tends to be overdrawn. There are three reasons why it is likely to be an exaggeration. The first reason is that the very term *power structure* suggests to the reader or listener that a group of persons, or a segment of society, is able to impose its preferences on the rest of the citizens. But the

reality is often disagreement, even fragmentation. The notion of power structure fails to suggest possible conflicts and disagreements among the persons who possess resources that can be put to political use in a dispute.

The second reason why belief in the existence of a power structure is likely to be exaggerated is that some, perhaps many, of the resources available for use by a power structure will be depleted by use. Issues arise in connection with many different topics, and since resources are quite varied in type, it is almost certain that some of the resources available for use by a power structure will be diminished by the very fact of their use. Time is a resource, for example, and as any student knows all too well, time spent studying for tomorrow's exam cannot also be used to study for the exam to be held the day after tomorrow. The same point can be made about money. Dollars tend to be used up as they go to pay for advertising one's argument in the newspaper, on radio, and on television, or perhaps to pay for the campaign expenses of one's preferred candidates or to support the lobbying activities of an interest group one supports. Sometimes a desired outcome may be obtained simply by display of a large amount of money, as Mark Twain showed in his story "The Thousand Dollar Bank Note." In the story, the bill was never spent; in fact it was counterfeit. But displaying it was enough to persuade many people to extend credit, hospitality, and even friendship. Thus it can be seen that the problem of sorting out the effects of "anticipatory behavior" by persons who defer to wealth or other resources (whether real or illusory, as in the story of the Emperor's New Clothes) is very difficult. Of course, more often than not the money must be spent if it is to achieve a desired purpose. The lesson to be drawn is that members of any power structure must calculate the possible gains and losses as they consider whether, and how, they wish to commit resources in the "game" of civic influence.

The third and final reason why beliefs about a power structure are likely to be exaggerated is that commentators often fail to understand that skill in employing a resource is, itself, an additional resource. Unskillful use of one's resources will hasten their depletion and thereby make the pursuit of power (or influence) more costly.

3. Resuming now the list of conclusions that may be drawn about power structures today, the third (and next-to-final) conclusion is that the distribution of resources is very uneven in U.S. cities. Moreover,

the skill used in employing those resources, which is in itself an additional resource, is unevenly distributed, too. Clearly, these uneven distributions are important to our efforts to understand patterns of influence in cities. Notice, if you will, that each of these preceding
statements is important for an understanding of agenda setting within
cities. And observers of politics often argue that the persons who control the agenda control the outcome. Thus, while it is true that the
head of a local labor union can gather signatures on a petition and
thereby gain access to officials to discuss the petition's concern, the
more pertinent question is whether he or she could get through to
those same officials by phone as easily as could a local factory manager or owner. Differences in ease of access (that is, the costs of access) may mean that some persons or groups must spend a significant
amount of their resources simply to obtain a hearing—to get on the
discussion agenda—while others need only pick up the telephone.
Thus, the owner of a local shoe store, concerned about inadequate
parking in the vicinity of the store, may have to put those concerns in
writing because a conversation with an official lies beyond reach of the
owner's resources—including the constraint imposed by the time the
owner must commit to operating the store. And if neither the owner's
name nor the name of the store will be recognized by an official to
whom a complaint is addressed, how would we evaluate that owner's
resources in comparison with the resources of a merchant whose past
activities have created a first-name acquaintance with the official?

4. The final conclusion to be drawn about power structures in U.S.
cities today is that democracy is not foreclosed; democracy is possible
despite all that has been written and said about power structures.
Skeptics may point to unequal distribution of resources as evidence of
democracy's failure, but the more important point is that democracy is
a matter of degree. Though democracy never is perfectly achieved, important questions must be asked about the degree to which a democratic ideal can be, and has been, approached. Though resources are
distributed unevenly, it often is possible to collect or accumulate a particular type of resource, as when owners of small businesses each contribute modest amounts to some political purpose, or when the head of
a labor union recommends contributions to a Political Action Committee. In addition, sometimes one type of resource can be used to oppose a different type of resource. An example of this could be when
the votes of a labor union are used to counteract the dollars spent to

advertise the political message of a local chamber of commerce. In *Camelot* there is no assumption of any pattern or degree of structuring other than what is stated in the city charter and in the role descriptions. But then you may ask, does not the absence of a clearly defined "power structure" hinder significantly the realism of *Camelot*? We believe it does not, and the preceding paragraphs may help you to understand and share this belief.

In sum, the presence of elites—persons who have a disproportionate amount of some valued resource, whether that resource be money, status, control over jobs or credit, education, or any of the other resources that one might identify as having some potential for community decision making—does not tell us whether, or how, those resources were employed in the past. Nor does that elite presence tell us whether or how those resources might be employed tomorrow. Perhaps certain resources will be used by their possessors in an effort to influence an outcome, or perhaps not. And if resources are committed to such a use, perhaps they will suffice; perhaps not.

Voters also have resources to commit when they enter their polling places. So the question raised in preceding paragraphs is not simply whether elites have some potential for intervention and control. They very definitely do. An important additional question is whether the citizenry has some potential for intervention and control, too. Here, also, the answer is that they very definitely do.

The basic questions remain: Who governs? And to what ends? But there is no single answer of general applicability to either of those questions. The answers are multiple and varied, for they depend on time and place, on the nature of the issues being examined, and on the interests and skills of the persons possessing resources, who must ponder resource needs and costs if they choose to become involved.

3

The Legal Authority of Cities: Constraints and Powers

The dividing and redividing of national decision-making authority was part of the grand design of the authors of the U.S. Constitution. The federal system, which further divided power, this time between the states and the national levels of government, fit perfectly into the scheme. And that is just about where the dividing ended. One might think that the states would eagerly follow what seemed to be the established trend and divide power once again, giving cities specific powers of their own, keeping some powers for themselves, and then blending or sharing a few between states and cities. Quite the opposite. States, for the most part, have jealously guarded state authority over cities, limiting cities' decision making to certain specified areas.

To many a harried mayor or perplexed council member the *limits* on city governments endeavoring to cope with community needs may appear greater than the legal *authority* to cope with those needs. This section describes the constraints cities experience and the consequences of those constraints. With the constraints in mind, the section then describes some of the powers the cities do have.

The first step toward understanding the legal authority of cities is to remember that the term *city* has two rather different meanings. As used here, the word *city* refers to a unit of government having a defined geographic jurisdiction and a relatively high density population. In the United States, a city in this sense of the word is called a *municipal corporation.* The second meaning of the word *city* is less precise, but an illustration or two may make it clearer. If you were to say that your family is going to move to Chicago, it would not be clear to a listener whether your family home will be located in the municipal corporation named Chicago, as contrasted to suburban municipal corporations such as Winnetka, Oak Park, Homewood, or Western Springs. If you were to announce that your family is going to move to Washington, not even the *state* of residence would be understood, for suburban Washington includes Arlington, Alexandria, and Fairfax, in Virginia; whereas Rockville, Silver Spring, and Wheaton lie north of the Potomac, in Maryland. Thus it becomes apparent that the word *city* may refer to a municipal corporation, or it may refer in a more general way to a metropolitan area by applying to the entire area the name of the municipality lying at the metropolitan core. Often the only way to know which meaning is intended is to infer it from the context, but in *Camelot* the word will refer to municipal corporations, or municipalities.

The second step in understanding the legal authority of cities is to examine the significance of municipal incorporation. Any corporation, whether it be General Motors or the City of Los Angeles, is a legal entity authorized by the state in which it resides. (The legal capacity of Congress to create corporations has been used only rarely and has been limited to public or semipublic purposes.) Whether municipal or private, an important purpose of a corporation is to facilitate collective action. In the case of the private corporation, aggregation of capital is the collective purpose served, and, in the process, the legal liability of stockholders for the debts of the corporation is limited, usually to the value of the stock shares owned by each stockholder. In the case of municipal corporations, the collective purposes are the capacity to make binding rules of behavior (called *ordinances*) and the capacity to collect taxes for activities such as fire protection and street maintenance that are undertaken for the benefit of all citizens. Both categories of corporation, municipal and private, are limited to those activities authorized by the incorporating authority—the state. For reasons that extend many centuries into English history, such a grant of authority is called a charter, and it is the city charter that establishes the city's legal existence and identifies the scope of its authority.

The parallel between private and municipal corporations ends when the notions of ownership and citizenship are compared. The stockholder purchases an ownership share and may later choose to sell it. However, you become a citizen of a municipal corporation simply by residing within its boundaries, and if you choose to move you cannot sell to someone else your fractional share in a fire truck or a police car.

In the nineteenth century, state legislatures often intervened in the detailed affairs of the cities they had created, so much so that many states adopted constitutional amendments forbidding "special legislation"—legislation having application only to a special situation or to a single city—and requiring that all legislation have more general application. This, in turn, brought the courts prominently into the picture to settle disputes over whether statutes were special or general. Moreover, the courts had an additional role to play in interpreting the grants of power to the cities. Unlike the grants of power to the federal government, which are interpreted broadly under the principle of "implied powers" first announced in the landmark case of *McCulloch* v. *Maryland,* the grants of power to cities are interpreted narrowly. The rule of interpretation was summarized many decades ago by Judge Dillon in his textbook on municipal law when he wrote that "any fair, reasonable substantial doubt concerning the existence of [the] power must be resolved by the courts against the corporation, and the power is denied." The application of Dillon's Rule, as it has come to be called because of the succinctness of his summary, has given judges and lawyers a major outlet for their energies; litigation has abounded, and city officials cannot be certain of the legality of innovative actions unless they have obtained a court decision on the particular ordinance or expenditure in question. In short, municipal corporations are constrained quite severely by their legal position as creations of the state.

There is, however, a complicating matter to pursue. An understanding of the complication can be obtained by recalling the history of urban reform at the turn of this century. Efforts toward urban reform included the notion of "home rule" for cities. Cities were to be given the capacity to determine their own scope of authority as long as municipal actions did not conflict with the state constitution or with general laws adopted by the state legislature. In some states—for example, Indiana—the idea of home rule, or more self determination for cities, never caught on. In some other states home rule was accorded the cities by state statute. In still other states, such as Ohio, attempts were made to grant home rule to cities by directive language in an amendment to the state constitution. But irrespective of the method employed, the cities found themselves substantially constrained by the spirit of Dillon's Rule, which the courts continued to apply. To illustrate, Ohio's Home Rule Amendment, adopted in 1911, specifies that each municipal corporation may exercise all powers of local government. Despite the apparent sweep of such language, the amendment is significant chiefly for conferring on municipalities the power to tailor the *form* of their government to the particular taste of that community and, within certain limits, to control land use within the community. Home rule did not repeal Dillon's Rule, and the state judiciary continues to have an active role in determining the limits of municipal authority.

Although this may seem to be a debilitating list of constraints on the legal authority of cities, cities do in fact have certain powers of some importance as they attempt to control their own destiny. By and large, most of these powers come not from constitutional grants of authority, but rather are either specific powers delegated by state legislatures or state-court approved activities. No attempt will be made here to provide an all-inclusive list of the powers of cities, but four important powers will be discussed. Two of these have already been mentioned: control over land use within the community, subject to the requirements of *due process of law* under the U.S. Constitution, and the power to determine the form of local government. In addition, a brief introduction will be provided to the housekeeping functions of cities. The final topic of local government authority to be discussed will be the expanded use of the right of eminent domain.

LAND-USE CONTROL

Ever since a U.S. Supreme Court decision in 1926 (*Village of Euclid, Ohio* v. *Ambler Realty Company,* 272 U.S. 365), there has been little question that local governments could, if they chose, decide how land should be used within their corporate limits. The usual process is for the city or village to authorize the mayor and council to appoint a planning commission, which body then develops a *master plan*. The plan will divide the city (or village, or township, or county) into zones of permitted uses: single-family housing, multiple-family housing, commercial (often subdivided into various specified categories), and industrial. This is a simplified sketch, and usually the zones are more numerous and more detailed, treating of such matters as height of buildings, required minimum setback from the street, minimum side yard, and so on. In addition to specific restrictions within each zone, uses permitted within the zone often are carefully described. Boston, Massachusetts, for example, once created a special zone for X-rated movie houses and bookstores, and sex paraphernalia shops. It became known as "the combat zone" because of the violence that occurred so frequently there.

Zoning can, of course, be abused. The theory on which zoning regulations originally were upheld by the courts is a theory of mutual protection. The zoning code may prevent you from operating a motor-cycle repair business in the garage of your home, but it also prevents the house next door from being turned into a disco bar specializing in half-price drinks every Thursday night. By each giving up a little bit of freedom, your investment in your home is protected against your neighbor's actions, and the value of your neighbor's home is protected against your actions. But sometimes the mutuality of benefits, the two-way flow of benefits, can be lost.

In the example just given, and in zoning codes generally, much weight is given to maintaining the lifestyles preferred by the property owners and fostered by the physical characteristics of the structures and lots in the neighborhood. Protection of the stability of values and behaviors is an important factor in the public's evaluation of a zoning code. But how far should that be carried? Would it be appropriate to cater to the lifestyle of a neighborhood populated predominantly by persons over age 55 by amending the zoning ordinance to limit the neighborhood to adults only? Could children be excluded for the convenience of owners if the majority of owners so wished and the city council concurred? We all understand that the courts of the land consistently hold that a zoning code attempting to exclude persons of a particular complexion, of a particular religion, or speaking a particular language would be unconstitutional. But what about fraternity houses? To exclude them from all sectors of the city in which a college is located probably would violate some constitutional provisions, but restricting them to streets proximate to the college attended by their members apparently is reasonable, and thus permissible.

Sometimes the regulatory action can be ambiguous, apparently lawful but possibly stemming from questionable motives. An example would be a rather common type of zoning provision, one that limits occupancy of any dwelling unit to no more than x (a variable) number of "persons unrelated by blood, marriage or adoption." This means that if x equals five in a college town, then an apartment unit or a single-family house could lawfully accommodate no more than five students, since it would be almost impossible to find a larger group of students, all of whom are related to each other by blood or marriage. The authors have experience with just such a zoning problem (one of the authors was a council member; the other was chairman of the planning commission). When a zoning code amendment in the authors' home town reduced the numerical value of five to four, the practical effect was that no more than four students could occupy any apartment. Families, of course, were unaffected since the members are related to each other by blood, marriage, or adoption. Even more restrictive was the action of a small community near the State University of New York at Stony Brook: the value of x was set at two (*Village of Belle Terre* v. *Boraas,* 416 U.S. 1, 1974).

Were these actions aimed at students as a class? Or were they aimed at landlords whose exploitation of an inelastic market led some students to accept living conditions that most readers would consider unacceptable from the standpoint of both safety and health? Or was each explanation a partial truth?

The law of zoning continues to develop in response to changing needs and circumstances, and it would be risky to base opinions about a new case on the few remarks that can be offered here.

CHOOSING THE FORM OF LOCAL GOVERNMENT

As stated earlier in this chapter, municipalities operating under home rule may choose their form of government. They can have a manager-council form of government, or the strong-mayor form, or something else. They may decide on the size of the council, the length of term of the mayor and of council members, and whether elections shall be partisan or nonpartisan (except in states such as California, where all local elections are nonpartisan), just to name some of the decisions they can make. Local governments can decide how power will be divided—that is, whether the mayor will have a veto power, whether the planning commission will have final approval authority (this is rare) or have its recommendations be advisory only (this is typical). If a manager-council form is chosen, more decisions have to be made at the local level. Shall the manager have sole power to appoint department heads, or is approval by the city council required? Can the manager fire these individuals without council approval? What is the relationship between the mayor and the manager? The decisions described in this paragraph are only a tiny sample of those that will have to be made when a local government is being established or reorganized.

HOUSEKEEPING FUNCTIONS

The traditional definition of the powers reserved to the states and the cities by the U.S. Constitution was that they had the authority to protect the health, safety, welfare, and morals of the citizens. These originally were called "police functions," but it is more useful today to think of them as housekeeping functions. It seems safe to state that there is little question about the authority of local governments in the areas of safety: street construction and maintenance, traffic regulation and control, and police and fire protection. More recently, local governments have added the safety of users and occupants of homes and commercial buildings to their responsibilities by means of the licensing of building crafts (carpenters, plumbers, electricians, and so on), occupancy codes, building codes and inspection of electrical wiring, plumbing, occupancy, and fire safety.

Almost all cities have health departments that now concern themselves with the fluoridation and chlorination of local water. Some cities add chemicals to the water to eliminate iron particles and soften the water. Under the same umbrella of authority, cities maintain restaurant inspection, and many have provided a response to the AIDS epidemic. In addition, local governments must attempt to find solutions to the problems presented by old sewer systems, and by the disposal of solid and hazardous waste. Local governments today carry out a multiplicity of functions never dreamed of by those who created the concept described above; for example, life squads, recreation programs, paramedics, historic preservation, recycling—the list goes on and on.

What about noise control, or open containers of alcoholic beverages carried on the street, or topless bars? Do cities have the authority under the "morals clause" to outlaw such activities? Neither state legislatures, state courts, nor the U.S. courts have provided consistent guidance over time to be able to answer that question with certainty. Yet local governments, even when they are unsure of their authority, try to respond to the demands of local citizenry by approving or disapproving various activities, behaviors, and businesses. Local legislators are expected to be experts on very difficult and very complex matters, and many of the decisions they must make on very technical issues require far more knowledge than most of us have.

One of the authors of this book regularly attends the meetings of the trustees of a local township. In spite of the limited powers of township trustees, he is repeatedly surprised and impressed by the range of specific knowledge a trustee should have if he or she wishes to be reasonably effective. Examples include knowledge about road maintenance equipment, including backhoes, trucks, and snow removal blades; banking practices relating to borrowing for major purchases; or building construction costs or preferred materials—to name a few examples in three different areas.

THE NEWER USES OF EMINENT DOMAIN

When the U.S. Constitution was written, the Founding Fathers had experienced firsthand the misuse of governmental authority, especially the taking of private property without any compensation. They were determined to protect citizens in the future from this kind of abuse. At the same time, they recognized that government, as the instrument of the citizenry, may sometimes need a particular parcel of land for a public purpose, to serve the public good. An example might be the need for some land on either side of a river to build a new bridge at that location. But even though the public good required that a particular parcel of land be available for public use, there is no reason why the public that is to benefit should not pay for the benefit by reimbursing the owner from the public treasury for the fair market value of the land. The alternative, having the landowner bear the loss when the land is taken for a public purpose, would violate our sense of fairness. Thus developed the concept of eminent domain, whereby the government may compel the transfer of property even though the owner is unwilling to sell. But if the government and the private owner cannot agree on a fair value, the value can be set by a jury. Thus the owner is protected against dollar loss, and the government is protected against the risk that private preference could block a public project indefinitely.

In short, the federal government, the state, or the city may take your property, but it must be for a public use and you must be compensated for the loss. However, two key phrases are left undefined: What is *private property*? And, what is *public use*? While it is not the purpose of this chapter to provide lengthy discussion of legal definitions, it is worth noting that the concept of eminent domain has been expanded in recent years in quite remarkable ways. Below are some illustrations.

We might think of the urban renewal program of the late 1950s and 1960s as a stepping stone to the present. Federal grants were combined with local government's power of eminent domain to achieve slum clearance and redevelopment.

More recently, and in a topic area further removed from our usual understanding of government, the owner of the Oakland Raiders decided to move the team to the Los Angeles area, and, in fact, did move the team. Needless to say, the City of Oakland was upset by the move and voted to use the power of eminent domain to buy the team in order to keep it in Oakland. This raised the legal question as to whether a city could use its eminent domain powers to buy a football team. The case went to court, and the California Court of Appeals ruled in December of 1983 that the City of Oakland had the right to acquire the Oakland Raiders professional football franchise under its power of eminent domain. The court stated, "The acquisition and, indeed, the operation of a sports franchise may well be an appropriate municipal function. That being so, the statutes discussed herein afford the city the power to acquire by eminent domain any property necessary to carry out that function."[1] The California court had given the City of Oakland the authority to use the power of eminent domain to buy the Raiders football team. Unfortunately for Oakland, the owners of the Raiders simply moved the team to Los Angeles before Oakland could complete the purchase. Neither the California court nor the U.S. Supreme Court would agree that Oakland had authority to force the Raiders back to Oakland.

While the situation discussed next never reached the state of a formal action, an op-ed article in the June 4, 1984, issue of the *New York Times* argued that the City of New York should buy the New York Yankees, using eminent domain, because of the demoralization of the team under the ownership of George Steinbrenner.[2]

---

[1] *New York Times,* Dec. 30, 1983, I, p. 20:5.

[2] *New York Times,* June 4, 1984, I, p. 19:3.

The June 10, 1984, issue of the *New York Times* noted that the mayor of New Bedford, Massachusetts, had stated that the city was prepared to use eminent domain to buy the Morse Cutting Tool division of Gulf and Western Industries if that would keep the plant functioning and save the jobs of the plant's 450 employees. The mayor claimed he had legal support for his recommendation.[3]

A federal judge ordered the City of Yonkers, New York, to buy private land through eminent domain in order to build public housing that would end discriminatory housing patterns.[4]

Missouri, in 1984, passed a law which stated that, in certain cases, after local governments have approved a developer's plan for a site, the local government power of eminent domain may be passed to the developer. For example, the Kansas City Plan Commission approved a developer's proposal to use eminent domain to acquire and demolish four apartment buildings because the buildings were "functionally blighted and because they do not have enough parking spaces and are economically blighted because they bring in far less revenue than the [proposed] office buildings would."[5]

The Impact of Federal and State Regulation on Cities

There is one other topic that must be included in this discussion: the increasingly rapid and dramatic changes in the relationships among the federal, state, and local levels of government. The familiar name for this is intergovernmental relations. But however familiar this term is to the student of politics and/or public administration, it in no way conveys the full complexity of current changes in the arena of federal and state regulation of cities.

There was a time when it was possible to discuss the powers of the federal government and those of the states as if there were a fairly clear distinction between the two. It was said that the federal government had the authority to carry out certain functions; was denied the authority to do certain things; and that authority not granted to the federal government "belonged to the states or to the people." That was long ago. The following chapter will include a discussion of federal

[3] *New York Times,* June 10, 1984. IV, p. 2:3.

[4] *New York Times,* December 25, 1987, II, p. 4:6.

[5] *Washington Post* National Weekly Edition, November 12, 1984, p. 33.

grants as a source of revenue for states and cities, and also will discuss the mandates (that is, federal requirements) that the federal government can impose on states and cities in order to receive the grants. For example, in order to receive sizable funds for highway construction and maintenance, the states had to agree to limit the earliest drinking age of all citizens to 21. If a state did not agree, funds could be denied. Of course, states could refuse to agree to the federal mandate, but, in fact, it is impossible for states to do without federal highway funds.

An even more significant federal extension of its authority has come as a result of civil rights and affirmative action laws, which now forbid discrimination based on race, religion, age, sex, ethnic origin, or physical disability in college admission, housing, and employment, just to name three areas of interest to students.

Some observers have concluded that the concept of federalism, that is of shared power between the states and federal government, either does not, or soon will not, apply. In their view, the states will simply become administrative units of the federal government. Others view the trend differently. State and local governments may have lost their exclusive control over certain areas of responsibility (civil rights and highways, for example), but they are not without *political* resources to resist at times or to modify programs. State and city agencies and political leaders have created national organizations. There are national associations of governors, mayors, city managers, city planners, and other officials whose responsibilities are even more specific in focus. For example, an author of this text once conducted interviews in many states as part of a research project for the National Association of State and Local Food and Drug Officials.

In practice, the federal bureaucrats who allocate the funds and the state and local bureaucrats who expend the funds in support of their programs become natural allies, especially when federal funds are involved. The federal agencies benefit from being able to establish fiscal priorities, the state and local agencies benefit from use of the funds, the political leaders benefit politically from having the funds spent within their states and districts, and labor and businesses benefit from the application of the funds to the economy. Everyone involved has a stake; everyone benefits; everyone is dependent on everyone else. The federal agencies need to keep the state and local people on their side simply because the political organizations, meaning votes and voters, are at the local level. And the national organizations of state officials, or city officials, or agencies, are not helpless pawns.

As one authority has noted, the term "intergovernmental relations" (IGR) describes a process of activity, not a condition involving spheres of power, that involves federal, state, and local governments. He elaborates as follows:

> Whatever directions IGR follows in the coming decades, one theme . . . seems likely to be applicable to any and all future circumstances. That lesson involves bargaining, negotiation, and exchange relationships. . . . The effective public administrator . . . will be like a skillful architect-builder who realizes that IGR in the United States is like a huge, complex building under continual construction and reconstruction. The edifice has no single deliberate overall design or consistent architectural motif. There is nonstop remodeling and renovation, plus minor and major interior repairs; there is even selective razing and often whole new floors and wings are added. But the old foundations of the original structure remain intact. They have been extended with reasonable ease to support many more occupants and many new, varied uses to which the building has been put. Barring catastrophes or calamities, it appears that the structure will survive and remain useful in the foreseeable future.[6]

---

[6] Deil S. Wright, *Understanding Intergovernmental Relations* (Pacific Grove, Calif.: Brooks/Cole, 1988), pp. 466–467.

4

Sources of Local Government Revenues and Their Constraints

Chapter 3 pointed out that each city (municipal corporation) is a creature of the state in which it is located. In no respect is this more true than in the matter of local government revenues. Without the authorization of the state legislature, cities can do nothing to provide financing for their own activities. The state legislature decides which revenue sources can be used by cities; it decides the amount or share of each source the cities can tap; and it may impose restrictions on the purposes for which particular revenues may be expended. The state may designate (or *earmark*) a percentage of the proceeds from a particular state tax to be used by local government. In the authors' home state of Ohio, the tax on estates of decedents is so shared with local governments, and with library districts in particular. Most, perhaps all, states specify the number of cents on each gallon of gasoline sold that shall be paid to local governments for building and maintaining streets and highways inside the city limits. But whatever the specifics, the more general point is that an American city is not master of its own fiscal destiny. And the city of Camelot is no different from any other city in the United States.

The next section of the chapter will review the several sources of local government revenues—taxes, user fees, intergovernmental transfers, and profits from gambling or a lottery. Borrowing, usually allowed only for capital improvements rather than for current operating expenses, is not considered revenue because it must be repaid. The final section of this chapter will be devoted to the problems encountered in using the several types of revenues, and it will examine the constraints thereby created for local governments.

REVENUE SOURCES

The Property Tax

Property is classified for tax purposes into two types, real and personal. Real property consists of land and all the structures and improvements thereon. Personal property consists of all other property. (A subclassification of personal property into tangible and intangible need not concern us here.) Real property has been a staple of local government treasuries throughout the history of the United States even though its dominance has declined significantly in the past five decades. The real-property tax actually consists of a number of different taxes earmarked for various purposes and packaged together into one total tax bill. Thus, a bill of $1,000 for six months of taxes on a home or place of business might include monies earmarked for the municipality's general operations, for the local school district, for a community college, for mosquito abatement, for public libraries, for operating the county government offices, for funding mental health and children's services within the county, and for interest and repayment of some of the principal on bonded indebtedness incurred when the local sports arena was built.

In many states, businesses are also subject to personal property taxes on the value of their inventories, and the income received by local governments from such a tax is prized by local governments. Some states exempt inventories for items held for resale, taxing only items such as the firm's office furniture and computers.

A third type of property tax is that imposed on all the assets of a person who recently died—an estate tax. Clearly, this is not a source of revenue for which local governments can plan with precision, and it will not be used in the simulation even though the arrival of such distributions from the county treasurer is a welcome supplement.

Of the three types of taxes mentioned in this subsection, only real-property taxes can be locally determined, and that is why the Camelot city council may have this as an issue.

"Income" Tax

The word *income* in the title of this subsection has been placed within quotes to remind you that, at the local level, the tax is seldom on all income. Rather, for reasons of administrative feasibility, it more often is a wage tax that makes no attempt to catch dividends from investments or interest on bank deposits in the net of taxation. Although fewer than one-fourth of the states permit local government to impose a wage or income tax, the authors of *Camelot* have chosen to give that city the authority to impose an income tax in the interest of fiscal flexibility. Where it is available, this tax quickly becomes an important element in the tax mix. Unless the legislature has forbidden it, the tax can be levied on *both* residents *and* persons who reside elsewhere but are employed in the city. Thus its popularity with councils straining to cope with the costs of commuter traffic is quite understandable.

Sales Tax

A tax based on the price of commodities when they are sold is widely used by states, but use of such a sales tax for municipal revenue is quite uneven across the United States. Nearly half of the states have not authorized municipalities to levy a sales tax, and the cities that do levy a sales tax vary greatly in the extent of their reliance on it. A recent trend among the states to extend the sales tax to services as well as to commodities has its counterpart in those cities that impose a sales tax.

Sales tax revenues are of two types. The state-imposed sales tax is usually a shared tax. The usual pattern is for the state to keep a percentage of the revenues generated for itself and share portions of the revenue with local governments—counties, townships, cities, villages, and so on. In addition, some states have authorized cities (as well as townships and/or school districts) to piggyback on the state sales tax a small sales tax for local use.

It should be mentioned that the states often impose a tax on the sale of a particular commodity. This is usually called an excise tax, though as a practical matter it is simply a sales tax limited to a particular commodity rather than applied to a broad range of commodities and (more recently) services. Examples of commodities so taxed are cigarettes, alcoholic beverages, and gasoline.

User Fees

Fees paid by those who choose to use or who must use a municipal service are being levied more frequently for several reasons. For services such as water and sewerage the price may be used as a rationing mechanism. Those who use more pay more, and presumably the cost of the service becomes a factor in the user's decisions about quantity and frequency of use. (For reasons of administrative convenience and economy, sewerage volume is usually assumed to equal the volume of drinking water flowing through the meter on each property within the billing period.) The costs of amenities such as municipal golf courses and swimming pools can be borne in whole or in part, depending on the preference of the community, by the clientele using the facilities.

Some activities of local government do not lend themselves to user fees because the distribution of the benefit is a *public good.* In other words, there is no reasonable way to exclude from the benefits of the service those members of the community who might choose not to purchase the "good." Police and fire protection offer examples of public goods not amenable to user fees. Parking meters offer an example of a former public good—street parking space—that now is rationed by the installation of meters.

Miscellaneous Fees

Local governments often receive a share of other state-assessed fees, such as motor vehicle license fees and liquor permit fees.

Intergovernmental Transfers

An excellent argument can be made for the proposition that the most important change affecting cities in the past four decades has been the proliferation of intergovernmental grants, and along with the grants have come terms and conditions tied to acceptance of the grants. To put it succinctly, the grants come with strings attached. And the strings are becoming more numerous and more varied in their purposes. Grants to the cities may come through a variety of channels. Some come from the states, from the state treasuries; some come from the federal government, from the federal treasury; and some come from the federal treasury via the states, which administer the details and parcel out the money to qualifying recipients.

Borrowing

Most cities are forbidden by state law to go into debt in their current operating budget. Typically, numerous strings limit the manner and the purposes for which a city may incur indebtedness. The indebtedness usually must be for some capital investment such as construction or land acquisition (rather than current operating costs), and often the voters must approve the indebtedness by voting on the matter at an election. In addition, the referendum proposal often is coupled to an earmarked tax whose proceeds will be used to pay off the indebtedness. Alternatively, the indebtedness may be for a revenue generating facility such as a stadium, in which case the rentals will be earmarked to cover the incurred debt (that is, the revenue from rentals will be the security for the bonds that were sold to raise the construction money).

Gambling and Lotteries

State and local governments have been experiencing severe fiscal strains from two sources in the years since the 1980 election. First, the federal government has cut back sharply on the amount of grant funds distributed to states and to local governments. This cutback seems likely to extend into the indefinite future, for the huge deficits of the Reagan–Bush years now claim such a large fraction of federal revenues to pay interest charges on the federal debt that there are not enough funds to restore earlier grant levels. Second, the cost of operating all governments has grown faster than either the inflation rate or the economy (measured by the gross domestic product). One response of many states has been the establishment of a state lottery.

Thirty-five states have established lotteries as of this writing, but in order to overcome political opposition to the lotteries many of the states have pledged (earmarked) the proceeds to support education. Unfortunately, it is often the case that although the lottery-generated funds are given to education as promised, state legislatures then deduct equivalent amounts from the general fund allocation for education. The net result is no gain for education. Yet the general public mistakenly believes that the lottery-generated dollars for education are *in addition* to the amounts from the general fund that education has received in previous years. (A lottery is not an option available to the citizens of Camelot.)

Even more recently, gambling has been experiencing a growth spurt. Nevada's reliance on casino gambling revenues has long been familiar, and the glitter of Las Vegas is now a symbol recognized internationally. In addition, for many years in most states, betting at race tracks through the parimutuel windows has been lawful even though bookmakers are not. But casino gambling, long confined to Nevada, may now be found in Atlantic City and is spreading to riverboats and some smaller towns. Iowa, for example, plans to have its casinos run by not-for-profit companies that will decide how the casino profits will be divided between the city in which the license is held, and charity.[1] Mississippi has given voters in each river and Gulf county the option of approving or disapproving local gambling, and Illinois has approved riverboat gambling. In a move evoking echoes of the days of Wild Bill Hickock, the voters of Deadwood, South Dakota, approved a return of legalized gambling by a vote of 690 to 112. By contrast, Ohio voters defeated a state referendum that would have permitted casino gambling in the depressed former steel city of Lorain, Ohio, although the state legislature is now considering permitting casino gambling on Lake Erie and Ohio River boats. Kentucky, Missouri, and Indiana also are exploring this source of revenue for their states and cities.

One should always remember that in any such proposal there is a risk that the revenue potential may be outstripped by the potential for political conflict over the issue.

TAXATION PROBLEMS FOR MUNICIPAL DECISION MAKERS

Financial constraints that restrict our freedom of choice in various ways are a fact of life for most of us in the United States, and much the same can be said of our cities. The fiscal capacities of municipal governments to undertake and maintain activities are limited significantly by several different types of constraints. In addition, there are certain practical problems related to raising revenues that cities must face.

[1] *New York Times*, April 2, 1991, p. A 10.

This section of *Camelot* explores the nature of those constraints and problems, and it also looks at some of their consequences.

The Fairness Problem

Probably most citizens would endorse the proposition that for a tax to be fair, it must treat in the same manner persons who are in similar circumstances. The difficulty comes in determining what is meant by "similar circumstances." A cluster of similarly circumstanced persons who will pay taxes imposed on land ownership will not correspond closely to a cluster of similarly circumstanced persons when income is taxed. Sales taxes on consumer spending for such things as clothing, food, and automobiles will yield a third pattern of clustering, while taxing a single commodity, such as gasoline or cigarettes, will produce still another pattern. Since personal income is so important in our society, a tax imposed on personal income is likely to seem fairer to more people than a tax on real property, for some persons of substantial income own no real property. The income tax, in other words, casts a wider net.

The matter does not end there, however, for many (though certainly not all) citizens believe that a tax rate of, say, one percent applied to all personal incomes will hurt the worker earning $20,000 per year more than it will hurt an executive earning $200,000 per year. The reasoning is that the basic needs for food, shelter, clothing, transportation, and medical care need not be ten times as costly for the executive as for the worker. Looking at it from the other side, the worker's wage goes mostly or entirely for the basics while the executive will have money left over after the basics are supplied. For that reason, a tax of one percent on the worker will cut more severely into basics than will the same tax rate applied to the high income of the executive. The economists would say that the executive has more discretionary spending power. The remedy, if one agrees with this analysis, is to apply a *higher percentage* rate to the higher income. This will target the discretionary spending power of each taxpayer more accurately. In other words, the tax rate will be *progressive:* it will impose a higher percentage rate on higher-income persons.

Now we have the information to see two problems of fairness in connection with municipal "income" taxes. First, since municipal income taxes are almost always flat rate taxes, they lack the progressivity that many persons believe to be necessary in a fair tax program. Second, since most of the municipal income taxes are really single-rate taxes on every dollar of wages (there are no deductions), but do not include capital gains, royalties, interest income, and dividends, they clearly become regressive rather than progressive. Thus they are thought to discriminate against wage earners.

There is another fairness problem in the estimate of many (though, again, not all) persons. The real estate tax once was thought to be a tax that was passed on to the consumer, but recent writings have challenged portions of that view. Farmers clearly cannot pass a real-property-tax increase on to the consumer when the market for farm products is a highly competitive international market. Tax increases on farm land in the United States in recent years seem to have become in part taxes on capital rather than on income. If that is the case, virtually everyone would agree that this alters the intended effect of the tax, and many persons would argue that the alteration is unfair; that taxation should aim chiefly at income, not at capital. Our purpose here is not to argue that the real estate tax is unfair, for that involves questions of personal values, but we do argue that whenever there is a widespread perception of unfairness in the operation of a tax, that tax policy is in difficulty. An excellent example of this point occurred in California in 1978 when the voters approved by a two-to-one margin Proposition 13, a citizen-initiated referendum that cut back real-property taxes in that state.

User fees also create problems of fairness. The question of fees for emergency ambulance service is a bone of contention in many communities today. In small and medium-size communities the prospect of profit may be too slight to attract private ambulance contractors, and if the municipality chooses to provide the service a subsidy is almost certain. But should the subsidy be total? Should the users get a free ride in the fullest sense of the term? Or is it appropriate to impose a user fee to defray part, but only part, of the expense? Since a user fee will serve to some degree as a rationing mechanism, is it wise social policy to impose such a calculation on persons of limited means who face a medical emergency? The question is even more complicated because some citizens have medical insurance that could pay part, or all, of the ambulance fee. Are taxpayers who pay for ambulances in effect giving the medical insurance company more profit? Is such cost shifting desirable? Or should emergency ambulance service be a public good? These are some of the practical questions facing council members today.

The Competition Problem

All governments have boundaries that, among other things, limit the geographic scope of any tax that may be imposed by a particular government. This becomes especially important to the policy makers of states and municipalities, for the competition to attract new industry, new commercial development, and affluent retirees can be fierce. For example, a high tax on real estate may discourage retirees; the absence of a state tax on decedent's estates may encourage retirees. A high tax on real estate will be a factor, though seldom the sole factor, in the location decisions of industry. Indeed, many cities and states have policies that allow certain new businesses a real-property-tax abatement (reduction) for some stipulated period in order to attract new investment. Probably you have noticed middle-class housing located outside municipalities in order to take advantage of the lower tax rates available, since counties and townships usually provide fewer services than do municipalities of comparable population.

The consequence of this potential for competition is that municipalities are limited in their capacity to tax. Although there are a few exceptional cases of cities that wish to avoid or sharply limit population growth, most cities are constrained by the risk that a tax rate too far out of line with taxes of other municipalities could limit the opportunity to attract and retain businesses and citizens having substantial tax-paying capacity.

The Enforcement Feasibility Problem

Policy makers must give thought to the enforcement feasibility of any tax they consider. To illustrate, a tax might be widely hailed as extremely fair, but if the collection costs amounted to 75% of the total revenue produced, the tax would be a very poor bargain indeed. A tax that is easily evaded can corrode citizen morale, for it rewards dishonesty and penalizes lawful conduct. Taxes on personal property items that are undocumented fall into this category, which in turn explains why legislators prefer to tax securities, bank deposits, and automobiles—all of which carry title documentation—rather than furniture, watches, and jewelry, as was done in the past. By contrast, real property cannot be concealed or moved out of the taxing jurisdiction, which helps account for its importance as a revenue source through several centuries of our history. Nevertheless, there is an administrative problem in assuring that evaluations are accurate and the tax fair: there must be an appeals process for persons who think the tax assessor was in error. While relatively few appeals are carried forward by the citizenry, the potential for doing so tends to hold down all of the valuations. (If you think you received the benefit of the doubt, whether from a tax assessor or from a professor grading an exam, aren't you less likely to appeal?) Some states, such as Ohio, where the authors reside, have a formal policy of undervaluing, probably to encourage each property owner to accept the tax assessor's evaluation rather than challenge it.

Enforcement of income taxes is relatively easy because the administrative costs of withholding and collection can be placed on each employer in the same way the federal government requires federal withholding. Since the tax almost always is flat rate, with no deductions and no exemptions, the administrative costs are only a small percentage of the revenues generated.

User fees and licenses usually are easily enforced, provided that one is not dealing with a public good. Delinquent accounts may have the water shut off, people unwilling to pay admission fees are excluded at the doors, and licenses must be displayed for easy inspection.

Sales taxes are costly and troublesome to enforce at the local government level unless they can be "piggybacked" on an existing state sales tax. If they can, administration is easy, but the risks of competition discussed earlier may inhibit the magnitude of the tax rate.

The Problem of Earmarking

Earmarking a tax for a particular activity or cluster of related activities is a time-honored method of increasing the chance of enactment, whether the enactment is by a legislative assembly or by the citizenry in a referendum, but earmarking creates several problems. It is feasible for the more popular and appealing types of government activities, such as emergency ambulance service or parks and recreation. But other activities, perhaps unglamorous though important, are unlikely to be able to benefit from it. Garbage collection, street sweeping, and snow removal spring to mind as examples of this point.

The second difficulty with earmarking is that it tends to be inefficient and inflexible. It sets aside funds according to a certain formula but not in accordance with any current estimate of need. Usually the funds cannot be transferred elsewhere, even in an emergency. Moreover, if it should happen that the earmarked funds become inadequate with the passage of time, there may be some hesitation about increasing them, because, after all, the funded activity already has a special tax dedicated to it.

The Problem of Preemption and Mandates

Elsewhere in *Camelot* (see Chapter 3) we examined the legal position of municipalities and noted their subordination to the state in which each is located. A further illustration of this subordination is found in the doctrine of preemption, the doctrine that a state's entry into a particular field of taxation excludes municipalities from collecting a tax on the same subject unless the state legislature specifically authorizes the municipal tax.

Compounding the fiscal problem for the cities is the fact that the state can, and very often does, mandate a certain activity or responsibility to the cities without bothering to furnish funds to implement the mandate. One can only sympathize with mayors who may feel that they have the worst of both worlds: they are required by the state to spend scarce fiscal resources for a particular purpose, yet the doctrine of preemption may inhibit severely their city's opportunity to find additional revenue.

The Problem of Terms and Conditions in Grants

Some of the strings tied to grants may seem unlikely to chafe. Accounting requirements, for example, seem innocuous enough, but many municipal officers, especially in moderate-size cities, will contend that the cumulative cost of compliance with federal reporting standards, no matter how reasonable they may appear, is nevertheless a perceptible fiscal burden for the reporting city. Other strings may be welcomed because of their worthy purpose. To take an example that is not municipal but is likely to be especially pertinent and familiar to many of the people who read these words, Title IX (of the Education Act Amendments) was instrumental in opening up more opportunities for women to participate in intercollegiate athletics. That particular "string" was attached to the broad array of federal grants, contracts, and scholarships that connect colleges and universities to various federal agencies. Affirmative-action requirements respecting hiring, retention, and promotion are placed on some employers, such as universities, by federal-grant strings, even though the majority of employers in this country are regulated by Congressional legislation based on the federal power to regulate interstate commerce.

A second consequence of the increase in grants is that, paradoxically, the cities are losing some of their spending discretion. One must be careful not to exaggerate this point, but when a grant requires, as do many, a fiscal contribution by the city to pay some portion of the total cost of the endeavor for which the grant is awarded, then the pressure to give top fiscal priority to the grant "match" is felt keenly by all officials. The consequence, in other words, tends to boost the priority ranking of the grant's objectives, and some competing claims on the city treasury may have to be postponed.

Other Administrative Costs

To the casual observer, real estate property taxes would seem to be simple to administer. A value is placed on a property and based on that assessed value, the property is taxed. Unfortunately, in addition to the fairness problem discussed earlier, this tax is anything but simple to administer. The first problem is to get an accurate valuation of real estate. Property values are related to location. As every real estate dealer will remind both buyers and sellers, the three most important factors determining the value of a particular piece of real estate are location, location, and location. There is frequently a time lag in keeping assessments up to date. Assessed values are expensive to determine and thus surveys are often infrequent. In addition, the accuracy of such surveys may drift unless a recent sale has indicated the market value of a given property. These two factors—the cost of reevaluation surveys at regular intervals plus the inevitable risk of moderate errors of judgment in evaluating or reevaluating land and buildings—constrain the amount of revenue that it is feasible to raise through real estate taxation.

Problems of administration would multiply if the real estate tax were to be used by state government, because achieving reasonable accuracy in evaluations throughout the entire state would be much more difficult than achieving accuracy within a single county, as is now the case. The result is that the real estate tax in the United States is overwhelmingly a local tax, and a large portion of the revenues derived from it are earmarked for local education, K–12.

In summary, for American cities each of the several tax sources has its own type of constraint. Some taxes create problems of fairness and equity; some have problems of enforcement feasibility; others might have adverse consequences for local employers or merchants in a competitive market; and, lastly, the unavoidable risk of unforeseen consequences may dampen any impulse toward experimentation with a new tax.

The fiscal problem for cities is also complicated by the possibility that the state may preempt one or more of the cities' sources of income, while at the same time requiring cities to carry out state-specified activities to be funded by cities. Finally, while cities may find it helpful to receive income in the form of grants from the state or the federal government, the grant money typically has numerous strings attached, strings that direct how the money shall be spent and conditions that must be met before the funds will be allocated or continued.

5

Organized Interests in the Decision-Making Process

It is a timeless image: the hero rides into town, single-handedly defeats the corrupt and ruthless villains, brings peace and justice, and rides on. In the political arena, the same myth often seems to prevail, only this time it is the lone citizen who defeats the evil (a) utility, (b) politician, (c) industry, (d) all of the above. This scenario is not impossible, but it is very unlikely in today's highly complex and organized world. The reality is that organization of some kind is almost always required to get anything done. Thus students of the political process speak of the activities of interest groups, or of organized interests.

What is an *organized interest*? Any group of persons who try to influence the decision-making process. And the reason many scholars today prefer the term *organized interests* is because it is a broader and more accurate descriptive term than *interest group*. In the past, the studies in this area of research concentrated on groups that had identifiable membership. Membership lists were maintained, members paid dues, and the members interacted. The group provided a sense of continuity to its members and to those it attempted to influence. In today's world, this may not be true. Today scholars find many nonmembership organizations, such as corporations, public-interest law firms, and governmental actors (domestic, foreign, intergovernmental) operating in the political world. Other organizations are composed exclusively of "checkbook members," that is, individuals whose participation is limited to paying dues. There is often now a fluidity of leadership and membership, of techniques used to influence political decision making, and of means of support that makes the term *interest group* less accurate. Hence the preference for the term *organized interests.*

Another view that tended to prevail in the past was the notion that *any* outside efforts to influence the public policy decision-making process were not quite ethical. The term *pressure group* was applied to organizations that tried to influence public policy, and often the newspapers of the day carried exposés of the activities of such groups engaged in bribery, kickbacks, and fraud. Even if the effort to influence decisions was perfectly legal, the impression often was conveyed that it was not quite right to use pressure tactics. Thus labor organizations were criticized for supporting "their" candidates for office and after the election for trying to persuade Congress or state legislators to pass legislation favorable to unions. Even now, police or teachers are sometimes made to look like villains because they organize and take actions to try to get higher salaries or benefits. At other times, corporations are criticized for contributing large sums of money to the political campaigns of people running for office, the allegation being that they are "buying elections." And what about religious groups that attempt to defeat candidates who vote "the wrong way" on sensitive issues such as abortion or prayers in public schools? The list is endless. Taxpayer rebellions are often merely the activities of property owners organizing to reduce property taxes. Are the property owners who want lower taxes good people and police and teachers who want higher salaries bad? It depends on which side you favor. Most of us, sooner or later, try to influence the political process, to maximize gains and minimize losses, to increase benefits and decrease costs. Unfortunately, there are no angels—or at least very few of them—in life generally or in the political process particularly. Who speaks for the entire community, the entire metropolitan area, the entire state, the entire nation? That in a nutshell is a problem of our system. There are not many voices to express concern or mechanisms to act for the larger needs. There are such voices and mechanisms—that is one of the tasks of elected or appointed leaders (mayors, city managers, governors, and presidents) who are responsible to the entire community. Still, voters often get very angry with leaders who focus on the larger societal needs and call for the sacrifice of our personal goals, or our wealth, or sometimes even our lives or our children's lives. It is not surprising that our leaders are frequently timorous, vacillating, or even defeated at the next election. Not many of us are very good at or very experienced in the art of gracious self-sacrifice. Our system is better at interest articulation than at interest aggregation.

Quite clearly, it is not enough to answer the question "Who are the organized interests?" by saying, "Everyone." Some people never join such groups, never try to influence the political process in any way. Other people are deeply involved. As suggested in Chapter 2, the more political resources you possess (education, intelligence, social class, occupational status, income, vitality, and energy, to name a few), the more likely it is you will be active. However, a scale that predicts activity in general does not necessarily predict activity in particular. The fact that you have the time and skills to be active politically doesn't mean that you will choose to be active, nor does the fact that most people like yourself are politically inactive mean that you will choose to be inactive. Obviously, it depends on the importance of the issue to you, what is called the *saliency* of the issue. Few individuals, regardless of potential for being active, would demonstrate in front of the White House to save the snail darters from extinction. But if someone proposes that property taxes be doubled, many normally quiescent, even submissive, citizens can become militant lobbyists. Issues vary in terms of the number of people affected, as well as how intensely each individual feels about the issues.

At all levels of government, it can be predicted that there will be a positive correlation between having a stake, real or imagined, in the outcome and a willingness to try to influence the political decision-making process. Moreover, the greater one's political resources, the more likely one is to join an organized interest and be active in its efforts. The irony is that those who have the most to gain from organization, the poor, are least likely to organize, to join organizations, or to try to influence political decisions.

The next question that should be addressed is "How do organized interests influence political decisions?" The word that immediately comes to mind is *pressure*. Social scientists used to refer to the organized interests as *pressure groups,* as described above. This term conjures up scenes of lobbyists calling in political IOUs, demanding that legislators vote this way or that way. Yet the evidence does not support this stereotype. What does influence legislators? Are they persuaded by a deluge of letters and telegrams? By an angry delegation of constituents in their outer office? By threats of organized opposition at the next election? Assume that you are a legislator. What would influence you most? Would not your response be based on something like the following two points:

1. *Having a stake in the decision.* What is the nature of the issue being considered? Is it an issue you really care about because of your personal values? Do you think it is a good public policy? Or is it an issue on which you have no strong feelings? Is it one that *most* of your constituents care about so that a "popular" choice would help your reelection prospects? For example, if the prolife group is demanding that you vote to prohibit abortion clinics, but you are an officer in a women's rights group, then you probably will not care how many letters and telegrams you receive demanding regulation of abortion. But if the issue is a request for permission to build a restaurant in a middle-class, single-family zoned area of new homes, you probably will listen to your constituents no matter how you feel about the issue. If they protest, it becomes more probable that you will oppose the restaurant's request. This suggests that *legislators at all levels may have a stake in many decisions.* In addition to your own policy preferences, you, as a member of a legislative body, like almost all legislators everywhere, will be concerned about your constituents and your city (or state or nation).

2. *The importance of accurate information.* Another factor to be considered when analyzing the impact of influences on legislators is the complexity of the problems they face. Imagine that you are a legislator trying to resolve these examples of complex, though not unusual, issues:
   a. Should you support the request of developers to rezone a downtown tract so that a high-rise hotel and office building plaza can be built there? The building will bring tax revenues and jobs to the city, but it will absorb one-third of a public park and cause a historic church and cemetery to be moved.
   b. Should the police be permitted to use the more powerful .357 Magnum handguns, or perhaps 9-millimeter semiautomatics, rather than the familiar .38-caliber police special revolvers?
   c. Should a home for mentally ill men be permitted in a residential neighborhood?

These issues are not unfamiliar in city politics. All of them are complex and difficult, and all require complex answers. Here are some typical questions that need answering before any legislator could vote intelligently: What will be the impact of a high-rise downtown hotel plaza on central city businesses? Will the gains in tax revenues and jobs justify the losses of park land and the relocation of a church and cemetery? How does one weigh the costs and the benefits? How does the pain of seeing an ancestor's grave disturbed compare to the value of jobs created or revenue generated that can be used for social services? Who will benefit and who will be harmed by giving the police weapons that possess greater stopping power? Will the home for the mentally ill depress the land values in the surrounding neighborhood? How much do the patients benefit from a less institutional living arrangement? *The point of all this is that the main reason an issue is controversial is because it is complex (it affects different people positively and negatively), and when facing a complex issue, the first thing a legislator is going to need is information—accurate information.* Above all else, information is the most powerful weapon of any group. This is not to say that every letter or telegram of protest is ignored, nor that every angry delegation of constituents is completely discounted, but rather that a legislator is more likely to be persuaded by the group with the best data to support its position. In this increasingly complex world, it is the expert whose words command most attention.

Finally, there is the question of how important are organized interests? The answer to this question depends on the answer to two other questions: (1) What kind of group is it? (2) What kind of an issue is it?

TYPES OF ORGANIZED INTERESTS

Different authors have different typologies or classification schemes of organized interests. The one that follows may or may not be the best, but at least it will help you to see (1) that there are different types of groups and (2) that both the governmental level and the kind of issue will determine to some extent which type or kind of organized interest will most likely get involved.

Admittedly, all classification schemes are arbitrary. The categories created are never as precise as one might wish, but no one wishes to create a classification scheme so precise that a separate category is created for every example. The classification system presented here focuses on why the group exists: what is its reason for being, and who or what created it.

Institutional Groups

An *institutional group* is an organized interest that is intimately tied to the political system; it is a functioning part of the system. The army fits this category, whether we are talking about right-wing dictatorships, left-wing totalitarian regimes, or democratic societies. Maybe the Luxembourg army or the Swiss navy do not try to influence the policy process, but armies almost everywhere else are institutional groups of considerable influence. It is often the case that the army is the most powerful of the organized groups in a society. The local police force in our own country is also an institutional group, although it is, of course, far less powerful than its counterpart in authoritarian regimes. It is not merely their weapons that make such institutional groups powerful; it is that they typically have the support of the state or the society behind them. As with all organized interests, institutional groups such as the police may have particular goals of their own, some of which may be good for the police but not for the community. How much should the police be paid, for example? The police have dangerous jobs, no question. The police are essential to our internal peace or order, undoubtedly. Police officers get killed in the line of duty. Very true. But in the matter of compensation for the police, the police themselves are not exactly disinterested bystanders. Yet, as an institutional group, they are in a crucial position when it comes to bargaining. Their *inputs,* that is, their salary increase requests (or demands), can be included directly in the following year's proposed city budget, which is prepared by the mayor (or city manager). Institutional groups, therefore, have a distinct advantage. Police departments and fire departments, to name just two, are automatically included in each year's budget. Their requests for new equipment, personnel, salary, or space will go on the agenda of the city. Groups outside the system do not have that advantage. Their first task is to convince someone in the system (mayor, city manager, members of council) that their request deserves to be heard, let alone considered or acted on.

Note the rather effective bargaining chip of the fire fighters. The crucial nature of their power became very clear to the citizens of Dayton, Ohio, when, several decades ago, there was a dispute over salaries. Fire fighters refused to put out any fire in which human life was not endangered. Many buildings burned, and the Dayton City Commission quickly got a crash course on the topic of the power of an institutional group.

Associational Groups

Unlike the institutional groups, which have been described as part of the political system, *associational groups* are for the most part outside the system's official institutions. They are what their name implies, voluntarily associated groups of individuals who have joined together in an attempt to influence the decisions of the political system. While they are often quite unalike, they follow several basic patterns. And the methods they use to influence decisions also fall into patterns, although there will be some overlap.

One pattern is manifested by those associational groups that have economic orientations, that have a financial stake in the outcome. At the national level the financial stakes will be enormous, involving governmental regulations that can either encourage or hinder economic activity, as with FCC television franchises or FDA bans on certain food additives; or subsidies to build merchant ships, to carry the mail on airlines, to build locks on rivers for the barge lines, or to encourage farmers to plant more or less of certain crops. At the local level, there are economic associational groups that act much as do their state and national counterparts. They may be as large as a giant electric power company or as small as a local real estate agent or developer. When the electric utility rate franchise is up for renewal, no city or village is too small to consider from the point of view of the utility company. The utility representatives will appear on the scene again and again to try to win the most favorable rate from the city council. Land developers or real estate agents will watch local council and planning commission agendas carefully and continuously to make sure that their interests do not go unrepresented. The consistent theme is that of an economic stake in the decision. Rarely do these groups take an interest in or a stand on social issues or political issues unless there are economic implications. Real estate agents, for example, generally do not care whether the local form of government is strong-mayor or council-manager unless the choice somehow affects them financially.

A second pattern of organization and tactics is evidenced by associational groups with a philosophical or psychological orientation. As with all associational groups, membership is voluntary; however, commitment is usually emotionally charged. The groups may be national or local. Some, such as the NAACP, may operate at every level. But within this large associational group category, several subtypes may be noted: general-cause groups, single-issue groups, and ideological groups.

General-cause groups.   What sets these groups apart from the other associational groups is that their interest is reasonably large in scope. Within the confines of a category, they are interested in anything that affects that category. Environmental groups, consumer groups, ethnic and racial groups, women's groups, and so on, all take stands or try to influence policies whenever an impact can be identified in any aspect of their areas of concern. The concern of women's groups, for example, is not limited to equal pay for equal work. Nor is it merely the economic aspect of an issue that motivates them. Rather it may be the experience of discrimination and the principle of equality that motivates individual participation. Thus the range of topics addressed by women's groups will be diverse indeed: women's colleges, their role and their future; sex roles in the family; socialization of female children in schools; medical conditions unique to women. Whenever these, or any other topic that seems to touch on the concerns of women, are introduced into the political decision-making process, you may be certain that one or more of the women's groups will be heard from.

The examples listed above could easily be used to indicate the concerns of racial or ethnic groups. Note how many of the listed examples are valid if Native American, or African American, or Hispanic, is substituted for women. While the topics listed obviously do not fit environmental groups, they too have broad lists of concerns and can be heard taking stands on air pollution, protection of spotted owls, pesticide residues in foods, and preservation of the wilderness.

Though general-cause groups operate at all levels of government, ordinarily their involvement at the local level will not be extensive. The size of the city likely will determine the degree of their involvement, with large cities the site of more of their efforts simply because more local chapters exist in large cities. The primary focus of their efforts, however, will be at the national level because of the greater effectiveness for their concerns of national legislation and the possibility of media attention.

There remains at least one other subtype of general-cause group. What makes these interesting and different from the others is the way their agendas are determined and the range of their concerns. They are, in fact, probably the most democratic of the general-cause groups, and they have the broadest list of topics of concern of any organization. One of them is Common Cause, which has as its announced objective that of extending the scope of citizen influence on the decision-making process. The widespread acceptance today of sunshine laws, which require (with only a few exceptions) that meetings of public bodies be open to the public, is due primarily to the efforts of Common Cause. The organization also addresses other concerns, and the range seems to be widening, due apparently to past successes and to the membership's votes on agenda priorities.

Another such group, the League of Women Voters, is somewhat similar in method of determining priorities, but not in structure. Common Cause is a national organization, which began as a result of the inspiration and efforts of a remarkable leader, John Gardner. Its state and local chapters are very uneven in influence and in distribution. The League of Women Voters, on the other hand, has a highly decentralized structure with a very large number of local chapters on which are built state organizations and a national organization. The League's agendas reflect this pyramidal structure, for they are set by members at the local level or by their representatives at the state and national levels. Thus Common Cause has a dominant national bureaucracy, while the League of Women Voters is more of a grass-roots organization. The topics the League will consider can be of any kind. If there is a prevailing theme, it would have to be described as primarily middle-class and roughly middle-of-the-road. Thus, both organizations eschew issues that reflect extreme ideologies, and concentrate on agenda items that do not challenge the "system." The democratic system and the major contours of the economic system are accepted as givens.

Single-issue groups.   The most obvious characteristics of single-issue groups are their zeal and their singleness of purpose. They may or may not have structure, organization, membership lists, dues, and so on, but if there is one feature all such groups hold in common, it is their vociferously and continually repeated statement that "we are all doomed unless _____ (fill in the blank)." Single-issue members and groups decide everything on the basis of this one criterion. Candidates for public office are judged by this issue alone. The issue might be prayers in public schools, or the right to life, or the elimination of nuclear power. But it will always be this single topic that becomes the be-all and end-all of the organization. One joins such a group as an act of conviction; discussion, reason, and compromise become irrelevant. Single-issue groups operate at all levels of government. The passage of the 18th Amendment in 1919 by the Prohibition

Movement required tremendous organizational effort at both national and state levels. But Prohibitioners had been organized at the local level by church leaders long before the 18th Amendment came into existence, and local groups had for many years pressured city councils to pass local laws forbidding the sale of alcoholic beverages. Today's single-issue groups have also tended to call for action by national or state legislative bodies, although city councils can also find themselves in the middle of such struggles, such as when prolife groups urge local ordinances against abortion. One thing seems clear about single-issue groups. When they are led by determined individuals who are sustained by other institutions in the society, as with clergy leading the Prohibition Movement or the current antiabortion campaign, they have a staying power that should evoke respect (and perhaps concern) from all who survey the political scene.

Ideologically extreme groups.   A political ideology is an internally coherent patterned way of thinking about politics and government. Every social system is built on an ideology, including contemporary America, which is based on a combination of classical liberalism and capitalism. Ideologically extreme groups do not want particular policy changes; they seek revisions, often basic revisions, in the system itself. Since the reforms they desire are so fundamental, ideological groups have difficulty creating much impact on a society that is reasonably at peace with itself. Right-wing extremists, such as the Nazis, or left-wing extremists, such as the Communists, have been able to capture little support in the United States. Only when the cleavages in a country are so deep and irreconcilable that compromise is impossible and the ruling authorities cannot maintain essential services and order will ideological groups exert much influence. During the Great Depression in the 1930s such conditions did exist, and it is not surprising that ideological groups developed and flourished until programs of the New Deal began to capture the hopes and ease the fears of the American people. Most ideological groups are authoritarian by nature. They thrive on faith, especially faith in a future that will somehow be better than the perceived present. They thrive on media attention and, since they begin with a rejection of the present system, concentrate on either conspiratorial or dramatic actions. Trying to influence the political decision-making process is an irrelevant concern for them. Their goal is to destroy and replace the present system.

Ad-Hoc Groups

These are groups that spring up, flower briefly, and then disappear, usually never to be heard of again. They epitomize the term *organized interest.* They lack structure, permanent leadership, and organization. An issue brings them forth, invariably one that is emotionally charged. They are most commonly found at the local level. In fact, there they are probably the principal form of interest group activity. A group of neighbors gets together to protest a zoning change or to ask for one; other groups are formed to save a building or to stop a restaurant from being built; a different group tries to have revisions made in the city charter. Examples can be found in your local paper almost every day.

At the national level ad-hoc groups are not unknown, but they are not common. During the antiwar demonstrations in Washington, D.C., in the late 1960s and early 1970s, ad-hoc groups appeared on the scene, and they appear at times during congressional hearings when controversial issues are being debated, for ad-hoc groups are composed of concerned citizens who often are very knowledgeable.

Since this is a democracy, it would be comforting to report that the testimony of these ad-hoc groups is taken seriously and that they have an important impact on the policymaking process. At the local level this may be true, for an ad-hoc group may be the only group to testify. But at the state level, and even more at the national level, ad-hoc groups are listened to politely, treated fairly and respectfully, and are usually ignored. (An ad-hoc group needs to be differentiated from an ad-hoc coalition, which is a temporary collection of established interest organizations that band together to work on a particular issue.)

The reasons why local ad-hoc groups are more influential than their national counterparts are quite easy to understand. First, it is easier at the local level to gain access to political decision makers. Ad-hoc groups, therefore, have a sense that they can have an immediate impact at the local level. Second, a local level ad-hoc group may be composed in part of friends, neighbors, or acquaintances of the members of council, which means that the councillors may have fairly frequent contact with individuals who possess similar values and status. In some communities, all may be part of the same social circle. The ad-hoc group members, therefore, are not individuals who can be dismissed easily.

A third reason for the greater influence of ad-hoc groups at the local level has to do with the scale of decision making. In most cities

policymaking is a far less complex process, there is a smaller bureaucracy, and one can more easily identify who is in charge than is the
case in the massive agencies of the national level. One can understand
the feeling of helplessness that must overwhelm most citizen groups
who, as amateurs, seek to influence the political process at the national
level. A fourth reason is the widespread use of nonpartisan elections in
local elections. Without political party organizations to recruit and support candidates for election and reelection, to identify the salient issues and provide public discussion of and the setting of priorities for
the salient issues, and to protect the party members with an effective
organization, an individual representative is all alone. There is no party
organization to blunt the opposition's attacks or to rush to one's support; thus nonpartisan elections increase the vulnerability of elected
officials at the local level. At the national and state levels, the political
parties may not be robust, but they exist, and ad-hoc groups will find
legislators more concerned about organized interests that persist over
time, especially at election time. Legislators are less concerned about
groups that appear to lack staying power.

To summarize, the organized interest that can provide the best information usually will be the most influential. Legislators at all levels
have to live with and justify their decisions. Accurate information is
the coin of the realm in such situations. When a member of Congress
or of a city council is heard explaining to the media the reasons for a
vote, it is certain that behind the vote was a set of effective arguments
provided by one of the affected interests.

Legislators usually have great difficulty determining what is in the
public interest. Only rarely is it really clear, and when it is, probably
the issue is not very important. Most issues, after all, are fairly routine.
When there is a difficult decision to be made, most decision makers
will attempt to assess the stake that either they or most of the contend-
ers have in the decision. This is undoubtedly a more important factor
for local decision makers, where amateurs normally run for office, than
at the national and state level where the legislators and executives are
likely to be professionals concerned about reelection.

6

Implementing Democracy

POLICY INITIATION

The word *policy* in this section's title has a larger meaning than just a law. Technically, it includes anything from amendments to the U.S. Constitution, the Executive Orders of the president of the United States, administrative rules of a government agency, acts of Congress, city ordinances, to the mayor's orders to the police to put down a riot. However, the scope of this brief review of comparisons and contrasts between federal and local processes will be limited to the initiation of legislation, that is, to enactments of the legislative branches of the different governments.

Policy initiation is a somewhat forbidding phrase which actually means nothing more than discerning the need for a remedy or response to some problem or circumstance within the society and then proposing a particular course of governmental action intended to alleviate or remedy that need or circumstance. The most common descriptions of democracy usually describe only one type of policy initiation, that which comes from citizen concerns and desires and is then transmitted by the citizens to legislators for effective action. But there is a second type of policy initiation, a type which springs from sources lying within the apparatus of government. Both types of policy initiation will be examined below.

Citizen-Initiated Policy Proposals

At the local level, an example of a citizen-initiated policy proposal might be a zoning problem. Such an initiative may come from local interest groups, perhaps developers who want to build a housing development, a mall, or a gas station. Or perhaps an individual entrepreneur sees an opportunity for personal gain through rezoning, seeking permission to open a restaurant, a massage parlor, or a fitness center in an area that currently does not permit such activities. Possibly a group of homeowners wish to preserve the residential character of a neighborhood by making their area more restrictive than it currently is. The thread that runs through these examples is that the decision does not require either the city administration or city council to address the ugly question of "How do we pay for this?" The proposed policy may indeed force the city council to have to choose among contending groups of local constituents. That will be painful enough. But at least the issue will not involve the additional problem of having to find new money through higher taxes or through the reduction of an existing program.

Citizen-initiated policy proposals that do not involve money and therefore have minimal budgetary implications are less common at the national level of government than at the local level. Examples usually appear in the form of protests, such as ones to "save the spotted owl." The most noticeable aspect of such activities usually is their inability to win much more than media attention. While it is true that such proposals do not appear to have budgetary implications, it is also true that they tend not to be taken very seriously, or perhaps they are taken seriously only to the extent that, and as long as, they have media attention. That is the principal weakness of citizen-initiated proposals at the national level.

Administration-Initiated Policy Proposals

Many of the proposals at the national or local levels will not come from individual citizens or from interest groups, and many of the proposals do in fact involve money. If an equal rights policy is adopted to eliminate discrimination based on race, sex, religion, or national origin, then an agency must be established to determine whether the law is being followed. If we want to have unadulterated foods, safe and effective drugs, clean water and air, then we must establish testing laboratories and hire agents to enforce the standards. The same impact occurs in areas of occupational safety and automobile safety. Examples are in the hundreds—and so are the agencies.

The point of all this is that every need, every problem to be addressed by government, requires a specific proposal that can be considered, perhaps amended, and then approved or rejected. Where will the specific proposal come from? Most citizens in need will be better able to articulate their needs and their fears than they will be able to articulate the details of a workable remedy for those needs and fears. Where will detailed remedies come from? Who will develop and propose them?

Increasingly the answer to this question is, the staff members of the executive offices of all levels of government. Moreover, the staff members of the executive offices are responsible for most of the second type of policy initiation, the type that springs from sources lying within the apparatus of government. How does this occur?

The popular image of governmental bureaucracies is that their chief activity is regulatory, but administrative offices actually perform very significant information-gathering functions. This information gathering tends to become intertwined with the budget-making process in a way that merits close examination. When the annual budget (request for funds) is being prepared it begins at the lowest echelons. Each operating office prepares estimates of its needs for the coming year, personnel costs (including both the cost of additional staff, if any, and raises for present staff); supplies such as postage and stationery; equipment such as computers, desks, chairs, and filing cabinets; funds for telephone and fax machines and for transportation to meetings or conferences; and other items perhaps distinctive to the office and its mission. This request for funds is transmitted upward to the next echelon of the administrative pyramid, where it is reviewed alongside similar requests from other offices. Priorities are established by the supervisor, who then transmits the revised and consolidated recommendations for the several offices upward to the next higher echelon where these consolidated recommendations must compete with other consolidated recommendations from other supervisors in other parts of the administrative pyramid. And so it goes, ever upward, until the increasingly consolidated requests reach the apex of the pyramid—the central clearance point—the point to which all budget requests flow, be it the desk of the mayor, the manager, the governor, or the president.

But there is more to it, for if the request were to travel upward without supporting documentation, chances of the request being fulfilled would be slender. To increase the persuasiveness of the request, the administrative office will send along a description of its recent activities, its successes, its hopes for the future, and an explanation of how the larger budget request will help to realize those hopes. In short, the budget request will be reinforced by an annual report pointing with pride to the agency's accomplishments, pointing with alarm to the unmet needs, and suggesting useful ways in which money should be spent to meet those needs. The budget preparation process, therefore, pushing upward, as it does, information about needs along with suggestions for meeting those needs, is a tremendously important source of policy initiatives. Information and suggestions for program innovation or modification are thrust upward along with the requests for funding, until all reach the desk of the chief executive, the central clearance point.

The consequence is that the chief executive, the head of this administrative apparatus, has important resources of information, ideas, suggestions, and expertise. This in turn has led increasingly to the dominance of policy initiatives by the executive. At the same time, the legislature's role has become one of reacting or responding, not one of innovating. The chief executive has the resources that produce the new ideas, plus documentation of the need to take action. And this dominance—this near monopoly of policy initiatives—by the chief executive is one of the most important, perhaps *the* most important, fact of political life in twentieth century America. Thus it is that legislative agendas, at both national and local levels, have come to be responsive more to the priorities and policy preferences of chief executives than to citizen groups who are outside the government.

AGENDA SETTING AND THE POLICY PROCESS

While the preceding sections identified several sources of initiation of specific policy proposals, it should be noted that in the past several decades a somewhat broader set of concerns has claimed the attention of political scientists as they have pondered the question of how public agendas are constructed. How do issues become recognized as issues?

How do they make their way toward achievement of the recognition essential to getting a place on the public agenda for possible action and then, perhaps, move through successive stages of the policy processes of government? Here the focus is on how certain problems become political issues that claim the attention of government while other problems never become issues and never obtain that attention. Or, to change the perspective slightly, it is important to ask, who has a right to participate in the process of determining what issues will be addressed by government? Who will define the terms employed in discussion of those issues?

Perhaps the most commonly offered answer to those questions is that agendas are created by the interactions of groups of citizens, or *organized interests,* in the more common terminology. The term *pluralism* often is used to describe that interpretation. In a series of works culminating in his study of New Haven, Connecticut, Robert Dahl argued that resources are neither evenly distributed nor heavily concentrated. He advanced the notion of "dispersed inequalities" to moderate somewhat the impression of an interest group free-for-all that one could derive from the writings of some of the most thorough-going pluralists. But the difficulty for many observers was captured by E. E. Schattschneider in his remark that "the flaw in the pluralist heaven is that the heavenly chorus sings with a strong upper class accent."[1] He went on to argue that the majority of citizens don't or can't get into the system of interest groups.

In a highly influential book about agenda setting, Cobb and Elder offered an even broader view as they suggested that an issue first must gain recognition within the society as a problem, a recognition that may come in response to changes such as in demographics or technology; then it must get onto the discussion docket of governmental institutions, perhaps in response to the activities of interest groups. Last, it must receive enough attention within government to reach the stage of policy action or decision.[2]

Once a problem has moved onto the agenda, there are additional stages to be passed through as the policy process unfolds. The most widely used formulation of those stages describes a six-fold sequence

[1] E. E. Schattschneider, *The Semi-Sovereign People* (New York: Holt, Rinehart & Winston, 1960), p. 35.

[2] Roger W. Cobb and Charles Elder, *Participation in American Politics: The Dynamics of Agenda Building,* 2nd Edition (Baltimore: The Johns Hopkins University Press, 1983).

FIGURE 6-1   Forming Public Policy

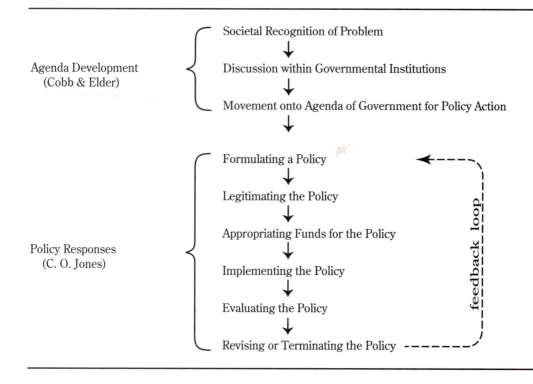

after agenda setting[3] (see Figure 6-1). First, *policy formulation—* articulating goals and drafting strategies to attain them; second, *policy legitimation*—gathering political support and achieving formal adoption through legislation, administrative rule, executive order, or some other means; third, *appropriating* (funds) *for the policy* in order to have available the necessary financial resources; fourth, *policy implementation*—day-to-day administration through use of the institutional resources of government; fifth, *policy evaluation*—determining whether the goals are being attained and analyzing cost benefits; and finally, *policy termination or revision*—revision that could occur through modification of goals or of methods for pursuing those goals.

Perhaps the most important point to be derived from an understanding of the process is that policy making is an ongoing process. Like the treads on a tank or a Caterpillar tractor, it is in constant motion, yet endless.

---

[3]Charles O. Jones, *An Introduction to the Study of Public Policy,* 2nd Edition (North Scituate, Mass.: Duxbury, 1977).

POLITICAL RECRUITMENT

Who Runs?

Political scientists speak of "political recruitment" to describe the processes by which a citizen is selected and persuaded to run for elective office. Sometimes it is a matter of self-selection and self-persuasion. Sometimes others urge the citizen to run in the name of civic duty or of concern for the party. Of course, not all government officials at all levels are recruited in the same way, but it seems that members of Congress and U.S. Senators display less diversity in that regard than do the council members of this nation's municipal corporations. Space limitations preclude an extended discussion, but at least the more pronounced contrasts will be discussed.

The most striking contrast between federal legislators and city council members is that, in all but the largest cities, service on the municipal council is likely to be by volunteers, by noncareerists. Most members of Congress hope to remain as members unless they have an opportunity to run for the Senate, but most council members see themselves as citizen volunteers serving a stint of limited duration, perhaps four to eight years. The council post typically is not a stepping-stone to bigger things; it is not the first rung on a political career ladder.

The congressional careerist can live reasonably well, even in Washington, on the salary that goes with the office, but most council members receive very modest salaries, in some instances merely token salaries. Why should they receive any more? Most council members in most U.S. cities spend only a modest number of hours each week on official responsibilities. Even in a city with a population of 250,000, annual compensation may be only a few thousand dollars—an income supplement, at best. As a rough rule of thumb one can say that the larger the city, the larger the amount of time that will be spent by council members on municipal affairs, but the relationship between those time demands on the one hand and salary on the other is very crude and includes some sharply deviating instances.

The time of day used for council meetings and the frequency of those meetings furnish useful clues to just how strongly the spirit of volunteerism imbues the council. Fortnightly meetings in the evening make it easy for the typical wage earner in the community to consider running for council, but afternoon meetings one or two times each week will discourage volunteerism and promote professionalism. (The word *professionalism* is used here to refer to the commitment of relatively large amounts of time, skill, and energy to council activities. Professionalism may be of limited duration, in contrast to careerism, which suggests a long-range pattern of activity.)

How are these candidates "recruited"? That is, what happens to them, or what do they do, that results in their names being on the ballot on election day? There is no single answer, but perhaps several answers can be arranged in such a way that a pattern emerges.

Individuals do not simply decide in the privacy of their rooms to run for office. Even the most ambitious and brash are likely to discuss the possibility with friends, with persons of political experience and judgment, and with persons who might be called on to help in the campaign. But often candidates are sought out by persons who wish to strengthen the quality of competition at the next election.

One reason why greater strength may be sought is for the purpose of filling a party slate with quality candidates. Candidates for the U.S. House of Representatives and the Senate run on partisan ballots, and so do many council candidates. But the majority (more than two-thirds) of the council members in the United States run on a nonpartisan ballot. By nonpartisan is meant that the party preference or affiliation of the candidate is not printed on the ballot. Does this mean that in more than two-thirds of U.S. cities (that is, in the nonpartisan cities) prospective candidates are solitary travelers across the political countryside? Not necessarily. In some cities, to be sure, a candidate's decision to run is unsolicited and is made in solitude. But in many cities there can be found solicitation and persuasion by some type of slate-making group which tries to identify able citizens and encourage them to run. That slate-making group can be a political party operating behind the scenes even though the form of the printed ballot omits the party label. Or it can be a group of citizens organized for some other purpose but possessing a civic interest. Examples might be a chamber of commerce, a community improvement association, or a labor union. Still another possibility is that the group may be organized especially for the purpose of creating a local slate of candidates. As an example, the authors of this simulation encouraged the establishment of a local slate-making group limited to former members of council, and one of the authors was active in that group for a number of years.

Whatever the foundation, it can help to structure the political process and make the selection of candidates for office less haphazard.

How Are They Selected?

The two-stage elections of Members of Congress and United States Senators—nomination in primary elections and then final election in November—are too familiar to require description. City elections are in many respects similar, but in three respects there are significant differences.

The first difference is that many of the smaller communities use nomination by petition instead of the primary-election nomination. Most of the time in a city of, say, 20,000, there will not be so many candidates that the screening (or winnowing) effect of a primary election is needed. A petition requiring 50, 100, or even 200 signatures will suffice to weed out the most frivolous or eccentric persons, and as for the rest, they can be screened by the electorate in the November election. Savings of time, effort, and money result from using this simple procedure.

The second difference is that nonpartisan elections give advantage to incumbents. Without a party label to assist the voters' decisions, the name-recognition advantage of incumbents is considerable. Another way of putting it is that nonpartisan elections reduce the ability of the political system to organize conflict around socioeconomic class differences or interests, and as a consequence the value of name recognition (and incumbency) rises.

The third difference pertains to protest voting and stems from the fact that most cities elect some or all of their council members at large. That is, the entire city is the constituency rather than a portion of the city. In addition, most cities use the at-large election to create a list of vote getters ranked according to the number of votes received. If, say, four seats are to be filled, the top four vote getters are victorious, while all the remaining candidates are defeated. This system permits voters to combine to elect someone they prefer, but voters would find it very difficult to organize to defeat a particular candidate. The only way to defeat Jones, for example, is to ensure that four others are elected instead. That is unlikely to happen. For that reason, minority groups may prefer the designated seat method of selection, where each at-large candidate must choose a particular seat to contest, or else minority groups may prefer elections by wards or districts.

The foregoing paragraph helps to explain two recent developments concerning at-large elections. First, when cities have occasion to review their method of selecting council members, there is a clear tendency for any changes in the method of representation to move in the direction of a hybrid plan. That is, the cities tend to choose a mixture of some council members elected by districts and other members elected at large. The number of changes in the past decade has not been large, but among that modest number of changes the tendency toward a mixed plan has been clear. The second development is that recent lawsuits have challenged at-large elections in some cities on the ground that minorities (and in particular, racial minorities) have been disadvantaged by at-large elections. The eventual outcome of this line of litigation is not entirely clear at the time this is being written. In those cases where there is evidence to suggest that there was a deliberate choice of at-large elections for the purpose of reducing the political influence of minorities, courts have found such behavior to conflict with the 14th Amendment's Equal Protection Clause. But as of 1993 there has not been a ruling that at-large elections are racially discriminatory under all circumstances. Thus far, at-large elections seem to be permissible unless adopted for reasons of racial conflict. What the future holds remains to be seen.

LOCAL GOVERNMENT ISSUES

A novice student of government quite promptly discovers that the processes of decision making will vary depending on the type of the issue or the problem to be addressed. Awareness of that fact suggests the utility of examining issues and problems typical of city governments.

At the risk of overgeneralization, it can be argued that the activities of government at the local level cluster to a significant degree around two major concerns: The first concern is to maintain the personal health and safety of the citizens; the second concern is to assure the security of property belonging to the citizens and to their organizations and institutions.

Of course, the human tendency to stick labels on things and put them into categories may lead to oversimplification, as can be seen in the case of municipal water supply. It is apparent that several different types of needs are met by water. The *quality* of the water is of critical importance to *health*. Through proper treatment of the water typhus and cholera are controlled, and in many cities the dental health of children has been improved through fluoridation. Water also is important to the *safety* of the citizens and of their property, because the *adequacy* of the supply and of the delivery system affects fire fighting capabilities in the city. (In addition to considerations of health and safety, the adequacy of the supply also affects the city's capacity for economic development through the establishment of new industry and through residential construction, both of which add to the demand for water.)

In addition to water quality, some other municipal undertakings that have important consequences for the health of the citizens include sewage collection and treatment; garbage and trash collection; hospitals in many cities; and clinics, particularly in target areas of widespread poverty. Ambulance service, at least in emergencies, is coming to fall pretty much within the domain of local government.

Personal safety is promoted through police enforcement of laws, through traffic engineering and enforcement, through inspection of new construction (often performed by local inspectors even when they are enforcing state building codes), and through inspection of rental property for compliance with fire and safety regulations. Property security is promoted through police enforcement of laws, through fire protection and prevention, and through regulation of land use so that one's own property will not be jeopardized by a neighbor who wishes to use land in a way that would depreciate the value of one's own.

Local government issues are smaller scale than are those at other levels—that is to say, the territorial scope of an issue is necessarily quite limited. Citizens are quick to express their concern about the appearance of a neighborhood or about a perceived threat to the lifestyles of the neighborhood when the use of a parcel of land is to be changed by the owner. However, many local issues, though geographically of smaller scale than the issues at other levels, are too large for a single municipality. Many issues extend throughout the entire metropolitan area. The authors recall, for example, an instance in which a city built a major new street that ended at an intersection with the street that formed the boundary line between the city and a suburb, but the suburb refused to improve the intersecting street because it opposed greater traffic flow through the suburb. Who can and will coordinate in such circumstances? Sometimes the answer is, no one. Sometimes the answer is that the central city, possessing the major share of a problem, will take some remedial steps even though you might think it better if a metropolitan areawide effort could be launched. Occasionally, in some metropolitan areas, government reorganization has been undertaken in order to address such problems: Nashville, Jacksonville, and Indianapolis are examples.

The topic "urban issues" tends to evoke images of conflict and debate, but it may be more instructive to think about the kinds of stakes involved in issues, comparing the stakes involved in municipal political issues with the stakes involved in national or state issues. For example, many of the stakes are more immediate in time at the local level than at the national or state levels, for the time span between decision and implementation tends to be short. A second characteristic of the local level stakes is that they are low most of the time for most people, in contrast to the national or state level stakes. (Students of public opinion would say that the "salience" of local issues is less than that of national or state issues.) For one thing, many of the stakes involve delivery of some municipal service to the citizens, and often only a single sector of the community will complain concerning the quality of the delivery.

It also is true that some categories of issues with which local government must cope seem to cut across the activities just mentioned. Race relations offer one example, and concerns for civil rights and liberties constitute another example. The problem then may be, not whether a service is to be provided, but whether its provision is distributed evenly and fairly. Such problems are common yet difficult to solve in many instances. They spread across the broad range of government activities. For example, should this parcel of land be used for middle-class housing or for housing that offers a subsidy to the poor? Do the police and fire departments try to recruit from minority groups as well as the majority? Are decisions concerning promotions for city employees made on a "color-blind" basis? Are the streets in poverty-ridden neighborhoods swept as frequently as the streets in middle-class sections? Are the police courteous to all citizens? These questions and issues arise one by one, in piecemeal fashion, in the real world, and it is only when we step back and try to understand them that we see the more general pattern that we label *race relations,* or *socioeconomic class rivalries.* Because the Camelot issues appear one by one, we have chosen a "direction of cut" for our analysis that parallels those issues. The question is rather like the question of how one chooses to slice a block of cheese: vertically with the knife pointed north, vertically with the knife pointed west, or horizontally. Thus you will find race relations considerations in some of the issues and not in others, but there is no package composed solely of race-relations issues.

Another way of thinking usefully about the contrast between municipal issues and issues at other levels of government is to examine the citizens' opportunity for access to decision makers and the decision-making process. Access at the local level is much easier and more open than at the state or national level *if* you are reasonably well educated and moderately skillful in interpersonal relations. But as can be seen, this suggests a class bias in the responsiveness of local government, for if a person is not so well educated or not so skilled in dealing with others, then access is, for practical purposes, closed unless that person can find an interest group in which to participate.

A final way to compare issues and decision making at several levels is to look at the responsiveness of government to citizen complaints and demands. As might be expected, responsiveness is significantly affected by city size: the large cities seem to have almost as much difficulty responding to citizen complaints and requests as have the state and national governments, but the medium-size and smaller cities often are much more adaptable and responsive.

By way of contrast, a large number of issues at the national and state levels cluster around income security—inflation, unemployment rates, unemployment insurance benefits, Social Security, and labor regulations spring quickly to mind as examples.

Another way of getting at the contrast is to point out that income redistribution is a significant consequence of national policies, but it is of only slight significance in local government policies. The national government has many programs that result in transfer payments. That is, taxes are paid in by some persons, or by most persons, and program benefits are paid out to others. Social Security is a good example of this; so are Medicare and Medicaid. Numerous welfare programs for persons in categories of need enlarge the list of examples. The point is that, in contrast to the local level where direct services (not cash) are provided to taxpayers, the federal government makes cash payments to the hundreds of thousands of persons, in some instances several million people, eligible for benefits. (In some cases the cash is channeled through another level of government that administers the day-to-day process of determining eligibility and authorizes payment to each individual.)

The reason why the federal level can promote income redistributive policies while local government cannot is that the federal government, unlike the cities (and the states, too, for that matter), has available to it progressive taxes—taxes that take money at a *higher rate* from the more affluent citizens; not just *more dollars,* but dollars collected at a *higher percentage* of total income. The personal income tax is the best example of this.

This, in turn, explains one of the most significant and apparent contrasts between national and municipal level issues. Cleavages, or political alignments, based on socioeconomic class are quite important in state and national politics but are much less so in local politics. Indeed, many cities have adopted ballots with no political party designation next to the name of the candidates (the nonpartisan ballot) precisely so that they can insulate city affairs from political parties, which are the primary instruments for engaging in conflicts based on socioeconomic class differences and preferences.

When the "stakes" of national politics are examined, it can be seen that often those stakes are quite high; however, they often are more remote in time and are likely to be more durable than local level decision stakes. For example, such goals as equality of opportunity or equal protection of the law can be implemented more effectively at the national level than at the local level. Any pressure toward equality will have a tendency to move in the direction of the national government's decision-making apparatus. Thus it is that ideological stakes are more prominent at the national than at the local level.

As for citizen access to national decision making, it is fair to say that direct access is virtually nonexistent for citizen-voters. Most people must make their wishes felt through interest group activity and through support of their political party. Responsiveness of the national government to individuals is negligible, so much so that when it does occur, it will appear on television or in the newspapers as an example of "the unusual instance that shows that democracy really does work."

7

Forms of Local Goverment

Nothing is very tidy in municipal politics. Thus, the forms (or plans) of municipal government include enormous variation. However, patterns do exist. It is important to understand that the descriptions that follow are only patterns—the political arrangements discussed are not carved in stone. You should also be warned that the phrase *form of municipal government* means the same as *plan of municipal government*.

The four forms (or plans) of municipal government to be discussed are weak-mayor and council form, strong-mayor and council form, commission form, and council-manager form. The description provided for each of these forms shows the typical arrangements (see Figure 7-1). An attempt will be made to give examples of the variations that have occurred.

The council-manager form was chosen for Camelot. It is a popular choice for small and medium-size cities, and each year witnesses an additional number of such cities selecting the council-manager form or a variant thereof. It seems quite probable that a basically middle-class community, with an educated electorate and a stable economic base (such as a major state university) would select the form of municipal government that stresses professionalism, good management practices, and the providing of city services. These qualities tend to describe the council-manager form. But before providing a detailed review of the council-manager form, it will be useful to discuss the principal features of each of the forms identified earlier.

FIGURE 7-1 Forms of Government

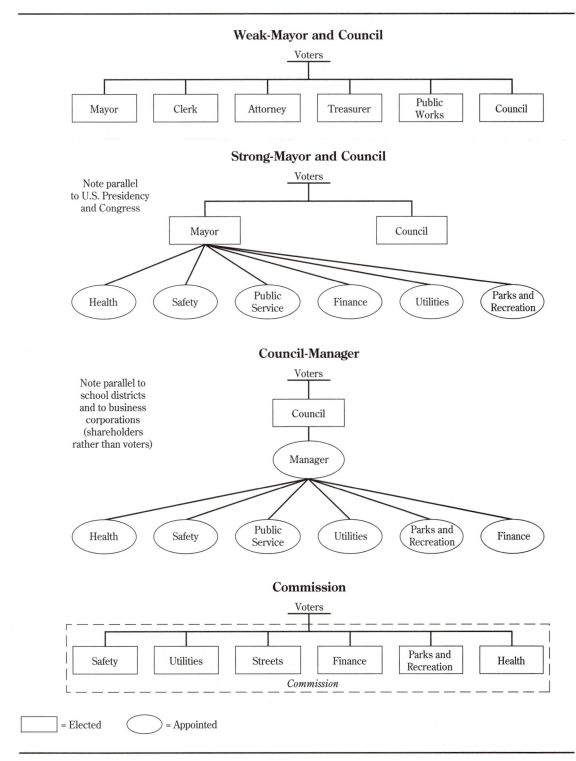

WEAK-MAYOR AND COUNCIL FORM

As part of the lingering legacy of Jacksonian Democracy, the weak-mayor and council form remains a widely used, but decreasingly popular, arrangement of local government powers. Its most apparent features are dispersal of authority and frequent elections. In practice this means that everyone (that is, every member of council and the mayor) has to decide *everything*. When carried to its logical extreme, this has required council approval of (and these are actual examples) the purchase of a dozen pencils, two flashlight batteries, a broom, and so on. The mayor has *no* independent powers. He or she may preside over council but has no veto power and no authority to develop a budget; he or she cannot hire anyone or fire anyone. The mayor may not even be able to prepare the agenda for the next council meeting! *Everything* is done by the mayor *and* council, which in practice means that a committee of council (probably including the mayor, although not necessarily) makes a recommendation to the full council for final approval. Who shall be hired to fill a clerical vacancy? A committee of council reviews the credentials of the applicants, handles the interviews, and makes recommendations to the council, where a majority must approve. The same is true for the hiring of a police officer or a fire fighter, the purchase of a water meter, or the resurfacing of a street. Members of the council thus have to make decisions that require a level of expertise that far exceeds that of the typical citizen. The result is what one might expect: amateurs are constantly making decisions on very technical problems, and supervision of the day-to-day operations of government is at best inconsistent and at worst nonexistent. The entire community pays the price. It is not simply inefficiency which results—that at least would be tolerable. It is often chaos. As an example, in one community the head of the water department knew where every water line and control valve was. The diagram was in his head. He had never put anything down on paper, even though council kept urging him to do so. One day he dropped dead of a heart attack. To this day, the city water department is still trying to find out where all the shut-off valves are. And it still is being surprised, especially when there is a water-main break. There you have the principal weakness of the weak-mayor and council form: the inability to fix or even locate responsibility. When everyone is in charge, no one is in charge. Decision making runs the gamut from infrequent to capricious, and is often prone to cronyism.

When the city or village is small, the inefficiencies are tolerable. In fact, the tax base may be so small that the citizens cannot afford to do anything but try to run everything themselves. There is nothing wrong with that. Government does not have to be efficient. It does, however, have to work, and when it no longer works, the citizenry begins to look for ways to correct things. After all, under this form of local government, the mayor and the members of council are, almost by definition, amateurs at running a city. Typically they are full-time something else: businesspeople, professionals such as doctors, dentists, lawyers, homemakers, skilled or unskilled workers. If the city or village is too small to be able to afford hiring professional administrators, it then is obviously too small to be able to hire a full-time mayor and members of council, pay them a living wage, and have them run the city. So amateurs run things.

As the city grows in size, the problems of running the city become more difficult. As the problems become more complex, specialists are needed to deal with them. In some cases, the citizens may decide not to alter the form of government in any basic way. All that is revised is the actual practice of running things: a city administrator will be hired to handle the day-to-day administration of the city, but the mayor remains a ceremonial leader and a leader of public opinion. Council and council committees remain as the real power—or absence of it. Thus when impatience with divided and limited authority becomes prevalent, the citizenry demands a restructuring of the authority in the city. One of the revisions could be the strong-mayor and council form.

STRONG-MAYOR AND COUNCIL FORM

One way of focusing responsibility in city government is to give the mayor more power. And this is exactly what the strong-mayor and council form does. Once again it must be stressed that there is not a checklist of items that must be met in order for the strong-mayor plan to be achieved. One looks for a pattern. Typically, in order to strengthen the authority of the mayor, and thus better to hold him or her responsible for what happens (or does not happen), in a city, one or more of the following powers will be granted:

1. Authority to develop and propose a budget (council continues to have authority to approve, disapprove, or modify).

2. Power to hire and fire department heads and immediately subordinate staff personnel (within the limits of the city's civil-service laws).
3. Veto power over actions of council; but council can override the veto by a two-thirds or three-fourths majority.
4. Authority to prepare agendas for council meetings.

There are other powers, of course: ability to reorganize the administrative departments of the city, authority to appoint investigatory task forces, creation of a separate budget for the office of mayor, and so on. As can be seen, the total impact of these items is quite significant. Possession of even several of them will strengthen the leadership ability of the mayor and enable him or her to identify goals and perhaps achieve them. The mayor is far from a dictator, however. Council still controls the purse strings and legislative authority, and must be persuaded by the mayor of the wisdom of any proposals. But at least the mayor should not have the feeling that she or he is hamstrung at every step of the way. Leadership is possible and, depending on the amount of authority granted, the city's programs can be administered in a coherent and responsible manner.

What are the weaknesses of the strong-mayor and council form? The people, of course, are the final authority in this as in the other forms of municipal government. They elect the mayor and the members of council independently of each other. And in their wisdom, the people often elect a council whose goals or personalities are in conflict with those of the mayor. Who, then, leads? The answer may be everyone and no one. Or more correctly, everyone tries to lead. Unless the mayor leads a strong party organization, capable of winning a majority of council seats and maintaining discipline over council members, there is a real likelihood that the diversity of the forces in the city, not to mention the independent nature of the independently elected council members, can result in conflict rather than consensus, in stalemate rather than objectives attained.

COMMISSION FORM

In 1900, a devastating hurricane hit the city of Galveston, Texas. Several thousand people died, and property damage was extensive. When the city government proved unable to meet the needs of the emergency, the state legislature appointed a commission of five local businessmen to run the city. The five men divided up their responsibilities and acted as heads of departments, but collectively they acted as a city council. The result of their efforts was so successful that the commission idea was widely adopted across the country. Unfortunately, what worked well in a crisis under the leadership of able and cooperative individuals failed to achieve the same results in the absence of crisis. The individual commissioners, with responsibilities as department heads, focused their attention and energies on their departments. Thus the design of the commission plan tended to create conflict and departmental parochialism, and it encouraged commissioners to run for reelection on the basis of their success as department heads. The needs of the entire city got lost in the process.

Interest in the commission plan declined, and increasingly cities turned either to variants of the strong-mayor and council form or the council-manager form. Some cities retained the commission name but changed the way the plan worked, giving increased authority over the day-to-day administration of the city either to an independently elected mayor or, in other cases, to an appointed city manager.

COUNCIL-MANAGER FORM

The remaining form of municipal government is the council-manager plan. It too attempts to concentrate leadership responsibility, but unlike the strong-mayor and council arrangement, which concentrates leadership in the hands of an independently elected mayor, the council-manager form removes the executive power and day-to-day administration from the direct control of the voter. This aspect is probably the form's greatest asset and greatest weakness. The voters choose, often by nonpartisan ballot, a city council in whose hands rest all legislative authority, whether it be approval of city ordinances, city budgets, or city planning and zoning. Ordinarily, the mayor has chiefly ceremonial powers and also presides over council meetings. Agenda setting for council meetings may or may not belong to the mayor. In addition to presiding over council meetings, the mayor does get to cut ribbons at the opening of new highways or city parks, hand out keys to the city to distinguished visitors, accept awards for the city, and announce officially recognized celebrations, such as the 14th Annual Pickle Harvest or the 125th Anniversary of the Landing of the Pioneers.

It is the city manager who has the real executive and administrative authority in the city. Appointed by a majority of council, he or she serves at the pleasure of council. It is literally true that the manager can be fired by a majority of council at any time, in fact at any council meeting. No notice need be given, unless the city ordinances or charter state otherwise. While it is not a common occurrence, it does happen that council will fire the manager without warning, as happened in the city of Cincinnati during the winter of 1993.

There are compensations, however. The pay generally is good. The city manager of Cincinnati earned $141,913 in 1993. *City and State*'s annual salary survey showed city managers averaging $111,654 in 1992.[1] And the job includes the authority to get things done. True, there is no veto power over actions of council, but the manager can hire and fire department heads and his or her immediate staff (subject only to civil-service rules), develop the city budget, and have a major influence (if not total authority) on preparing council's agenda.

As an aside, there is another source of influence possessed by city managers that is not often mentioned. Council is forever asking the manager to make recommendations concerning solutions to problems. The typical response of a manager is to suggest several alternative solutions, each of which has advantages and disadvantages. There is an old saying: "Whoever develops the options, rigs the game." Surely this is true. Whether intentionally or not, the options described and evaluated by city managers cannot help but reflect their values and, implicitly (if not explicitly), their preferences.

THE STRONG-MAYOR AND COUNCIL FORM VERSUS THE COUNCIL-MANAGER FORM

When the citizenry has agreed that the weak-mayor plan is no longer functional, why would they choose the strong-mayor and council form rather than the council-manager, or vice versa? There is no hard-and-fast answer, but there are some generalizations one can suggest. The council-manager form seems to be adopted more frequently by small and medium-size cities than by large cities. Does this mean that the council-manager form cannot work successfully in truly large cities?

[1] *City and State,* September 21, 1992, p. GM7.

Not necessarily. It does mean that the citizenry in very large cities seems to believe that this form will not meet their needs.

With only one exception, no city that had a population of more than 500,000 has ever adopted the council-manager form and kept it. That exception is Cincinnati. Other cities adopted the council-manager form when they were small cities and retained it as they grew in size. As of the 1990 Census, the largest council-manager cities are (in thousands, rounded off) as follows:

San Diego, Calif.	1,100	Fort Worth, Tex.	440
Dallas, Tex.	1,000	Kansas City, Mo.	440
Phoenix, Ariz.	980	Oakland, Calif.	370
San Antonio, Tex.	930	Cincinnati, Ohio	360
San Jose, Calif.	780	Fresno, Calif.	350
Austin, Tex.	460		

Another generalization we can make focuses on the diversity and the socioeconomic traits of the population. As a general rule, the more homogeneous the city population and the higher its education and income, the more likely is the council-manager form to be adopted and retained. The converse is equally true: where educational achievement and economic level are lower and heterogeneity is greater, it is more likely that a change will utilize the strong-mayor and council form. Why should this be true?

There is no single, definitive answer to the question, but one of the most important reasons seems to pertain to the process of building a majority coalition in a democracy. In any representative democracy a majority coalition must be achieved in the legislative assembly on each issue, and this process of coalition formation seems to be facilitated when the legislative coalition is in turn supported by the presence of a large coalition of voters, preferably a majority. (It is worth noting in this connection that a political party is an important instrument for building an electoral coalition and linking it to a legislative coalition.) The task of electing a mayor, like the task of electing a U.S. president, is an exercise in coalition building, and mayoral candidates spend much of their energy and skill piecing together the largest possible electoral coalition. Thus it can be stated that some cities, because of their ethnic, economic, and social diversities, appear to *need* a mayor-council form of government to help get agreement on anything at all. Other cities, less divided on basic values and priorities, can devote relatively more attention to problems of means, implementation, and administration. It is a difference of degree.

A second possible reason has to do with the perceptions of the citizens concerning their ability to gain access to the political process. Because managers (in council-manager cities) are appointed by council rather than elected by the voters, the several groups (whether religious, or ethnic, or class-based) may resent the apparent remoteness and insulation of the manager from the elective process. They want an *elected* mayor in order to retain the sense that they have direct access to the chief executive they elected. But this is only speculation, not fact. Even though it is very easy to demonstrate that managers are often better educated, better trained, and more skillful in obtaining compromise among contending groups than are most popularly elected mayors, it is nevertheless true that when there is conflict in a city, people seem more content with the system if they can go to the office and pound the desk of the person "they elected." This is true even if they didn't vote for the individual. It is also true that minority groups are particularly sensitive to this point. In a council-manager city they can never have the sense that a block of votes can be translated into a set of achieved goals.

Are council-manager cities more efficient than strong-mayor and council cities? Are they more businesslike? More professionally led? Less expensive? Are taxes lower? Services better? The council-manager form is often so advertised, and there are examples of it being true. Yet the reason may be attributable to the particular qualities of the citizenry rather than to the political structure. It is government's job to reflect the values and aspirations of its citizens, and if efficiency is what they want (and the community is relatively homogeneous), then that is what they will probably get. It is more likely true that a community will use the council-manager plan as a means to the end of gaining the objectives of better services, more professional leadership, and so on, rather than that the council-manager plan will guarantee that certain patterns will develop following its adoption. A community divided over its goals and values will not suddenly become united just because it adopts the council-manager plan.

8

Land-Use Planning, Planning Departments, and Planning Commissions

Many responsibilities of cities, such as police and fire protection, water supply, sewerage, and street maintenance, are carried out by administrative departments reporting to the chief executive, but one important activity uses both a more complex process and a special commission to assist the city council. The process is called *land use planning,* and city council is assisted by the policy-making deliberations of the *city planning commission.*

Questions about how land may be used are important for everyone. An owner would like to maximize the income from the sale or rental of the land. The more intensive the use of the land, the higher the potential rent or sale value. By "intensity of use" we mean the degree to which the value of a particular use approaches the theoretical maximum value under any conceivable use. Thus, duplex housing is a more intensive use than single-family dwellings, and a supermarket is a more intensive use than housing, even when that housing is a multi-family structure. Conflicts may arise when one owner sees opportunity for a more intensive use that would diminish the value of neighboring properties, such as a gas station being placed next door to your home. Economists would say that the gas station imposes "negative externalities" (that is, spillover effects) on the properties around it.

Generally speaking, municipal corporations have substantial powers to regulate and influence land use within their boundaries, and substantial economic stakes can hinge on those decisions. To assist in the decisions, a city such as Camelot will have both a Planning Department and a Planning Commission. The *Planning Department* collects and analyzes information about such matters as population trends, economic activities within the city and region, skills within the labor force, water supply quantity and quality, electricity costs, and centrality to markets. Information of that sort can be useful in economic forecasting, helping to attract or retain jobs and investment capital for the city. The department's professional staff also maintains data on the use for each parcel of land within the city boundaries. From data on the present uses of land and data on economic and population trends, the professional staff estimates growth rates and patterns. The city government then is in a better position to assist and shape the growth patterns. The two most important ways of shaping growth and development are through *public capital investment* and through *land-use zoning*. Public capital investment can be used for purposes that may include upgrading of major street arteries, new streets, improvements and extensions of water supply and sewerage, locations for parks and recreation, sports arenas, and convention centers.

In addition to public capital investment, development patterns within cities are influenced through zoning regulations. The zoning code (that is, the assembled regulations) describes the various ways in which land may be used within a particular sector, or *zone,* of the city. Uses that are omitted from the description of a particular zone are, by implication, prohibited in that zone.

In addition, to clarify our meaning, the zoning code at times may explicitly prohibit a particular land use in a particular zone. Along with identification of the types of use permitted, zoning codes often specify minimum dimensions for lots, minimum and/or maximum dimensions for structures, minimum dimensions for yards in residential districts, parking spaces, and other desired matters. Of course, zoning codes restrict the "right" of property owners to use property in whatever way an owner may wish. The U.S. Supreme Court has upheld such restriction against constitutional challenge by pointing out that zoning can stabilize property values within the zone by enabling all owners to ascertain the range of uses possible in the zone. Thus you can be assured before you break ground for your new house that the lot owner next door cannot construct or operate a laundromat there (unless, of course, you chose to build in a commercial zone). When each owner gives up some freedom, the remaining freedoms to use and enjoy one's property are reinforced.

It is clear that the process of determining what types of uses should be permitted in which sectors of a city involves policy issues of great sensitivity around which may swirl strong interests and concerns. It is too important and sensitive to be left to the administrative professionals in the city's planning department. At the same time, the already crowded agenda of city council has little room for the numerous zoning and planning matters that come up for resolution. Establishing a *city planning commission* is the response that has been most widely used in the cities of this nation. The planning commission, typically composed of citizens appointed either by the mayor or by the council, is in effect a screening committee for the council. Through concentration on one type of issue, the citizens on the planning commission develop a degree of expertise and understanding that the council, with its broader responsibilities, cannot attain. For that reason, planning commission recommendations to council are adopted much more often than not.

The overall process of planning for the city's future calls on the resources of the planning department as well as the planning commission. The major tasks of the planning department include assisting the planning commission and the council in goal setting and standard setting, and applying those goals and standards to particular situations. The role of the planning department staff is especially important in developing the information on which long-range goals can be based. Those goals, and more detailed identification of means for attaining those goals, will go into the city's *comprehensive plan.* The comprehensive plan includes a description and assessment of present economic and social conditions, geographic circumstances, resources available and resources desired (such as cultural, educational, transportation, health, commercial), and any other matters that may be pertinent to the particular situation of the city. One important purpose of the comprehensive plan is to match those strategic resources to the goals of the plan and, in the process, identify other needed resources. The comprehensive plan includes a *zoning map,* which actually is part of the zoning code, showing the zone (that is, land-use category) for every portion of the city. Suggestions for alteration of the zoning map may develop as the master plan is considered and prospects for growth and change are identified.

Enforcement of standards of the zoning code is an administrative process lodged somewhere in each city's administrative structure, though usually not in the planning department. The most important tool of enforcement is the requirement that a building permit be required for any construction or remodeling of any structure in the city. Since failure to obtain a permit may place both the property owner and the construction contractor at risk, and since the permit will not be issued by the city's permit office until the plans are checked against the zoning code for adequacy of lot dimensions, building dimensions, legality of proposed use, and any other pertinent constraints, the permit process is very useful for enforcement.

Finally, a word about possible exceptions to the operation of the zoning code is in order. Every piece of land on this earth is, of course, unique. No other parcel has precisely the same location, and few parcels have identical buildings placed on them. That being the case, how should claims for adjustment of the zoning code be handled when only a single parcel is affected? "Spot zoning," that is, changing the zone boundaries for a single parcel, is widely condemned. An alternative procedure is to allow for the possibility of a *zoning variance* whereby a specific, narrowly defined adjustment of the zoning regulations, as applied to that parcel, can be made. Such adjustments often are quite minor, as for example a reduction of the sideyard minimum requirement by six inches so that a car port of standard size can be built. But some requests for a variance may be quite significant, even to the point of generating substantial opposition from owners or renters in the affected area.

In many cities the consideration of applications for variances will be the responsibility of a special board, often called, simply and accurately, the Zoning Appeals Board. The ZAB may consider requests for variances because of "hardship," except that decisions based on *economic* hardship usually are forbidden by the city charter. Otherwise, the greed of some property owners could give the zoning map the appearance of Swiss cheese.

PART TWO

Simulating Political Decision Making

WELCOME TO CAMELOT

You are about to enter a magic place. "That's ridiculous," say the cynics among you. "It is just a game of some sort. A mixture, no doubt, of the high school 'mayor for a day' and Monopoly." You may be in for a surprise. This is a simulation of a part of a city government. It has been developed and revised over a twenty-year period, and the consistent response has been enthusiasm by those who have participated. It is called *Camelot,* after the city of King Arthur legends, the difference being that it is a city of the present and future, not the past. In describing the features of the city of Camelot (middle-class, integrated, and of medium size), the possible future is being predicted.

The question frequently asked in any city is: "Who is running things around here?" During this simulation of local politics in Camelot, *you will run the government.* Within a few constraints to be described later, you can do as you think best.

9

Introduction to Simulation

WHY A SIMULATION?

A persistent complaint by students is that the classroom does not seem to provide a sense of reality. "This theory is well and good, but what *really* happens?" is a familiar criticism. And that is exactly where a simulation comes in. It is the nearest thing we have to a laboratory. It is an attempt to create a situation that is like the real world, to simulate reality. You may have had experience in a simulation before, or perhaps you have played a game that was an attempt to provide an illustration of the real world. But Camelot is different from a typical game and different from a gaming simulation. It is a role-playing simulation. It involves a city council and a planning commission in a medium-size city integrated in race and socioeconomic class. The simulation requires you to play a particular role as realistically as you can. More on this topic will be presented later in the instructions. For the moment, it is important for you to understand the difference between a game or gaming simulation and a role-playing simulation. In a game there are prescribed boundaries, there are set rules, there are winners and losers, each of whom knows what can be won or lost. The combination of luck and skill, used within the parameters and rules of the game, determines who wins. And winning is not ambiguous. One knows whether one wins or loses.

In a role-playing simulation, as in real life, things are never quite that simple. Sometimes it isn't clear who are the winners and who are the losers; sometimes you lose by winning, or win by losing; sometimes you don't know whether you won or lost. It is this ambiguity that makes Camelot so realistic.

Of course, there are limits to what may be simulated. For example, most simulations rule out criminal behavior, as does Camelot. There really is no way to simulate the passions and intensity of fear that swirl around criminal transactions. Similarly, friendships and longstanding loyalties cannot match in the short span of a simulation the importance that they sometimes carry in real-life behaviors. Thus, although we cannot simulate passions, and although we choose not to try to simulate criminal behaviors, we can and do simulate the pursuit of interests by lawful and rational means. The interests, or stakes, will be varied, and the resources available to various members of the community as they pursue those interests and stakes will be diverse.

There is one other aspect to which we should alert you: Camelot is not only like reality, *it develops a reality all its own.* The decisions one must make, the responsibilities that come with the role, the duties of the office, the pressures of one's constituents—all are real. Truly real. You don't play at being a member of city council, you are *in fact a member of council,* and you have duties and obligations, just as everyone else in the simulation has. Camelot, you discover, *exists!* And the consequences of this discovery are always exciting and sometimes painful. There is no such thing as escaping from the pressures of a role.

Each year, the unanimous reaction of participants has been surprise at how much they learned about how city governments really operate.

The only constraints are the following:

1. One cannot violate the laws of the state and nation.
2. One is constrained by the city charter and city ordinances (especially the budget and zoning ordinances).
3. One must remain within the bounds of realism.
4. One must remain within one's role.

Thus, you cannot solve city budgetary problems by having the police agree to a pay cut or by winning the state lottery! Your instructor serves as the judge at all times, to halt the proceedings if things become illegal or unrealistic. But fear not. These constraints only make the simulation more real, and the inventiveness of the human mind and the variety of human activity are quite remarkable. Following are just a few illustrations to dramatize the kinds of things that have happened in previous simulations.

In one simulation, the city manager just disappeared! Literally! It was the day the budget was to be presented to council, and there was no sign of the city manager. Council went on to other business while other members of the class made frantic phone calls, and the assistant city manager (understandably) even went to the apartment of the city manager. There was no sign of him. So, the assistant city manager was named acting manager by city council, and then he struggled to become familiar with a budget from which the manager had excluded him during the preparation. Of course, *The Camelot Daily News* had headline stories, suggesting everything from foul play to embezzlement of city funds. But the assistant city manager had a learning and growth experience he will never forget. (The city manager, by the way, never did appear in class again. We later learned that he had withdrawn from school and didn't bother to tell anyone.)

In another instance, the newspaper reported that a councilwoman and the fire chief had shared a table for two at a local bistro. The councilwoman found to her surprise that she was quite angered by the story.

Still another time the police wanted a pay raise, and the chief reported a very high incidence of planned absenteeism. The newspaper then called attention to a wave of burglaries taking place in the central business district, with the merchants demanding more police protection, while at the same time the residents of the poorer neighborhoods were complaining about the inadequacy of police protection! Can you guess how that episode turned out? What would you have done, if you had been on the city council?

These are just three examples of the kinds of unexpected events that occur in *Camelot*. There are dozens of other equally intriguing episodes created by members of the class. They reveal dramatically how unlike a game this role-playing simulation is. Remember the four basic constraints, and then use your imagination. The simulation will become very real for you if you work hard at playing your role.

WHAT TO LOOK FOR

Textbooks and lectures can never fully convey to you how things really work in a democratic society. All the words used to describe organized interests (or pressure groups), the role of mayor, powers of council, duties of the city manager, influence of key leaders, are just that—words. It is easy for citizens to view events in city affairs as all predetermined, or rigged, if you like. It is probably difficult for you to believe that planning commission recommendations and council actions are rarely predictable and may seem to defy explanation.

As the simulation progresses there are several questions that you should ask yourself constantly, for they will help you to understand the process in which you are involved.

a. What is it that I am seeing?
b. What is going on here that I did not expect?
c. Is this simulation like real life? If not, how does it differ?
d. Why are things happening the way they are?

OTHER THINGS TO KEEP IN MIND

The most important ingredient in the simulation is you. The simulation is like life. It will be as good as *you* make it. If the simulation succeeds, it will be because you made it succeed. If it fails, you are the cause. You will, to your astonishment, make a difference. That is the most exciting, yet perhaps sobering, aspect.

It is absolutely essential that you stay within your role. You are not playing yourself. You are playing a role. Thus Camelot is no upper middle-class suburb, where all "us good citizens" live. It is heterogeneous, especially in terms of race and ethnicity, but also in terms of class. In short, different kinds of people are living in one city, having to face the realities of conflict in values. In order to dramatize this, there are various types of people in the simulation. *Read your role description very carefully.* Ask yourself how that person would think, how would he or she respond to the issues you have to face? Remember: You are *not* playing yourself. Read and reread the description of the person you are playing. You are constrained by that person's value system and by the responsibilities resulting from your official capacity, whatever it is.

The descriptions of each area in the city are very important, and so is the map. Read both of them carefully and refer to them. The newspaper will keep you informed about zoning changes under consideration or proposed. You must decide whether the proposed change will have an impact on where you live or work.

If you are chosen to play one of the more important roles, your presence in class is essential. As in real life, when key people are missing, things happen or sometimes fail to happen. A council member in one simulation was casual about attendance. A recall election was held, and he was voted out of office, but not before causing many problems for officials and citizens by his absences! The City Charter, in fact, states that a council office is automatically vacated by two consecutive, unexcused absences by a member of council (Section 2.02).

As you plan your strategy to achieve some objective, whether it is to obtain increased funding for a city program, a revision in the zoning of an area, or approval to permit waitresses in your bar to be topless, you should ask yourself who might support you. Politics is the art of the possible, and what is possible is typically determined by coalitions. Think about who would be a logical ally, talk with him or her, and find out if support can be gained.

10

Starting the Simulation

HOW TO USE THE MATERIALS

1. Role Request Form (p. 209). Your instructor may ask you to fill out the form and return it in order to match student interests to simulation roles.

2. Role Descriptions (pp. 182–207). Become thoroughly familiar with the description of your role in the simulation. Look at the other role descriptions to get a sense of what the other citizens of Camelot are like, where they live, and where they work. There may be some role descriptions that are not used in your simulation, but by referring to the set of role descriptions, you can find the role of each class member.

3. Maps (inside the covers), Economic and Demographic Data (pp. 162–163), City-Area Descriptions (pp. 163–167). Here you will find the basic information about the community, its geography, economic base, and social composition. You will note that the information is organized by named city areas, and, of course, these areas are likely to have significance during the simulation.

   Before the simulation begins you should read through the descriptions of each city area and find the map locations described. The map is drawn approximately to scale, and you will be able to use it to estimate distances and compass directions. You will want to be especially aware of the characteristics of your own area.

4. Council Proceedings (p. 101). This page of information is of special importance to council members, the manager, and the clerk, all of

whom should become thoroughly familiar with it. The page will be of passing interest to council observers. Planning commission members probably will find it a useful guide for their own meetings.

5. Nominating Petition (p. 211). Your instructor will announce a date for elections to council and also will identify the council members whose terms are expiring. *Each candidate, whether incumbent or not, must be nominated by a properly executed nominating petition.* Information about eligibility and procedure is to be found on each petition form. There is no limit to the number of candidates who may run for council. Also, there is no limit to the number of petitions a citizen may sign.

   Petitions must be deposited with the city clerk no later than the close of the last simulation session before election day.

HOW TO BEGIN

To begin the simulation, the council members take their seats at the front of the council chamber, the instructor designates a mayor pro tem to preside until council has selected a mayor, the mayor pro tem calls the meeting to order (see p. 101) and proceeds to follow the agenda (see p. 104) until such time as he or she is able to transfer the gavel to a duly chosen mayor.

Agendas for the first two meetings of council are included in the simulation package (see pp. 104–105). Thereafter, each agenda will be prepared by the clerk in consultation with the mayor and the manager and distributed to city officials and posted on the municipal bulletin board. (If no clerk has been appointed, the manager will prepare agendas.)

Simulation Time and Real Time

Two weeks are presumed to have elapsed between simulation sessions, regardless of how much real time has passed.

The newspaper's publication schedule requires the players to exercise their imaginations a bit. Since the newspaper can publish only one issue between council meetings, that issue must be presumed to cover all pertinent events and matters of the simulated fortnight, but the coverage *is in the style of a daily paper.* The same is true of the radio/television news reporters.

SAMPLE ROLE-REQUEST FORM

[Use the tear-out located on page 209.]

NAME_____

In the simulation, I prefer:

1. *An active role.* I understand that this role may well involve some time out-side of class as well as public activity in class. I also realize that if I accept an active role, it is necessary that I attend class regularly on simulation days. (Examples are city manager, mayor, member of council, clerk of council, the newspaper roles, the newscaster.)

2. *A semiactive role.* I understand that these roles could also involve some time outside of class, but less than that of an active role. My activities in class will not be so public, except when I am involved in a particular issue. These roles also require my presence during days of simulation. (Examples are chief of police, city planning commission, the ministers, the attorneys, the developers.)

3. *A more modest role.* I understand that these roles will not require much out-of-class time, unless I choose to be involved. There is generally much less public involvement, but I will not be anonymous. My presence is essen-tial when there is a particular issue that involves me, but otherwise my pres-ence is desirable but not essential to the simulation.

4. *A small role.* I understand that these are roles that will make me part of a group of which someone else may be leader and spokesperson. My pres-ence will be useful, but not essential. However, if I find a particular issue important to me, there is no reason why I cannot feel free to participate to any extent I wish.

If any of the above-mentioned roles sound interesting to you, please list below as many of them as you wish:

_____

_____

_____

_____

_____

_____

_____

100

The Camelot Daily News

OFFICER DIES IN SHOOTOUT

For the second time in 18 months a police officer was shot and killed in the line of duty yesterday. Officer Dennis Murphy, responding to a report of a robbery in progress at the College View Liquor Store, 1327 Robert Street, at 9:23 P.M., arrived just as the gunman ran into the street. In an exchange of gunfire the robber was hit three times and died at the scene, but not before mortally wounding Murphy, who died of an abdominal wound five hours later while undergoing surgery at Camelot City Hospital.

Witnesses stated that when Murphy called for the gunman to halt, the gunman whirled and fired a shot which went wild, and in the exchange of gunfire which followed, Officer Murphy was struck once and the gunman was hit three times. The gunman emptied his six-shot, .32 caliber revolver at Murphy. Murphy fired only three times, wounding the gunman in the left arm, the left lung, and the abdomen.

Murphy, a four-year veteran of the force, is survived by his wife, Linda, a son, Kevin, age 5, and a daughter, Julie, age 2. The family resides at 3082 Westerfield Drive. Funeral arrangements were incomplete at press time.

This latest tragedy is expected to give new impetus to the drive of the Police Benevolent Association for greater protection for officers on duty.

HOTEL FIGHT LOOMS

Crown Developers yesterday announced plans for Pioneer Plaza, a 24-story office and hotel complex along the west border of Pioneer Park. The multipurpose structure also will house restaurants, shops, and an underground parking garage. The president of Crown Developers emphasized the favorable impact this project will have on revitalization of the downtown business district. The hotel will offer first-class accommodations to business and university visitors, among others. Remaining floors will be devoted to business and professional offices. Crown Developers expects the development to attract additional business to the downtown area. In particular, they point to the attractiveness of the Plaza for headquarters operations that have been located at the edge of the city, near the interstate, in recent years.

The focal point of the project will be an eight-story, glass-enclosed atrium facing Pioneer Park. Plans call for purchase of a hundred-foot strip of the Pioneer Park border from the city in order to complete the project.

Alison Stanbaugh, vice president of the Camelot Historic Preservation League, criticized the project in a telephone interview yesterday. She pointed out that a strip of land 100 feet wide would encroach upon land now occupied by First Presbyterian Church and its historic cemetery. To complete the plans as announced, the church would have to be demolished or else moved from its original, historic site. She estimated that as many as 25 graves of early settlers in the region also would have to be moved if the developer's wishes were met.

Crown Developers stated that the Camelot Planning Commission will receive the plans and a petition for the necessary permissions and land sale at its next meeting. Planning will consider the petition and report its recommendation to council.

GAY RIGHTS BEFORE COUNCIL TOMORROW

Selection of a mayor will be the first item of business as council meets for the first time since the recent election. Council is expected to turn then to a proposal aimed at prohibiting discrimination against gays and lesbians in housing and in employment.

AN EDITORIAL

As the Camelot City Council continues to wrestle with budget questions, it is worth remembering that the city's largest employer, the university, probably has reached peak enrollment and may well experience significant decline in enrollment during the coming decade. Today, even more than in the past, each expenditure must be weighed not only for its impact upon this year's budget but also for its impact upon future budgets. In saying this we do not intend to take a position at this time on any budget item. We wish only to counsel a cautious approach to the matter.

COUNCIL PROCEEDINGS
A SAMPLE MEETING

I.   Mayor: "The Camelot City Council will please come to order."

II. Mayor: "Will the Clerk please call the role."
     Clerk: (Calls roll and announces number present and absent. A quorum is three [3] councillors if council has five seats, or four [4] councillors if council has seven seats.) "A quorum is present, Mr. (or Madam) Mayor."

III. Mayor: "Will the Clerk now read the *Minutes* of the previous meeting."
     Clerk: (reads *Minutes*)
     The *Minutes* should record:
     1. Date of meeting.
     2. Names of those on council present and absent, and who is presiding.
     3. All actions taken. Thus *all* motions are included. *No* debate is ever included in the *Minutes*.
     4. a. All actions, *except* procedural (close debate, amendments, adjournment, refer to committee, recess, etc.) require a roll call vote.
         b. Procedural motions require a simple majority of those present and voting. Voice or hand votes are all that is required. The *Minutes* will simply say "motion passed" or "motion failed."
         c. *All actions* of council, including ordinances and resolutions, require three [3] affirmative votes if council has five seats, or four [4] votes if council has seven seats. (Emergency ordinances require a larger majority. See the Charter of the City of Camelot, section 3.02.)
     5. Announcements.
     6. Time of adjournment.
     Mayor: "Are there any corrections or additions to the *Minutes* as read?" (Pause) "Hearing none, the *Minutes* stand approved as read." (Note: Some councils will require the *Minutes* to be approved by a majority or even a roll call vote.)
     If there are corrections or additions, the Mayor will then say ". . . approved as corrected."

IV. Mayor: "Are there any committee reports?" (such as treasurer, or city manager).

V.   Mayor: "Will the Clerk please advise us if there is any old business?" (This will be motions left on the floor at the time of adjournment at the last meeting, or previously tabled motions or motions scheduled to be discussed at this meeting.)

VI. Mayor: "Is there any new business?"

VII. Announcements.

VIII. Adjournment.
     (The proceedings listed above are also applicable to a planning commission meeting.)

Rank Order of Commonly Used Motions

Highest Rank on Top*	Needs Second?	Debatable?	Vote Required
1. To adjourn	Yes	No	Majority
2. To recess	Yes	No	Majority
3. To table (i.e., to postpone temporarily)	Yes	No	Majority
4. Previous question (i.e., to vote immediately)	Yes	No	Two-thirds
5. To limit debate	Yes	No	Two-thirds
To extend debate	Yes	No	Two-thirds
6. To postpone motion to particular day	Yes	Yes[†]	Majority
To postpone motion to a particular time	Yes	Yes[†]	Two-thirds
7. To refer to committee	Yes	Yes[†]	Majority
8. To amend	Yes	Yes	Majority
9. To postpone indefinitely (i.e., to kill a motion)	Yes	Yes	Majority
10. Resolutions (proclamations, appointments, recognitions)	Yes	Yes	Majority
11. Ordinances	Yes	Yes	Majority
12. Emergency ordinances	Yes	Yes	Three-fourths

*Example: If a Rank 9 is "on the floor," only motions of higher rank can be proposed until the Rank 9 motion is disposed of.

[†]Subject to restricted debate. That is, one can debate such items as what limits on debate, or what day or time to which to postpone a motion, or special instructions to the committee (size, composition, and so on), but the main motion cannot be debated.

Incidental motions can be introduced at any time. They have no rank order. Examples are:

Incidental Motions

	Needs Second?	Debatable?	Vote Required
Appeal the decision of the chair	Yes	Yes	Tie or majority
Point of order	No	No	No vote
Withdraw a motion	No	No	Without objection or majority if there is objection
Suspend rules of order (i.e., to revise agenda)	Yes	No	Two-thirds
Object to consideration (applies only to main motions)	No	No	Two-thirds negative
Division of the question (into segments that will be voted upon individually)	No	No	Decided by the chair. If there is objection, then majority vote.

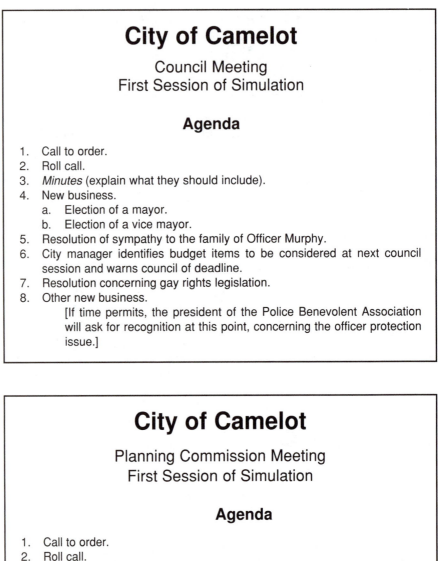

City of Camelot

Council Meeting
First Session of Simulation

Agenda

1. Call to order.
2. Roll call.
3. *Minutes* (explain what they should include).
4. New business.
   a. Election of a mayor.
   b. Election of a vice mayor.
5. Resolution of sympathy to the family of Officer Murphy.
6. City manager identifies budget items to be considered at next council session and warns council of deadline.
7. Resolution concerning gay rights legislation.
8. Other new business.
   [If time permits, the president of the Police Benevolent Association will ask for recognition at this point, concerning the officer protection issue.]

City of Camelot

Planning Commission Meeting
First Session of Simulation

Agenda

1. Call to order.
2. Roll call.
3. *Minutes* (explain what they should include).
4. New business:
   a. Election of a chairman or chairwoman.
   b. Election of a vice chairman or chairwoman.
   c. Appointment of a secretary by the chairman or chairwoman.
   d. The downtown Hotel Plaza issue.
   e. Beauty salon zone variance issue.

City of Camelot

Council Meeting
Second Session of Simulation

Agenda

1. Call to order.
2. Roll call. Mayor's warning to members of council regarding absence. (See Section 2.02 of The Charter of the City of Camelot.)
3. *Minutes* of meeting of first day of simulation.
4. Old business.
5. New business.
   a. Officer protection program issue. [If the Officer Protection Issue was introduced during the first council meeting, it should appear under "old business," above, at this second council meeting.]
   b. Consideration of budget items.
   c. Consideration of planning commission actions.
   d. Announcements.

City of Camelot

Planning Commission Meeting
Second Session of Simulation

Agenda

1. Call to order.
2. Roll call.
3. Minutes.
4. Old business
   a. Downtown Hotel Plaza Issue.
5. New Business.
   a. Beauty salon zone variance issue, petition to rezone from R-4 to C-1, _____ _____, petitioner.
   b. The Massage Parlor Issue.

11

Issues

INTRODUCTION

It is a truism that life is an unending series of choices. For city governments this is a fact of daily life.

You will find two types of issues in this simulation: those involving money trade-offs and those involving people trade-offs. Both present very difficult choices. Money trade-offs focus on the city budget. If you increase one service or program, you must either increase taxes or reduce another program, or do a combination of both.

The second kind of issue involves people trade-offs, such as when conflicts exist between and among people over lifestyle preferences or when people disagree as to how land shall be used. Only indirectly will the city's budget be involved. Shall the city pass an ordinance which protects gays and lesbians from discrimination in hiring and firing? Shall a piece of land be zoned so that Mrs. Smith benefits by being able to use her property for a beauty salon, while her neighbor discovers that his single-family home has lost value because no one wants to live next to a business? Or suppose developers want to build a strip mall on land currently zoned for residential use. All they ask is that the lot be zoned for commercial enterprise and they will pay for everything, plus generate additional property tax revenues for Camelot. Everyone benefits, no one loses. Or do they?

Some of the roles will provide clues as to what stand the individuals might take on certain issues. No one is precluded from taking positions, pro or con, on any issue. In fact, each of you, whether an elected official, an appointed official, or an ordinary citizen, is urged to consider every issue carefully in terms of whether you have some stake involved. Whenever you find yourself concerned about how an issue will be resolved, it is important to speak up and attempt to convince others (council, planning commission, or fellow citizens) of the wisdom of your point of view.

As you read the issues and consider your involvement in them, there are three matters of law to be called to your attention. Additional details about each item are provided in the sections indicated.

1. *Initiative.* If there is an issue which has been ignored or defeated by council and you are not willing to accept this action, you can use the initiative petition procedure. If you obtain a sufficient number of signatures on a petition, the question will then be voted on by the citizens of Camelot. For details, see the Camelot Charter, Section 7.01, Chapter 12.
2. *Referendum.* There may be instances when you are quite opposed to an action by council, in which case you have the option of forcing a referendum on the matter. This procedure requires the securing of a specified number of signatures on a petition, followed by the approval or disapproval of the voters. For details, see the Camelot Charter, Section 7.02, Chapter 12.
3. *The sunshine law.* With only a few exceptions, all discussions and voting by elected or appointed public bodies must be carried out in public. For details and exceptions, see Chapter 12, page 176.

RESOLUTION OF SYMPATHY

The councillor from Madisonville (the former chief of police) will present the following resolution immediately after the election of the mayor and vice mayor.

Resolved: That the City Council of Camelot express to the family of Officer Dennis Murphy its deepest sympathy and regret at the death of this brave member of the Police Force of Camelot, killed in the line of duty while attempting to arrest a robbery suspect.

That all flags on municipal buildings be flown at half-staff for seven days out of respect for Officer Murphy.

That an appropriate Certificate of Commendation of Officer Murphy be prepared and delivered to his family.

That these actions be recorded in the official *Minutes* of the City Council of Camelot.

THE GAY RIGHTS ISSUE

This will be presented to COUNCIL on the first session of the simulation.

The councillor from College Town, a professor at Camelot State University, has requested that the following item be placed on the agenda for the first session of the simulation.

> *Resolved:* That the city attorney shall be directed to draw up legislation which will (1) prohibit in the renting, leasing, or sale of housing any discrimination based on sexual orientation or preference; and which will (2) prohibit in the employment, promotion, or dismissal of any person by any employer of ten or more persons any discrimination based upon sexual orientation or preference.
>
> Violation of the ordinance shall be a Class III misdemeanor, punishable by a fine of not more than Two Hundred and Fifty Dollars for each offense.

The State of Huron has no parallel legislation.

OFFICER PROTECTION PROGRAM ISSUE

This will be presented to COUNCIL on the first session of the simulation by the president of the Police Benevolent Association (PBA), time permitting (probably not sooner than the second session if class periods are 60 minutes or less).

As was reported in yesterday's issue of *The Camelot Daily News,* a police officer was shot and killed in the course of responding to a report of a robbery of a liquor store. The president of the PBA will present the following demand to council on the date indicated.

Summary of Costs of Officer Protection Program

Shotgun Racks for Patrol Cars	
80 racks @ $140	$ 11,200
Kevlar Body Armor Jackets	
200 @ $400	80,000
Stun Guns: handheld, battery	
200 @ $54	10,800
Total	$102,000

(continued)

Summary of Costs of Officer Protection Program *(continued)*

Officers' Weapon Replacements
    Either (a) or (b):
        (a) .357 Magnum stainless steel
              revolvers, 210 @ $330
              (net with trade-ins)
              $ 69,300
        (b) 9-mm Smith & Wesson (semiautomatic)
              210 @ $430 (net with trade-ins)
              $ 90,300

Holster Replacements
    Safety Holster
      210 @ $52 = $ 10,920
           Grand Total Using .357 Magnums $182,220
           Grand Total Using 9-mm Semiautomatics $203,220

    This is a one-time conversion cost, not a recurring annual expense. (There will be additional ammunition expense each year to maintain officer marksmanship.)

    Background information. The present service revolvers are .38-caliber Specials. The difference between the .38 Special and either the .357 Magnum revolver or the 9-mm semiautomatic lies in the shocking power, the stopping power, of the bullets. Much larger powder loads in the cartridges propel the Magnum bullets, which in turn means that a person struck by a Magnum bullet is less likely to be able to flee or harm anyone else. The 9-mm bullets are nearly as fast, but they are lighter, thus producing less shocking power than the Magnum but significantly more than the .38 Special revolver. The contrast may be seen in the table that follows, which sets forth the comparative ballistics for the preferred bullets in the various calibers.

    The semiautomatic pistol has several points of superiority as compared to either of the revolvers. First, the semiautomatic has a larger magazine capacity—fifteen shots as against six for either of the revolvers. Second, the semiautomatic can be reloaded very quickly by replacing the magazine clip. This replacement can be accomplished in about four or five seconds if the replacement clip is easily accessible to the nonshooting hand. Third, the trigger pull of a semiautomatic is much lighter (easier) than a revolver in rapid-fire situations, which means a greater chance of hitting the target with a greater number of bullets. The effort required to squeeze the trigger is minimal, which reduces the likelihood that squeezing the trigger will pull the aim of the gun off target.

The proposed holsters are available to fit the presently used weapons or either of the proposed alternatives. The purpose of the safety holster is to prevent an officer's gun from being withdrawn by someone else, especially from behind the officer in the course of a struggle. The holster is designed so that the weapon can be inserted conventionally and easily, but to withdraw it the butt of the weapon must be pushed forward about one-quarter of an inch as it is withdrawn by lifting upward. Otherwise, the holster securely grips the gun and prevents its withdrawal. Inasmuch as officers are killed in the United States each year during struggles in which the arrestee pulls the officer's gun from its holster, this device will reduce the risks borne by officers in Camelot. The forward push and upward pull on the weapon comes naturally to the officer wearing the holster but is quite awkward for anyone else.

Comparative Data for Three Weapons

	Muzzle Velocity Feet-per-Second	Muzzle Energy Foot-Pounds (Shocking Power)
.38 Special (Revolver) 150 grain Super-X + P (6-shot capacity) Cost: on hand	910	276
.357 Magnum (Revolver) 158 grain Super-X (6-shot capacity) Cost: $330 each net with trade-in	1235	535
9-mm Parabellum (Semiautomatic) 115 grain STHP (15-shot magazine; quick replacement of magazine clip) Cost: $430 each, net with trade-in	1225	383

It is possible to use .38 Special cartridges in a .357 Magnum weapon, but Magnum cartridges are too long to fit the .38 Special weapons. (Interchangeability of ammunition may be a concern when several different enforcement agencies are cooperating in a fire fight.)

The body armor jackets are made of a densely woven fabric using incredibly high tensile-strength, artificial filament for the thread. These jackets are impervious to penetration by handgun bullets; they diffuse the force of the bullet impact in such a way that, though a large and severe bruise will be inflicted, there will be no penetration of the body. They can be worn under regular uniform shirts.

The stun guns are handheld devices about the size of a pocket transistor radio. Operated on a 9-volt transistor battery, they produce a high-voltage crackling spark between two electrodes located about two inches apart. When the electrodes are pressed against a person's flesh or clothing and the switch-button is activated, the resulting high-voltage shock is designed to incapacitate the target person completely for a period of three to four minutes. The voltage operates against major muscle groups to produce a temporary paralysis. Cardiologists have tested and pronounced the stun gun completely safe, thus making it safer than chemical mace or a wooden nightstick, both of which pose some risk of injury.

If any of these proposed expenditures is authorized, you should note the implications for "The Budget Issue" which will be considered later.

THE DOWNTOWN HOTEL PLAZA ISSUE

The following issue will be presented to the PLANNING COMMISSION on the first session of the simulation, time permitting. If there is not sufficient time, it will be placed on the agenda for the second session

The map of downtown Camelot (see inside covers) shows a small finger of land in the Central Business District (CBD) fronting on the north side of the river and abutting the east side of Robert Street. The space involved is approximately 315 feet on each side. Its eastern boundary looks out on Camelot's Pioneer Park. The commercial area is filled with mostly nineteenth-century buildings, housing some small retail stores, including several restaurants, a bank, a music store, two antique stores, a furniture store, an old hotel which caters mostly to transients, and a large building, now empty, which formerly was a department store. The tallest building is the hotel, which has 12 stories. Thus none of the buildings exceed the height limits of the zoning code, which for the C-3 zone (the CBD), is 15 stories. Most of the other buildings in this area are three to five stories high, with some as low as one story. With one exception, the buildings are of rather poor quality, lacking architectural grace or distinction. The exception is the bank, which dates back to the 1920s and is considered to be a fine example of the Italianate period, with its domed ceiling and elaborate brass interior railings and marble staircases. For years there have been complaints about the general ugliness of this area, but no renewal plan has ever come to fruition.

Pioneer Park, on the other hand, is viewed by almost everyone as a green jewel surrounded by the concrete hulks of Government Square and the Central Business District. Its dimensions are 315 feet (north to south) and 700 feet (east to west), totaling about five acres. Given the nature of the area, it tends to be used mainly during the day. The First Presbyterian Church, an architectural gem that is intertwined with the history of the early settlers in this region and is located at the southwest corner of the park, is still very much in use, and the Pioneer Cemetery which adjoins the church is the final resting place for 78 of Camelot's early settlers. Many of the descendants of those early settlers live in Camelot and regularly attend the First Presbyterian Church of their ancestors. It should not be surprising, therefore, that any threat to the church and its cemetery will evoke a vigorous response.

The Crown Real Estate Development Corporation, arguing that Camelot is long overdue for a more impressive use of the commercial area described above, has presented an innovative proposal for a downtown hotel plaza. The developer's plan for the plaza includes a 24-story, high-rise tower, with a glass-fronted hotel facing the park. The street level will contain boutique and gift shops, and the first seven floors will be commercial, including such activities as law firms, accounting firms, engineering consultants, brokerage offices, and regional offices of various national corporations. The eighth and ninth floors will house the lobby and convention facilities for the hotel, plus a prestigious restaurant. The hotel will occupy the remainder of the floors. A parking garage is also included in the plan.

The developer's architectural team, one of the best-known commercial development firms in the United States, has submitted a design that calls for more land than is available in the tract. More specifically, the plan calls for the acquisition and use of 100 feet of land to the east of the present tract, land owned by the city of Camelot and comprising the westerly portion of Pioneer Park. The parkland needed for the development plan includes a portion of a pond (known as Camelot Lagoon) which hosts ducks in the summer and ice skaters in the winter. Also included in the plaza plan is the space now occupied by the First Presbyterian Church and the small Pioneer Cemetery adjacent to it. Both the church and the cemetery would have to be moved if the plaza plan were to be implemented.

The developer has been told by the architect that the private tract held by the developer under an option to purchase simply is not large enough for the project, and other consultants called in to discuss the question confirm that the project would have to be canceled rather than scaled down to the inadequate size that would be imposed if the development were squeezed into the acreage presently under option. The consultants do not believe the project would be economically viable if scaled back. Therefore, the developer now wants to purchase the needed parkland from the city, at a price that would be sufficient to include the cost of moving the church and cemetery to another portion of the park or to any other location requested by the city officials.

The planning commission and city council of Camelot now face a difficult decision. There is no question that downtown Camelot has been decaying for many years. Regional malls located along the interstate highway to the north and the south of Camelot, and outside of its jurisdiction, have weakened severely the viability of the Central Business District. Thus many of the buildings in the tract under discussion are not only underutilized, but some have been empty for some time. It has been estimated that the assessed value of the plaza will be $50 million, an increase of at least $40 million over the assessed value of the present structures. Not only will the plaza bring in a much needed increase in property tax revenues, it will also increase the likelihood of a revitalization of adjacent areas of the Central Business District. The plaza itself will provide new employment for an estimated 175 individuals and encourage the return of both tourists and individuals visiting Camelot for business reasons, both of which groups have stayed overnight in motels located along the interstate highway rather than stay in the now quite seedy hotel.

As can be imagined, the proposed development has its detractors. Emotions are running high. There is a "Save Pioneer Park" group, headed by the minister of the First Presbyterian Church (Role 48), which has been outspoken in its opposition to what is viewed by them as a surrender to crass commercialism at the price of precious open space. The group has many supporters, including the junior high school teacher (Role 43), whose grandparents and great grandparents are buried in the cemetery; the owner of the delicatessen (Role 26), who will be forced to relocate since the business would be unable to afford the much higher rent to be charged in the new structure; and the copywriter (Role 45), an outspoken supporter of "Save Pioneer Park" and a persistent and staunch conservationist.

Supporters include the director of the Planning Department of Camelot (Role 33), the editor and publisher of *The Camelot Daily News* (Role 19), and the owner of the large business (Role 25), whose real estate holdings include the now closed department store. Naturally, the developers (Roles 38, 39, and 40) are in the forefront of the struggle to get the high-rise approved.

Two individuals are finding the proposed development particularly troublesome. Both are members of the First Presbyterian Church and have ancestors buried in the cemetery, yet both also are concerned about the future of Camelot's decaying Central Business District and the resulting decline in employment opportunities and property tax revenues. The individuals struggling with the dilemma are the councillor who is vice president of the local Chamber of Commerce (Role 4) and the planning commissioner who favors rapid growth for Camelot (Role 13).

The planning commission and council have three decisions to make:

1. Should the city sell part of Pioneer Park to be used for the high-rise development? Neither body need concern itself with the amount of money involved, for if agreement cannot be reached between the parties on this aspect, the matter will be resolved in court. This is a land-use issue, but one that has real costs involving loss of open space and dislocation of important human symbols and values. Yet these costs must be balanced against equally real benefits of increased employment opportunities and tax revenues, not to mention the revitalization of a decaying Central Business District.
2. Should a zoning variance be allowed to permit the construction of a 24-story high-rise in this C-3 area? There is no question but that this building would dominate the skyline of Camelot.
3. Will council approve vacating Union, River, and Church Streets? The automobile and pedestrian entrance to the hotel plaza, the office building, and the parking garage will be from Governor Modred Boulevard.

FIGURE 11-1   The Downtown Hotel Plaza Issue

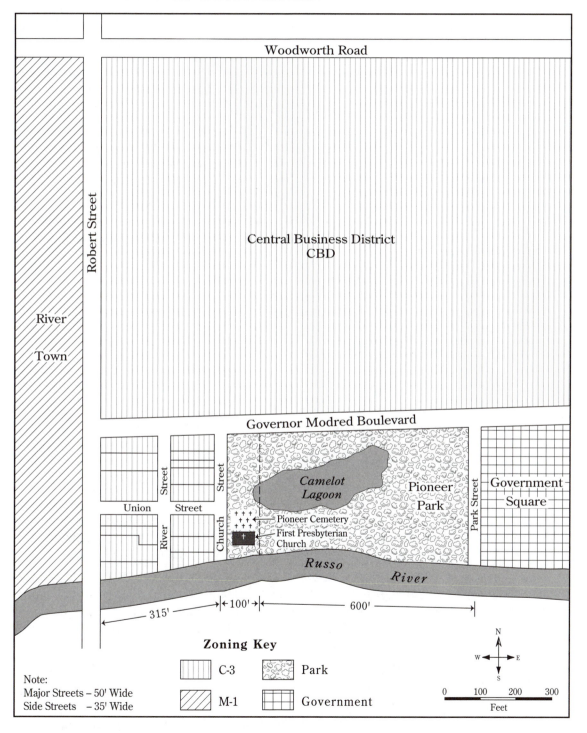

THE BUDGET ISSUE

At the first session of council, the city manager will alert council members that this issue will be on the agenda for the second session.

The following paragraphs include an abbreviated version of some aspects of Chapter 4, "Sources of Local Government Revenues and Their Constraints." The reader is urged to review that chapter in order to gain a fuller understanding of the problems surrounding the income generation side of city budgets. The emphasis of "The Budget Issue" will be on the expenditure side, with some necessary references to income generation aspects. However, the focus will be on questions such as: What services should cities provide? How should these services be paid for? No attempt will be made to review all the services which cities might provide. The problems presented here emphasize the difficulties involved in making decisions as to which services should be approved and paid for out of public funds.

Every year the city manager's staff, or the mayor's staff, depending on the form of city government, prepares a proposed budget for the following year. A budget is a set of proposed expenditures for the next fiscal year. It is, in effect, a message from the chief executive officer to the legislative body (in this case the city council) requesting operating funds for the various municipal departments, and the response of that legislative body will be in the form of an appropriation for the coming fiscal year. The chief executive's staff must struggle to balance the proclaimed needs of city departments for staff and facilities (assertions of need often reinforced by demands of citizen groups for services from those departments) with the projections of revenues to be received by the city from various sources. Those sources include transfers of funds from the federal government and the state government, but most importantly those funds are derived from taxes on the local citizens and businesses. Inevitably, the requests for funds exceed projected revenues: more police officers and equipment are desired; the streets need to be repaired or widened or rebuilt; the health department needs more staff and the equipment must be modernized; citizens demand new services (a new swimming pool, additional recreational facilities); they also complain about the poor quality of existing services (inadequate refuse collection, potholes in streets, sediment in the drinking water), and on and on.

Of equal importance to the demands on government for services is the fact that city governments, unlike the federal government, are almost everywhere prevented from engaging in deficit spending. Expenditures for services cannot exceed income. Bonded indebtedness is permitted only for capital improvements, such as building a new city hall, a water treatment plant, or a swimming pool. And bonded indebtedness may require the levying of a special assessment or a special tax so that the bond purchaser (the lender) can be assured of repayment when the bonds come due.

The simplistic response might be to tell citizens they must pay for the services they demand. For some services this does occur, and a user fee is utilized. For example, in many, if not most, cities the resident pays for the water consumed, the swimming pool enjoyed, and the refuse collected. Here the person using the service pays for all or most of the service. The city can estimate how much service is needed because use and users can be counted and then charged for the service.

Yet some services are what economists call "a public good," meaning they are available to everyone and cannot be denied effectively to anyone. Police and fire protection exist all the time—are "consumed," if you will, constantly by everyone. In this case everyone pays for a service and everyone benefits from the availability of that service. But how do we know how much of this service to provide? Or how much to pay those who provide the service? Or what facilities are really needed? In the 1960s, during the period of civil unrest, some police departments were of the opinion that armored vehicles were necessary. It was even suggested in some cities that tanks should be purchased! Today, police departments regularly request protective body jackets and higher powered weapons. While there may be honest disagreement among us as to what equipment and how much of it the police need, or how many officers there should be, or how much they should be paid, it is quite clear that we cannot leave the final decision to the police, nor can we limit the service to those who pay for it. (Interestingly enough, in some rural areas fire departments have a contractual arrangement with citizens, and if a property owner who does not pay an annual fee then has a fire, the fire department will limit its service to making sure no person is endangered. The buildings will be allowed to burn to the ground.) For most of us, however, it is assumed that everyone will contribute through tax dollars for the police and fire service, and it is the elected officials, the city council members, who must make the final decisions as to what is the proper balance between agency requests and actual agency needs.

There is yet another category of budget expense, and it involves a *redistribution* of money. That is, by law it is decided to take money from one group of citizens and give benefits to another group. While some examples are obvious, others are less so. An obvious example occurs when city health departments provide free medical services for those who cannot afford it, or when certain city services are provided at no cost to those of low income or at reduced cost to the elderly. Municipal transportation charges are often reduced for school children or the elderly; rent subsidies may be provided to low-income individuals. The underlying assumption is clear. Certain services are provided at little or no cost to those we believe are less able to pay, and the cost difference will be borne through tax revenues taken from those deemed more able to pay.

However, some cities also build marinas and golf courses with public funds, and often the user fees are not set high enough to cover the total cost of building and maintaining these facilities. Again there is a redistribution; in this case tax money is taken from individuals who cannot or do not own a boat or play golf, and the money is spent for the benefit of other individuals who do own boats or play golf. In such situations the governmental funds are used to subsidize the more affluent rather than the poor, which suggests that the more affluent among us are not without political influence.

Finally, there is one more category of city expenses—economic development. It is apparent that not all cities are at a similar stage of development. Some are stagnating and decaying. Industries have moved and have not been replaced by new ones. The Central Business District looks as though nothing has been built or renovated in the last 30 years. Yet other cities, often in the same area, appear vibrant with new construction, new industry. Most likely you can think of examples from your own travels. Obviously, many factors are at work, including competence of city leadership, adequacy of water, quality of educational facilities and city services, availability of skilled labor, proximity to markets, attractiveness of the quality of life and climate, just to name a few. But in addition there is the factor of willingness on the part of political leaders to attract new businesses with such tangible enticements as property tax abatement (reduction) or deferral, construction of access roads and water and sewer lines, or even free land upon which to build. Cities have been known to purchase land upon which stand old buildings, raze the existing structures at city expense, and then sell the cleared land at below cost prices to developers. The new developments, it is believed, will result in increased costs for the city in the short run but will increase tax revenues in the long run because of the additional people employed and the new industries built.

It is obvious that the simulation cannot include the entire process of budget preparation and approval, nor can all the preceding aspects be built into the experience. Therefore, in order to make the budget simulation more useful as a learning experience, certain simplifying constraints have been built into it so that your attention will be focused on a manageable number of decisions. Here are the constraints:

1. The entire city budget has been approved except for the following items which will be described. Perhaps this may seem unrealistic, but in fact the problems facing the council will be the same whether the entire budget is considered or only these few segments. Choices must be made, priorities must be set. If council does x, then there may not be enough money to do y. If the requests for funds are greater than the projected income, then some projects must be reduced or eliminated, or else more funds must be generated.
2. An uncommitted excess of income over expenditures for the next fiscal year is estimated at $187,500. This amount is available to council to fund some of the following proposals.
3. Council can only reduce or eliminate expenses from among the items presented. You cannot "invent" program savings by eliminating programs not listed. (One city manager in one of our classes announced that he had a buyer for the city transit system and that the proceeds from the sale would cover all the projected increased program costs! Needless to say, the instructor quickly suggested that while this was a very imaginative solution, it would not be permitted.)
4. The total program costs of the following items recommended for the next fiscal year exceed projected income, as will be noted in the discussion which follows. Depending on how many of the recommended programs are approved, all program costs which exceed the projected $187,500 excess must be paid for by funds generated by increasing taxes or user fees. (Inventive solutions, such as winning the state lottery, will not be permitted.) Council has the

authority to increase user fees by ordinance. A tax increase will require approval by the electorate.

5. Action on the budget items listed must be completed no later than 5 minutes prior to the end of the third simulation session, assuming 90-minute sessions. (Or no later than the fourth session, assuming 50-minute sessions.)

6. The deadline listed in paragraph (5) includes *council approval* of the tax increase, if a tax increase is required. If council has indeed decided to increase taxes, the tax increase ordinance must schedule a special election for the next simulation session, to be held at the beginning of that session.

7. If the tax increase fails, council must again consider the proposed budget and determine before the end of the fourth 90-minute simulation session (the fifth 50-minute session) what must be eliminated or whether a different tax proposal is to be put before the voters at the beginning of the fifth 90-minute session (the sixth 50-minute session).

8. No deficit financing is permitted in the state, thus borrowing for the purpose of meeting current operating expenses is illegal.

9. It is assumed that Camelot has 50,000 families and that the median family income per family is $37,500, creating a total income base for tax purposes of $1,875,000,000. If the city income tax is increased, it will generate additional revenue as follows:

$\frac{1}{10}$% increase will generate $1,875,000.
$\frac{1}{4}$% increase will generate $4,687,500.
$\frac{1}{2}$% increase will generate $9,375,000.

An increase of one mill ($1 per $1,000 assessed valuation) in real estate property tax will generate $1,782,000.

10. Council will concern itself only with the issues presented. Council may increase the amounts suggested, decrease them, or eliminate them entirely. Council may not revise the facts as given. That is, it cannot decide that it can acquire some of the items for less money than that stated in the proposed budget. If, for example, council decides to purchase .357 Magnums, it may do so but only at the price stated per gun. Thus it may purchase fewer guns, or no guns (or more guns, for that matter), but the cost per gun may not be revised.

1. Proposal: Police Department New Programs

   a. Drug Enforcement Unit.

   In order to increase police capability to control the growing drug traffic in Camelot, the Police Department proposes the establishment of a Drug Enforcement Unit. The first-year start-up costs of this unit will be as follows: Personnel, equipment, and training for four additional officers: $255,000.[1] In future years it is assumed that the cost will be $163,000 each year (plus inflation).

   Addition to chief's discretionary account: $50,000. This amount will cover supplies, payments to informers, and money for drug purchases. *This is a first-year cost and will be a continuing annual cost.*

   > Total first-year cost: $305,000.
   > Total cost each year thereafter: $213,000.

   b. SWAT Team (team of 10).

   In order to increase the police capability in handling potential hostages, terrorists, and other situations requiring special police expertise, the Police Department proposes the establishment of a SWAT Team. These officers will not be additions to the force. They will be part of the regular force.

   Equipment start-up costs will be $15,000. This will cover the cost of high-powered rifles, telescopic sights, and automatic weapons; flak jackets (heavier than body-protection jackets, they protect more of the body and protect against higher powered weapons); battle dress (camouflage); and initial training.

   Vehicle start-up costs will be $34,000, which will pay for a van (one-ton chassis) specially equipped to carry the team and equipment. This is a highly desirable item, but is not essential.

---

[1]This figure assumes that the cost of one additional officer is about $63,750. This amount is based on a salary of $32,500, plus fringe benefits which amount to about 22%, uniforms, training, and equipment. The unit will consist of the equivalent of two full-time undercover agents (rotating) and two uniformed officers (specialists, supervisory level) who will be permanent. The larger first-year figure is necessary to cover the cost of start-up training and equipment. Training is essential and includes an extended period at the officer training school of the U.S. Drug Enforcement Agency. In order for the city to keep its governmental immunity from lawsuits, there has to be evidence that the training was maintained at state-of-the-art levels.

Annual costs (first year and each succeeding year) will be $8,000. This will cover the cost of special training at the National Guard Armory for three days each quarter, plus ammunition, plus continuous upgrading and repair of weapons and equipment. As with the Drug Enforcement Unit, the training is absolutely essential. In order for the city to keep its governmental immunity from lawsuits, there has to be evidence that the training is maintained at state-of-the-art levels.

Total first-year cost for SWAT Team: $57,000.
Total cost in succeeding years for SWAT Team: $8,000.[2]

2. Proposal: Health Department New Programs
The present Health Clinic, based in Madisonville, provides only pediatric services. It is open six days a week from 9:00 A.M. to 9:00 P.M. The services are for children and adolescents up to age 15 and include consulting, diagnosis, prescriptions, treatment of illnesses, referral, and physical examinations. It is not equipped to handle accident emergencies. Such cases are sent to the emergency rooms of local hospitals.

This facility is located in an old house converted to a clinic. The costs of the present facility are based on the assumption that it is open to the public for 72 hours each week (six days times 12 hours each day), for 52 weeks each year, a total of 3,744 hours per year.

Cost of Pediatric Services

Pediatricians—$85 per hour × 3,744 hours	$318,240
Nurses—$15 per hour × 3,744 hours	56,160
Receptionists—$7 per hour × 3744 hours	26,208
Equipment (minimal)	–0–
Supplies per patient (assumption: 12 patients per hour × $5 per patient = $60 per hour)	224,640
Fixed expenses (rent, utilities, janitorial service, maintenance) for an estimated 1,500 square feet, $1620 per month	19,440
Total cost for pediatric services	$644,688[3]

---

[2]This cost information was obtained from a police consultant and represents costs in midwestern cities of medium size. The authors are aware that regional variations occur in the United States.

[3]This amount is currently budgeted.

a. Proposal: Gynecologic and Prenatal Services
    In order to meet the needs of women who cannot afford to pay
    for such services, the Health Department proposes the estab-
    lishment of gynecologic and obstetric services for 36 hours per
    week, or 1872 hours per year.

Cost of Gynecologic and Prenatal Services

Gynecologist and obstetrician—$80 per hour	
× 1872 hours	$149,760
Nurse—$15 per hour × 1872 hours	28,080
Receptionist (no additional cost)	–0–
Equipment (one-time cost)	5,000
Supplies per patient (assumption: 2 patients per hour	
× $12 per patient = $24 per hour)	44,928
Fixed expenses (added costs for an estimated increase	
of 400 square feet, $540 per month)	6,480
Total cost for gynocologic–obstetric services	$234,248

b. Proposal: Planned Parenthood Services
    The increase in pregnancy among unmarried, very young girls
    has suggested the need for the availability of information and
    counseling. The Health Department is proposing the establish-
    ment of Planned Parenthood services. The minimum age for
    access to such services is 16, unless accompanied by a parent
    or guardian. The services will not include dispensing of contra-
    ceptives, nor will the services include any recommendation or
    referral concerning abortion. It is assumed that space will be
    made available within the present Health Clinic. The service
    will be available to the public for 72 hours per week, or 3,744
    hours per year.

Cost of Planned Parenthood Services

Counselors—$18 per hour x 3,744 hours	$67,392
Nurse (none needed)	–0–
Receptionist (no additional needed)	–0–

(continued)

Cost of Planned Parenthood Services *(continued)*

Equipment (one-time only—desk, chairs, files, answering machine, personal computer, and printer)	3,500
Supplies (phone, postage, paper, pamphlets)	1,500
Total cost of Planned Parenthood services	$72,392[4]

3. Department of Development
   Proposal: Camelot Shores Project
   The River Town side of the Russo River has been in a state of decay since the demise of the wheel foundry and other associated manufacturing plants. The rail siding is no longer used; the buildings are either unoccupied or used as inexpensive warehouses for marginal businesses. The Department of Development, in cooperation with the Parks and Recreation Department, has proposed that the land which abuts the river be developed into an attractive recreational area, with incentives to developers who would build upscale high-rise apartment complexes, restaurants, and marinas.

   This would be a 10-year development plan. The G. and W. R.R. has agreed to remove the no-longer-used tracks and donate the former passenger station to the city. The city's Department of Development hopes to generate interest in developers to build a high-rise office building.

Cost of Camelot Shores—First Year

Purchase of privately owned land	$2,700,000
Razing of present structures	600,000
Total first-year cost of Camelot Shores	$3,300,000[5]

[4]This cost information was obtained from a medical consultant and represents costs in midwestern cities of medium size. The authors are aware that regional variations occur in the United States.

[5]It is estimated that this same amount will be needed for each year for the next 10 years, for land purchase and clearing, for installation of water and sewer lines, and for the building of streets, curbs, gutters, and sidewalks.

4. Parks and Recreation Department
   Proposal: Camelot Marina Project
   In order to make the shore area more attractive to both tourists and residents, the Parks and Recreation Division is proposing the development of a marina along the north shore line of the Russo River in River Town. This project is not meant to compete with Camelot Shores, but rather to make the entire area more attractive. It is planned that once the marina has been built, user fees will cover the cost of annual maintenance. Architect and engineering fees in the amount of $75,000 were funded last year.

Cost of Camelot Marina Project for Next Year

Land acquisition		$ 550,000
Razing of present structures, grading, trash removal		130,000
Administration—service building, marina gas pump,		
sewage pumps, storage tanks, etc.		150,000
Docks: 200 for boats up to 20 feet long		
100 for boats up to 25 feet long		
50 for boats up to 40 feet long		
(Construction cost of docks averages $2,700 each)		945,000
Parking option for 100 more spaces		
Land acquisition	$550,000	
Preparation and paving	125,000	
		675,000
Total cost of Camelot Marina Project next year		$2,450,000

BUDGET WORK SHEET

	Budgeted	Revision
Issue: *Proposed addition of Drug Enforcement Unit*		
Four additional officers at $63,750	$ 255,000	_____
Chief's Discretionary Account	50,000	_____
Total	$ 305,000	

Notes: _____

Issue: *Proposed addition of SWAT Team*		
Equipment	$ 15,000	_____
Van	34,000	_____
Training	8,000	_____
Total	$ 57,000	

Notes: _____

Issue: *Proposed addition of gynecologic and obstetric services*		
Gynecologist and obstetrician	$ 149,760	_____
Nurse	28,080	_____
Equipment	5,000	_____
Supplies	44,928	_____
Fixed expenses	6,480	_____
Total	$ 234,248	

Notes: _____

Issue: *Proposed addition of Planned Parenthood services*		
Counselors	$ 67,392	_____
Equipment	3,500	_____
Supplies	1,500	_____
Total	$ 72,392	

Notes: _____

	Budgeted	**Revision**
Issue: *Proposed Camelot Shores Project*		
Land acquisition	$ 2,700,000	_____
Razing of present structures	600,000	_____
Total	$ 3,300,000	

Notes: _____

	Budgeted	**Revision**
Issue: *Proposed Camelot Marina Project*		
Land acquisition	$ 550,000	_____
Razing of present structures, etc.	130,000	_____
Administration—service building, etc.	150,000	_____
Docks	945,000	_____
Parking facilities	675,000	_____
Total	$ 2,450,000	

Notes: _____

	Budgeted	**Revision**
Total cost of all proposed programs and projects:		
Drug Enforcement Unit	$ 305,000	
SWAT Team	57,000	
Gynecologic–Obstetric services	234,248	_____
Planned Parenthood services	72,392	_____
Camelot Shores	3,300,000	_____
Camelot Marina	2,450,000	_____
Officer Protection (if previously adopted)	182,220[6]	_____
Grand total	$ 6,600,860	
Excess of income over expenditures in current proposed budget	187,500	_____
Shortfall	($6,413,360)	

[6]This figure assumes that the less expensive .357 Magnums were chosen. If the 9-mm weapons were chosen, add $21,000 to expenditures.

THE BEAUTY SALON ZONE VARIANCE ISSUE

This will be presented to the PLANNING COMMISSION on the second session of the simulation (third session if class periods are 60 minutes or less).

A divorced mother of four children has just received her cosmetologist's license. If she can open a beauty salon,[7] even on a very small scale in her living room, she will be able to remain off welfare, yet be closer to her children. Otherwise, she will have to continue being a part-time waitress, leaving her children either with baby-sitters or by themselves. However, she has a problem. Her home (located on a side street in North Madisonville, north of Woodworth Road) is in an R-4 zone, which does not permit any commercial activity.

Our would-be entrepreneur is now asking for a zoning variance to permit her home to be used for a C-1 activity, even though it is in an R-4 zone. Her neighbors are not sympathetic. They have hired an attorney, role 49, to represent their interests before the planning commission and the council. The neighbors fear a loss in the value of their property if commercial activities are permitted in this residential area. Also, they are troubled by the complete absence of any off-street parking spaces in this older part of town. They already have problems finding a parking space on the street near their home. The additional traffic generated by the proposed beauty salon would make the problem even worse.

THE MASSAGE PARLOR ISSUE

This will be presented to the PLANNING COMMISSION on the second session of the simulation (third session if class periods are 60 minutes or less).

The owner of Camelot Adult Bookstore (located in River Town on the southwest corner of Robert Street and Woodworth Road) is ambitious. Activities at the bookstore have been expanded, but there is a problem. The area is zoned M-1. Originally it was a religious bookstore, and as the character of the area changed, so also did the kind of books

---

[7]Some states no longer permit beauticians to open beauty salons in private homes. Your state may have such a law, but for the purposes of this simulation we have assumed that the state of Huron does *not* have such a law.

sold. However, as long as it remained a bookstore there was no problem. But the current owner of the bookstore expanded the enterprise to include a massage parlor, and the zoning administrator has said this change is not legal. As yet, the owner has not shut down the operation, nor has it been closed down by the city. The owner is now requesting a "special use" permit for the property from the planning commission and council, as is required by the M-1 section of the Zoning Code.

Although massage parlors have an unsavory reputation in some communities, the owner insists that the massage parlor in Camelot is not a front for prostitution and points out that no such arrests have ever been made. Critics concede that no arrests have been made but argue that male customers are given "massages" by scantily clad women, who are neither trained nor licensed. The owner's response is that no claim was ever made that the masseuses are trained and licensed, nor is this required either by state law or city ordinance. Thus they are engaging in a legal activity.

The question to be addressed by the planning commission is: Shall a special use permit be recommended?

When the issue reaches council, some councillors may wish to hear assurances from the city manager and the police chief that adequate investigation of the massage parlor has occurred and will continue to occur, and that illegal activities are not occurring.

The city manager and the police chief may wish to have council provide some guidance as to what kind of priority should be given this type of investigation. Since police resources are limited, does council plan to prefer that other activities, such as traffic enforcement or night patrols in the neighborhoods, be curtailed?

THE "OBSCENE PHOTOGRAPHS" ISSUE

The following issue will be presented to the COUNCIL at the simulation session indicated by your instructor.

Since it was established early in the twentieth century, the Camelot Art Museum has been well supported by the community, and it has provided important leadership in introducing young people to the world of the arts. It has a governing board of ten individuals, nominated by the mayor of Camelot, the nominations approved by Camelot City Council. Board members serve for five years, with terms staggered so that two members are chosen every year. The Art Museum, which is a not-for-profit institution, has a one million dollar annual budget and is funded by city tax dollars and by its own endowment on about a 50–50 ratio.

Two years ago, the position of director became vacant with the retirement of the incumbent director. The chair of the museum board was then, and still is, one of the most successful attorneys in Camelot (Role 49), who had for a number of years believed that any search for a new museum director must be national and open. As a result of the chair's efforts, a nationwide search was held and a person of outstanding credentials was chosen to be the new director (Role 61).

As mentioned earlier, about half of the monetary support for the Camelot Art Museum is provided by the City of Camelot. There have been no restrictions on the use of the money, and in fact there has never been any controversy in this respect. The citizenry in general (the few who are aware of it) and council members in particular have believed that support of the arts was a legitimate use of public funds.

Two events have brought the controversial budget item to the attention of the general public. The first event is the arrival of an exhibit of more than 170 photographs by a now deceased famous artist/photographer, William James. The exhibit contains photographs—often of stark realism but almost uniformly of exceptional beauty—of still lifes, nudes, and portraits. It is an impressive collection.

Included in the collection are seven photographs which clearly are different. Two are of children with their genitals exposed, one a boy and one a girl. While there is a definite sensual quality to the two photographs, there is *no* suggestion of any kind of sexual activity or behavior by the children. It is the way the genitals are exposed which makes the pictures sensual; it is the suggestion of sexuality that is indeed startling to the observer.

The other five pictures are even more extreme in topic, execution, and likelihood of triggering allegations of obscenity. The photographs are homoerotic and use exclusively male models. The topics include a finger inserted in a penis; a fist, an arm, a cylinder, and a bullwhip (respectively) inserted into a rectum; and a man urinating into the mouth of another man. These seven pictures (two of children and five homoerotic) were displayed in the Camelot Art Museum separately from the rest of the William James exhibit, and viewers of the main exhibit were alerted to the subject matter by a sign suggesting that some might find the seven photographs offensive.[8]

The second event was the reaction of the Presbyterian minister (Role 48) when given a description of the seven photographs in question. The minister was outraged and communicated the outrage to council by calling a member of council (Role 3) who, it was believed, shared the minister's views. The minister also wrote a letter to the editor of the *Camelot Daily News,* spoke at a council meeting, and gave more than one thunderous sermon to the church's congregation.

The conservative member of council (Role 3) did indeed share the minister's views and made these views known to council and to the public at a meeting of council. Both individuals believed strongly that the photographs were anything but art and should never have been included in an exhibit open to the public. The fact that the actual display of the seven photographs in question was separated from the remainder of the exhibition was, to these critics, irrelevant. They were not art, these critics declared, and did not deserve to be seen. These seven photographs were additional evidence of the total corruption of American society and of the necessity to "draw the line." To the critics, this was the moment and the example of when and where the line must be drawn.

The member of council (Role 3) has an additional complaint: "By what right does the museum have the audacity to display such garbage when public funds are involved? Even if the courts can't decide what is obscene, this council should have the courage either to reduce or to eliminate the taxpayer support for the museum if it is going to show such filth."

The simulation should concentrate on the second issue, the issue of taxpayer support. Whether or not the seven photographs are obscene, whether or not the entire exhibition is tainted by the presence of the seven photographs, and other possible legal questions will have to be decided by courts of law, not in this simulation. However, the

---

[8]These descriptions of homoerotic content are based on three articles that appeared in the *Cincinnati Enquirer:* "Seeing the Mapplethorpe Show," by William F. Buckley, Jr., May 9, 1990; "Contested Pictures Described," by Ben L. Kaufman, Sept. 26, 1990; and "After the Trial, Questions of Art," by Andy Grundberg, Oct. 21, 1990. *Thus the descriptions are of actual photographs* that were shown in the Contemporary Arts Center in Cincinnati, Ohio, and at several other galleries in the United States.

issue of the public funding of the museum is a matter for council to decide. While the Presbyterian minister (Role 48) and the conservative councillor will lead the opposition, they will be joined by other conservative members of the community. However, the museum is not without its defenders. The new director of the museum (Role 61) and the chair of the museum's governing board (Role 49) will lead the defense, and they will be joined by those in the community who believe that any attempt to reduce the public funding of the museum because of disapproval of part of one exhibit is a not very subtle attempt by a moralistic minority of the community to censor an artist's right to freedom of expression. (Each member of the class has to decide how he or she stands on this issue and, having made a decision, has an obligation to defend that stand publicly.)

Council (and the public) confront questions that include the following:

1. Should council continue to provide financial support for the museum?
2. If there is tax support for the museum, is it appropriate for citizens to participate in deciding what is proper to be shown in the museum?
3. If there is to be public participation, how should it be implemented?

THE AFFIRMATIVE ACTION ISSUE

The following issue will be presented to COUNCIL at a simulation session indicated by your instructor.

For many years it was standard practice within the Camelot city government that all candidates for promotion take an examination. Heads of Camelot city agencies were then allowed to select from among the three who scored highest on the examination. Also, the experience of the several candidates was considered an important factor in making the final decision. (Note: "Experience" is determined by reviewing length of service along with merit, which is defined by reviewing the candidate's annual effectiveness ratings made by supervisors.) An informal analysis of the selection results over the decade between 1970 and 1980 suggests that test score and experience were weighed about 50–50.

In 1984 the Huron State Legislature revised the state law regarding civil service appointments and promotions for the many public agencies of the cities of the state. Whereas prior to 1984 the choice could be made from among the top three applicants, with test score and experience weighing about 50–50, after 1984 the choice could be made from among the top six. In addition, the test score was to count as 40%, experience as 40%, and a new category, called "community needs," as 20%. "Community needs" was a term that was not defined in the legislation, but the purpose was to advance equal opportunity, especially for minorities and women. In fact, that seems to have been the result. Promotions since 1984 have gone to individuals of less experience.

However, the legislature added one other factor. "Home rule" cities were given the authority to set their own rules. Even though Camelot is indeed a home rule city, the city council has in the past not exercised its right to devise its own rules and has simply gone along with the state's 1984 rule changes.

The problem now has become more complicated for the council. A study by the Camelot affirmative action officer (Role 31) revealed the following:

Minority Appointments as a Percentage of All Promotions

	Top Three Test Score—50% Experience—50%		Top Six Test Score—40% Experience—40% Community Needs—20%	
	1970	1980	1990	2000
Minority appointments	8%	10%	15%	21% (est.)

The affirmative action officer also published the results of three other studies (see Figures 11-2 through 11-4). All dealt with the Camelot Police Department, one being a chart showing the percentage distribution of *all promotions by minority status and sex* for the police department for the period 1961 to the present, plus a projection of the trends to the year 2010 (Figure 11-2). (Note: Figure 11-2 percentages are based on *promotions,* not individuals. Thus, a person is tallied

Figure 11-2 Camelot Police Department Promotions by Gender and Race, 1961 to Present and Projections

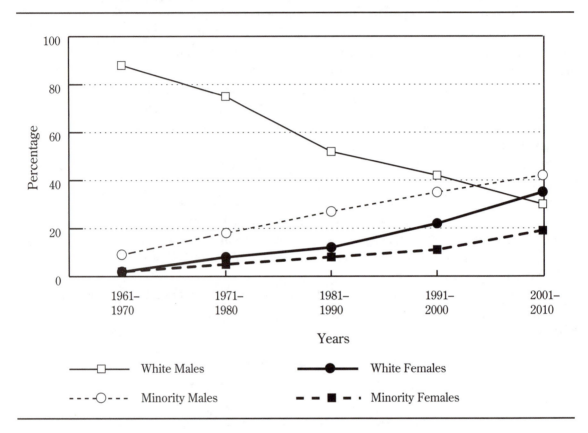

Camelot Police Department

each time he or she is promoted.) The trend line is based on the existing criteria for promotion: that is, test score 40%, experience 40%, community needs 20%.

A second chart (Figure 11-3) documents the *current distribution* of the sworn officers of the police department according to sex and minority status. A "sworn officer" is one to whom an oath of office has been administered and who has thereby sworn to uphold the laws of the nation, the State of Huron, and the City of Camelot. The "swearing in" authorizes the carrying and use of a firearm and confers the authority to make arrests. Six weeks of training at the Huron Police Academy are among the prerequisites to becoming a sworn officer.

The third table (Figure 11-4) reveals the distribution by sex and minority status of Camelot's police recruit graduates from the Me-

FIGURE 11-3   Current Distribution by Gender and Race of Sworn Police Officers in the City of Camelot

	Captains	Lieutenants	Sergeants	Detectives	Uniformed Officers	Sworn Officers, Total
White males	3 = 75%	7 = 70%	14 = 61%	23 = 55%	116 = 63%	163 = 62%
White females	0 = 0%	1 = 10%	1 = 4%	5 = 12%	17 = 9%	24 = 9%
Minority males	1 = 25%	2 = 20%	7 = 31%	11 = 26%	40 = 22%	61 = 23%
Minority females	0 = 0%	0 = 0%	1 = 4%	3 = 7%	12 = 6%	16 = 6%
Column totals	4 = 100%	10 = 100%	23 = 100%	42 = 100%	185 = 100%	264 = 100%
Percentages of the 264 sworn officers. (Read across.)	1.5%	3.8%	8.7%	15.9%	70%	100%

FIGURE 11-4   Distribution by Gender and Race of Camelot's Police Graduates for the Preceding Two Years

	Male	Female	Total
White	12	5	17
Minority	6	3	9
Total	18	8	26

tropolis Police Academy for the preceding two years. Camelot is too small a city to have its own police academy, and thus sends its recruits to the police academy of Metropolis, its large urban neighbor some 50 miles away. For each of the last two years, Camelot has had 13 graduates, and the table lists the two-year totals simply because the profile of each class was so similar.

One final piece of information has to do with the minority population of Camelot. Of Camelot's current 138,000 population, minorities make up about 23% of that total. The male-female division is approximately 50–50.

Individuals who have lobbied for increased promotion of minorities and women have not been pleased with the results of the 1984 changes in promotion standards, arguing that while the improvement in opportunities for minorities and women is salutary, it is disgraceful that the progress has been so slow. Promotions for minority males seem realistic to these critics. However, they point out that at the present rate of change, women and minorities will be experiencing serious discrimination well into the twenty-first century. This is true especially of women. Thus, women's groups have been outspoken proponents of still further revision of the standards, especially for promotion. They note that although women have received 21.7% of all *promotions,* the *current* percentage of *female officers* above the rank of patrol officer (that is, detective and above) is only 13.9%, and that of minority females is a mere 5%. (Note: Some critics have argued that the problem for women begins at the recruitment stage. While this argument may have merit, the central issue at this time is *promotions.*)

Critics of the 1984 state revisions, especially male police officers, have complained publicly and by means of the leadership of the Police Benevolent Association (Role 27) that the result has been and will continue to be an increased risk that the reduced emphasis on the importance of experience will surely come back to haunt the community. The conservative member of council (Role 3) and the councillor who was a former chief of police (Role 6) agree with these predictions. There will be, these critics prophesy, an increasing number of crisis situations where mistakes will be made by the officer in charge because of his or her lack of experience. The result will certainly be an increased risk of injury or loss of life to the citizenry in general and the police in particular. They argue that their stand is not an attack on true equality of opportunity, for they are supportive of the advancement of qualified minority and women candidates. It is, rather, a concern that law enforcement should always have the best qualified leaders.

Defenders of the 1984 rule change argue that these are simply red herring arguments. In the first place, say the defenders, the criticism is more of the tired old arguments by white Anglo-Saxon males who wish to retain the old rules in order to continue the unfair impact of the "Old Boy" network which ensures that especially women will be "kept in their place," at the bottom of the socioeconomic ladder.

The situation has been simmering for several years. Neither side in the dispute has felt any necessity to accommodate to the other side's position, and the public has been passive. Contrary to the arguments of the pessimists, there has been no evidence until recently that any member of the public has been harmed by the changes in the promotions standards. Those who have supported the changes, however, have been only partly pleased by the results and have argued for a further loosening of the rules.

Two quite disparate events have occurred. The first event was a proposal that has been sent to council to revise the standards once again. The new standards would reduce the weighting of experience to 30%, community needs would be increased to 30%, and test scores would remain at 40%. This, the proposers argue, will create the possibility that as many as 35% to 40% of the promotions will go to women and minorities by the year 2000. While that may not be nearly as many as are deserved, proponents argue, at least the new revisions will provide evidence of the city's good intentions and may get the federal government off the city's back so that a threatened loss of equal opportunity funds will not occur.

The second event was a hostage crisis. The police were called to a home in College Town where a domestic crisis was taking place. The husband had previously been ordered to stay away from his wife as a result of a conviction for abusing her and threatening her with bodily harm if she attempted to divorce him. In spite of this court order, the husband had returned to the house and begged for forgiveness and asked to be permitted to return to the family. The wife was adamant in her refusal to grant this permission, and she called the police. When she did this, the husband became violent, threw the television set out of the front window, and threatened to beat his wife again. She barricaded herself in the bathroom and locked the door. A neighbor, hearing the shouts, the threats, and the screams of the woman, dialed 911. Shortly thereafter, the police arrived.

As soon as the responding officers assessed the situation they called for backup, and a recently promoted female lieutenant arrived to take charge. Realizing the seriousness of the situation, she called for the assistance of a police psychologist, hoping that the psychologist could talk the husband into surrendering. If not, then a SWAT team from Metropolis would have to be called. Unfortunately, the shouts and threats of the husband, the screams of the wife, and the fear by all observers that the husband might break down the bathroom door and kill his wife caused the lieutenant to order the police to charge the house and arrest the husband. When the police entered the house and attempted to restrain the husband, he rushed the police. They, in turn, fearing for their own safety, shot at and killed the husband. When the officers examined the body of the husband they discovered that he was unarmed. All persons involved were white.

The aftermath was a demand for a thorough investigation of the event by a citizen review board, and angry charges of incompetence, of inexperience, of unnecessary use of weapons against an unarmed man. The defenders of the lieutenant were equally vigorous in their response, stating that her action was taken to protect the wife and that there was insufficient time to await the arrival of the police psychologist to negotiate with the husband, or for the SWAT team to arrive. Moreover, the defenders point out, even if she made a mistake (which they deny), she should not be condemned on the basis of a single example. In addition, no comparable study has been made to see if even more experienced officers have made similar "mistakes," assuming that this was a mistake. Nor is there a study of the less experienced, to note how many times a crisis was successfully handled.

The charges and counter charges, and the facts, will have to be investigated carefully by a team of investigators. *They are not the concern of council at the moment.* What is of immediate concern to council, to the head of the PBA (Role 27), and to the representatives of the National Organization of Women and the affirmative action officer (Roles 54 and 31) are the standards for promotion as they exist and as they are proposed to be changed.

The issue before council is: Shall the "community needs" criterion be increased from its current 20% to 30%?

THE STRIP MALL DEVELOPMENT ISSUE

The following issue will be presented to COUNCIL at the simulation session indicated by your instructor.

The City of Camelot has been growing steadily in the last six years. The newest subdivisions, Camelot Acres and South Ridge, are located to the south of the University Park area, and are accessed from Robert Street. There is a vacant field of more than 30 acres immediately south of University Avenue and north of Camelot Acres (see map inside front or back covers). Camelot Acres is immediately south of University Park subdivision and is the site of moderately priced homes, ranging in price from $125,000 to $200,000. While these are all very nice homes, the lots are small and modestly landscaped. About 75 homes have been built in this area, with space remaining for perhaps another 25 to 30.

At the southern boundary of Camelot Acres is Lancelot Creek, which runs east–west in this location, and which separates the Camelot Acres subdivision from the South Ridge subdivision. While the homes in South Ridge are not mansions, they are expensive, most of them falling in the $200,000 to $450,000 range. They are all beautifully landscaped. About 50 homes are sited in the area, with the potential for more homes being built there.

Crown Development Corporation (roles 38, 39, and 40) has proposed to build a 180,000 square foot shopping center (in strip mall style, that is, not an enclosed mall). Because of the size of the proposed mall, two things are essential: proximity to an interstate interchange and a site of no less than 30 acres of open land. As is typical of land use around a city, especially near an access road to the interstate, much of the available space west of the interstate has been filled in with motels, gas stations, and fast food restaurants. Houses have been built along almost all the roads because farmers have sold off lots facing the roads in the area.

One piece of land exists that meets the necessary criteria. It is very near the interchange, and at 35 acres it is large enough to hold the mall and a parking area. *It runs east–west just south of University Avenue and north of the Camelot Acres subdivision. It can be reached from both University Avenue and Robert Street.*

It so happens that Crown Development owns the land, having bought the former farmland three years ago, planning to build single-family homes. Crown Development requested an R-l zoning for the land, and this was approved by planning commission and council, but Crown Development did not proceed with the development because of uncertain economic conditions.

The developers now wish to have the zoning changed from R-l to C-3. They believe that what is now needed in that location is a shopping area that would be convenient to all the housing that has been built in the area south of town. In addition, they argue, the shopping area will reduce the amount of traffic cluttering the highways now caused by shoppers who must go into town to buy the needed products. The developers state that a mall of this size will be big enough for a large grocery supermarket, a major discount store, a hardware store, plus many smaller stores. Crown Development argues that a strip mall will be very beneficial to Camelot for several reasons:

1. It will benefit the property tax revenues by increasing the amount of taxable property in the city. A definitive figure is not yet possible; however, based on developments in similar locations, it is estimated by the developer that property tax revenues will amount to between $120,000 to $160,000 per year.

2. Approximately 400 jobs (some part-time, some full-time) will be created, which in turn will assist in reducing the 7% unemployment that exists in Camelot. The additional jobs will reduce the welfare burden at the same time that $50,000 of income tax revenues will be generated.

3. Perhaps the most appealing part of the proposal is that the city is not being asked to provide any tax funds to support the development of the strip mall. Quite to the contrary, the developers point out that building the mall will bring jobs and income to the city as a result of the construction of access roads, sidewalks, sewer extensions, and, of course, the buildings.

The city planning department director (Role 33) and the assistant city manager (Role 9) support the proposal.

The strip mall proposal is not without opposition. A coalition has been created by those who live in the newly developed Camelot Acres and South Ridge subdivisions. They have given their group the acronym S.O.S., for Save Our Subdivisions. These individuals feel threatened by the idea of a strip mall being built in an area not far from their homes. They can foresee much increased traffic on both University Avenue and Robert Street, which will be the main access roads both to the strip mall and to the subdivisions for traffic from the north and east. Thus there will be a major increase in noise, dirt, clutter, and traffic congestion as a result of the mall. This in turn will increase the number of automobile accidents and pedestrian injuries, and will pose danger especially to the children in the area. In addition, mall parking lots are notorious breeding grounds for drug traffic and crime, the critics argue. The residents have a very real fear that the property values of their new homes will be threatened.

Facts cited by opponents include the following:

1. Contrary to the statement by Crown Development, land already zoned C-3 is available to the west of River Town, and it is of a size sufficient for the strip mall. There is an interstate interchange at the northern boundary, and thus the mall could be accessed from both the interstate and Woodworth Road. (The developers object

to this location because they feel the area is not as desirable and is not as well located to the new subdivisions.)

2. Crown Development makes no mention of the cost to the city of sidewalk and road improvements required by the mall. For example, who will pay for the sidewalks that would enable pedestrians to get to the mall (estimated cost: $50,000), for widening the lanes on Woodworth Road, (estimated cost: $112,000), and for a new traffic signal (estimated cost: $38,000) that would be required?

3. The developers argue that Camelot needs the additional retail outlets. Yet some opponents suggest that this is not true. Several apparel stores, restaurants, and a grocery store have closed in the past five years because of declining revenues. (The developers argue that the reason was lack of adequate parking, poor management, and inconvenient location.)

4. The developer did not submit the traffic impact analysis that is customary for regional shopping centers. Based on studies made by the planning department, it is estimated that traffic on Robert Street will increase 17% northbound and 22% southbound. The potential need for additional traffic control personnel is not even mentioned by the developer.

5. Finally, opponents claim that if the mall is a financial failure, not only will the projected increase in revenues not be forthcoming, but in addition, the city will then face the prospect of a decaying and empty shopping mall next to the newest subdivisions. (The developers are particularly angry at this gloomy prediction, arguing that the there is no evidence to support it.)

The S.O.S. coalition members include:

Professor of Mathematics (Role 17)
Retired Professional Football Player (Role 29)
Director, CSU Institute for Applied Gerontological Studies
    (Role 36)
Attorney (Role 41)
President, Right to Life Society of Greater Camelot (Role 53)
High School Teacher (Role 58)

As a result of the opposition, the planning commission split three to three, with one abstention, on the zoning change. Commissioners 10, 13, and 15 voted "yes"; commissioners 11, 12, and 14 voted "no," and commissioner 22 abstained. The tie vote means that the planning commission submitted the proposal to the council without a recommendation.

Other voices have been heard on the issue. Letters to the editor have appeared in the *Camelot Daily News* claiming that the opposition to the strip mall comes from the well-to-do who care only for themselves, not the unemployed, and especially minorities, who feel acutely the need for jobs created by the new retail stores. In addition to persons mentioned earlier, the following individuals have announced their support of the strip mall proposal:

> Affirmative Action Officer, City of Camelot (Role 31) Minister of
>   the A.M.E. Church (Role 32)
> Insurance Agent (Role 35)
> Director of Urban Welfare Program (Role 37)
> Minister of the First Presbyterian Church (Role 48)
> Head of the Local Chapter of the NAACP (Role 50)
> Owner of the Firehouse Bookstore (Role 60)
> Executive Director, Camelot Chamber of Commerce (Role 62)
> Chairman of Camelot Hispanic Coalition (Role 72)

(Note: The list of proponents and opponents should not be viewed as exclusive. *Any citizen of Camelot should feel free to speak for or against this proposed zoning change.*)

The issue is: Shall council change the zoning from R-1, single-family homes, to C-3, commercial? Since no city funds are involved, the council must weigh the possible increase in tax revenues and job opportunities against the stated threats felt by property owners in the Camelot Acres and South Ridge subdivisions to the personal safety of themselves and their children and to the potential loss in value of their property, and then council must decide whether approval of this new commercial facility is appropriate.

THE HOME FOR THE MENTALLY ILL ISSUE

The following issue will be presented to the PLANNING COMMISSION at the simulation session indicated by your instructor.

Historically, adults suffering from mental disability or mental illness and who had no one to care for them were placed in state institutions established for that purpose. Many of these individuals were not dangerous to society or themselves, and investigations into the quality of their care often revealed conditions that ranged from unsatisfactory to appalling.

As criticism of the conditions of state institutions increased, as the attitudes of the health professionals toward the mentally ill or retarded changed, and as advances were made in the treatment of chronic mental disorders, particularly in terms of antipsychotic medication, a national trend developed, supported by federal law, to de-emphasize institutional care and allow people with mental disabilities to live in the least restrictive environment possible. As one professional put it: "We are in an era of community treatment of the mentally ill. We used to take them out of the community and put them in a warehouse. But the mentally ill are now in our community."

The Federal Health Care Finance Administration has mandated states to develop residential homes for developmentally disabled and chronically mentally ill people. Many of the people are covered by medicaid, and state agencies have been informed that if these individuals are not taken out of nursing homes or institutions and integrated back into home communities, support funds will be cut off. Thus the issue is no longer a matter of debate because the process of shifting from institutions to community living is taking place. To illustrate the trend, according to one 1986 report, the number of patients in Ohio's 17 mental hospitals had declined from more than 28,000 in 1960 to about 4,000.

It is important to realize that the courts have stated that mental health clients are not state wards. They have all the rights of every citizen. They have a right to choose where they live. They can refuse treatment. They can decide not to go to counseling. If clients cease to come to treatment, they are not put on a missing persons list. The law says that unless persons are judged to be a danger to themselves or to others, they may not be institutionalized against their will.

As a result of this change in both attitudes and law toward the mentally retarded and mentally ill, residential care homes have been established. Some of these homes are supported by state and federal funds. In some counties additional funds come from local mental health levies. The most striking trait of the program is the unevenness of the quality of the services provided, including counseling about how to find housing and jobs, and follow-up care. A lawyer for the Ohio Legal Rights Service has stated that "a lot of people do get lost, not that that's bad. People have a right to a certain amount of freedom." Yet there is criticism that the mentally ill are discharged from hospitals too soon, sometimes because third-party payers limit hospital stay; that they refuse to follow a referral to the local mental health center after discharge; and that they stop taking medication regularly.

The problem, thus, is that often there is great variability in the functioning level of clients in need of or eligible for residential facilities licensed by the state. It is clear that some need supervised care and some don't. The determination of who needs what kind and how much care is less clear.

The Health Department of Madison County has purchased a home in Crown Knolls several blocks north of Woodworth Road, west of the Interstate, in an R-4 zone. It is one of the "large, well-kept old homes with large lots," mentioned on page 165. The Health Department's plan is to convert the house into a home for 10 men with mental disorders. It is likely that this will be the maximum number to be housed at this time, but it is possible that the number could reach 15. In many ways it is an ideal location for the home. The neighborhood is quiet and crime-free, with minimal amounts of traffic. These individuals do not have a history of being dangerous to themselves or anyone else.

Several facts must be made clear. This facility will provide 24-hour supervision. Two psychiatric attendants will be on duty at all times. One of these individuals will be a nurse and thus qualified to administer medications. Should the number of residents be increased, there will be a proportionate increase in staff. A doctor will examine the men at regular intervals in order to monitor the dosage of the medication and to check on the general health of the residents.

In keeping with the deinstitutionalization of the mentally ill, the residents will be permitted to come and go as they wish. Indeed, this location was selected because of its proximity to shopping facilities and public transportation. There is at present no fence around the property, nor is there any plan to build one.

The neighborhood is most upset. The residents include some young families with children, a sizable number of older couples who have lived in the area for years, and a number of widows living alone. They have hired an attorney (Role 51) to represent them, for they are convinced that a special use permit should not be granted for the home for the mentally ill in their neighborhood.

The director of the Public Health Department (Role 44) argues that a home for the mentally ill is not a "mental institution," for these men are not dangerous individuals. The supervision they require is not to protect the community from them, but to assist them in living in the community. They are not prisoners in any sense of the word, for they have committed no crime, nor are they deemed mentally incompetent. The request by the Department of Health representatives, therefore, is to ask the planning commission and council to issue a special use permit for this activity in this R-4 zone.

Particularly interesting about the problem is the fact that there is support for the idea in the planning commission (Role 12 lives just two blocks away). However, councillor 4 and the junior high school teacher (Role 43) live only a few houses away. Their views reflect those of the neighborhood.

The problem of definition is now in the hands of the planning commission and council.

THE TOPLESS BAR AND GRILL ISSUE

The following issue will be presented to the PLANNING COMMISSION at the simulation session indicated by your instructor.

When the Camelot Bar and Grill went bankrupt, it was purchased by Role 59. Then the menu was extended so that lunch was served on a regular basis, Monday through Saturday, and the hamburgers, chili, hot chicken wings, and other menu items became enormously popular, especially when an additional feature was provided—topless waitresses. Business boomed. The new owner found that by remodeling the interior he could increase the space available for tables, and thus increase the number of patrons. However, the additional space for patrons will require additional kitchen space, for the present kitchen is already inadequate for the volume of business.

When the owner sought a building permit to expand the kitchen by adding on to the rear of the building a space measuring 15 feet by 20 feet, the application was denied because the restaurant does not conform to the zoning code. It now lacks four parking spaces that would be needed to bring it into conformity with the code, and the kitchen expansion would take away three additional spaces.

A word of explanation about nonconforming uses is in order here. When a zoning code is first adopted, or when it is amended in some way, there may be particular structures that fail to conform to the new standards. The nonconformity may be in the character of the current use—a rooming house in an area of single family homes, or a convenience store in a residential area. It may be in the dimensional requirements of the zoning code—a lot too small for a duplex, or side yards too narrow to meet the standard for single-family homes in that area. In such instances, the use may continue; the zoning code cannot extinguish an ongoing use that was lawful the day before the code (or its amendment) was adopted. *But a typical provision of zoning codes provides that a structure that is nonconforming because of present use or because of dimensional inadequacies of the lot, or for any other reason, cannot be enlarged.* That is, while interior remodeling can occur lawfully, the external dimensions of a structure cannot be increased without a zoning variance. A *zoning variance,* which can be issued by the Camelot Planning Commission, is a special permission tailored to a specific property and circumstance. In most cities a variance request would be addressed to a zoning appeals board, established to relieve the planning commission of some of its burden of decision, but for purposes of the simulation the authors have merged the functions of the zoning appeals board with the functions of the planning commission. As with all planning commission actions, council approval or disapproval is required.

The zoning law requires one parking space for each 200 square feet of floor area. The current space available for parking is four spaces fewer than is required, but the building is considered a *nonconforming use* because it was built before the parking space requirement was established, and is therefore exempt from the requirement *as long as no changes are made in the size of the structure.* The proposed addition would add fifteen feet to the building at the rear, in order to enlarge the kitchen and increase the seating capacity of the establishment. This addition would eliminate three more parking spaces. The building is already at the allowable front and side limits.

In addition to the problem of an insufficient number of spaces for parking, there is the matter of the topless waitresses innovation, which has not been without opposition. Opponents include an unusual coalition: the head of the Camelot chapter of the National Organization of Women (Role 54), the vice president of the Christian Revival Movement (Role 56), the copywriter (Role 45), the junior high teacher (Role 43), and the minister of the First Presbyterian Church (Role 48). They have circulated a petition that urges council to ban toplessness in food service establishments and then to order police action to close the restaurant. In addition, they have circulated a second petition that calls on the planning commission and council to deny the restaurant owner's request for a zone variance to enlarge the restaurant because of the restaurant's failure to have an adequate number of parking spaces. The city manager has referred the first petition to council and the second petition to the planning commission.

The immediate issue for council is whether to ban upper body nudity in public places, in particular in food service establishments, since there is no suggestion that prostitution is involved. But council must face not merely the immediate problem of this bar and grill with topless waitresses but also what it forecasts. Suppose more of the bars decide to go topless, what then? Suppose other businesses decide to have topless attendants? For example, the tiny New York State community of West Brighton, on Staten Island, recently faced the prospect of a topless car wash. Does Camelot want to face that prospect? The bar is located in the Central Business District, not too far from the location of the proposed new downtown hotel plaza. The area is zoned C-3 (see page 164 for a description of this zone).

The question of topless bars has simply never come up before in Camelot. Since the waitresses are all members of a local union, their attorney (Role 51) will represent them.

1. The issue for the planning commission is whether or not to grant the zoning variance to permit the bar and grill to expand even though the expansion will eliminate more parking spaces. The planning commission does not have to deal with the question of topless waitresses, although the coalition opposing toplessness will urge a denial based on this point. Council must review planning commission's recommendation on the variance issue.
2. The second issue, that of permitting upper body nudity in public places, does not require council to write a detailed ordinance. All that is needed is a resolution instructing the city manager to have appropriate legislation drawn up either to permit or prohibit upper body nudity in public places. However, the resolution has at least to be specific about what is to be permitted or banned. State law prohibits lower body nudity in all public places where food or beverages are served, so that is not at issue here.

It goes without saying that the opponents are adamantly against permitting any nudity in public places. Equally concerned, because of the implied exploitation of women, are the female councillors.

The problem is not as simple as it may seem, for the laws of the State of Huron provide definitions and limits to actions council may take. Following are extracts from the relevant sections of the Revised Code of the State of Huron.

2907.01   *Obscenity.* A performance is obscene if the dominant appeal is to prurient interest. [Note: *Prurient is* that which tends to arouse sexual desire.]

2907.32   No establishment shall produce or direct an obscene performance for commercial exploitation. [Note: *Performance* is defined as any play, show, skit, dance, or exhibition performed before an audience.]

2907.37   The operation of an establishment can be enjoined if 2907.32 is being violated.

Arguments for the operation of a topless bar:

1. The waitresses are not performing but rather serving the customers.
2. The dominant appeal of the establishment is the bar and the restaurant, not to prurient interests aroused by the employees.
3. No sex acts are performed, nor is prostitution or solicitation permitted.
4. The laws prohibiting obscenity are not involved, for nudity, especially toplessness, is not of and by itself obscene.

Concluding remark from *Huron Jurisprudence,* Vol. 19, p. 493: "An employer's right to carry on his business in any manner that seems best so long as it does not violate any law or infringe upon the rights of others is a constitutionally guaranteed property right."

THE HANDGUN BAN ISSUE

The following issue will be presented to the COUNCIL at the simulation session indicated by your instructor.

As reported in The Camelot Daily News, the death of Police Officer Dennis Murphy made him the second officer within the last 18 months to be killed in the line of duty by a gunman using a handgun.[9] This has evoked a public outcry against guns, in addition to the issues discussed in the Officer Protection Issue.

---

[9]The Handgun Ban issue is based on similar events that occurred in Morton Grove, Illinois, in June 1981.

The following proposed ordinance will be presented to council by councillor 2:

> *Whereas* the proliferation of handguns represents a significant threat to the citizens of Camelot, its business community, and its children, and
> *Whereas* the number of handguns in the community is increasing,
> *It is hereby ordered* that all handguns in the city of Camelot must be handed over to the police within 90 days. Anyone found in possession of a handgun after that date may be imprisoned for not more than six months. This provision does not apply to handguns that have been altered permanently to prevent their use as a firearm.

Section I

A handgun is considered to be any ballistic weapon of calibers ranging from .20 in. to .50 in., with a barrel 12 in. or less in length, with no shoulder stock, and firing a self-contained cartridge.

Section II

Within 90 days of the date of enactment of this ordinance, all handguns in the possession of citizens of the city shall be presented to the Police Department for inspection (at the expense of the owner) and subject to confiscation or proof of inability to fire. Exceptions will be granted for merchants, security guards, and other citizens who can demonstrate a need to own a gun. Rifles and shotguns will still be legal and residents will not need a permit to own such weapons. Any other handgun shall, following issuance of a search warrant, be seized by the police of the city of Camelot.[10]

It is not surprising that councillor 2 is a supporter of the handgun ban, as is the city manager and the police chief. Police departments and city administrators in general tend to be in favor of legislation that may reduce the danger faced by the police in their investigation of reported crimes. The owner of the Firehouse Bookstore has strong views in opposition to a ban. It is equally understandable that councillor 3 is outspoken in his opposition to the attempt to control handguns. Joined in this opposition is the editor of *The Camelot Daily News,* and one of the owners of Crown Real Estate (Role 39). These individuals, whose positions on either side of the subject have been stated publicly

---

[10]Automatic weapons are already illegal under federal law.

in the past, will very likely be joined by other citizens of Camelot as the occasion to speak out occurs.

Many defenders of gun possession cite the wording of the Second Amendment to the U.S. Constitution, which states: "A well regulated Militia, being necessary to the security of a free state, the right of the people to keep and bear Arms, shall not be infringed."

This argument overlooks the fact that the Bill of Rights of the U.S. Constitution was written to protect citizens from actions of the *national* government, not the state governments. The Founding Fathers assumed from their study of history that the greatest danger of violations of civil liberties would come from a central government.

Some decades after the 1868 ratification of the Fourteenth Amendment, the U.S. Supreme Court began to decide, on a case by case basis, that some of the limits on the power of the national government, created by the First through the Eighth Amendments, also created limits on the actions of the states. This extension of the Bill of Rights to the state level *occurred on a selective basis.* Bit by bit, the Supreme Court said that the states, as well as the national government, could not abridge the First Amendment freedoms of speech, press, religion, peaceful assembly, and so on. However, this selective incorporation by the Supreme Court of provisions of the Bill of Rights into the Fourteenth Amendment has not as yet included the Second Amendment's assertion of a right to bear arms. The states and localities appear to have broad range of powers to regulate guns without interference from the U.S. Constitution.

THE ABORTION CLINICS ISSUE

The following issue will be presented to the PLANNING COMMISSION at the simulation session indicated by your instructor.

The president of the Right to Life Society of Greater Camelot, speaking for citizens opposed to abortion, has presented to the Camelot Planning Commission the following petition:[11]

---

[11]In spite of the Right to Life Society statement, abortions in Camelot are legal. However, the petitioners are not challenging the legality of abortions. Existing hospitals would be classified as "nonconforming use" structures. Thus, if a licensed physician has been admitted to practice at an accredited hospital in Camelot and that physician prescribes an abortion, then the petitioners do not question the right of the physician to carry out an abortion. However, existing hospitals could not be enlarged for the purpose of establishing an abortion clinic. *As it is stated, this is a zoning*

Whereas the taking of the life of an unborn child is murder and therefore contrary to the laws of God and the State of Huron,

And whereas the attached petition signed by over 5,000 citizens of Camelot testifies to the widespread community support for this concern for the safety of the unborn,

Therefore, we do respectfully request the Planning Commission and City Council of Camelot to amend the zoning regulations of the city of Camelot to forbid the use of any structure located within the city of Camelot for the purpose of aborting the life of a human embryo. No exceptions should be allowed to this prohibition.

THE BUDDHIST TEMPLE ISSUE

The following issue will be presented to the PLANNING COMMISSION at the simulation session indicated by your instructor.

A group of Korean Buddhists has purchased a house in Forest Acres, to be used as a temple for holding their religious services.[12] The house happens to be located in one of the most affluent sections of Camelot, the area west of Robert Street and north of Patricia Road (see description on page 165). The services involve chanting, singing, and tapping on a coconut-sized wooden instrument called a mok tak. The service lasts for about three hours, beginning about 8:00 A.M.

There are two problems involved. One is that the neighbors (represented by their attorney, Role 41) are disturbed by the noise created by the service, by the traffic created by those coming to the service, and by their fear of loss of property values. One neighbor, who lives several doors away from the home, commented that "I don't care what the religion is. It's just not a place for a church." Another neighbor, who lives next door to Buddhists, said, "The noise they make is driving everyone batty."

The second problem is that, according to Camelot zoning restrictions, no church is permitted in an R-1 area without a special use permit. Apparently the drafters of the zoning ordinance assumed that all

question. The legality of abortions is not the question, only the prohibition of it as a permitted use in any zone description. The target of the petitioners is abortion clinics.

Numerous cities have experienced difficulty with this issue. In particular, the authors have drawn upon the continuing controversy on this topic in Cincinnati.

[12]The Buddhist Temple Issue is based on events that occurred in Fulton, Maryland, as reported by Associated Press writer, Larry Rosenthal. The article appeared in The *Cincinnati Enquirer,* February 20, 1983.

churches would be constructed rather than remodeled from existing buildings. As a consequence, there are no dimensional requirements for churches in the zoning code, nor are there any parking space requirements.

The attorney for the Buddhists (Role 49) has submitted a request for a special use permit to the city manager, who in turn has placed the request on the planning commission's agenda. The attorney for the Buddhists will argue that failure to grant the special use permit is a violation of the "free exercise of religion" clause of the First Amendment to the U.S. Constitution and that a permit would undoubtedly be approved if those requesting it were Episcopalians. There are no other churches in this area. The Buddhist attorney also will stress that no one has suggested that the house will be used for purposes other than religious, that the number of people in the congregation is, at the present time, a maximum of 20, and that attendance at the temple and the resulting traffic will be limited.

THE GROWTH RATE ISSUE

This will be presented to the Planning COMMISSION at the session indicated by your instructor.

The master plan for the city of Camelot is being updated, and some two months ago a draft of the revised plan, prepared by the city's planning staff under the supervision of the assistant city manager, was submitted to the planning commission. Due to the pressure of current business, the planning commission has not been able to deal with the report, particularly the policy question raised by the report: For what growth rate should the staff plan project estimates?

Of course, the growth rate is not easily controlled, nor is it ever entirely controllable. Economic factors and climate may exert influences that overshadow the best efforts of planners. Still, one must begin somewhere, and the best way is to decide what the preferred growth would be if one had full control over the situation. Then subsequent steps in the planning process can take account of the latest economic forecasts and the most recent information concerning migration in and out of the region. Following that, the council will be in a better position to adopt implementing measures in pursuit of the previously identified preferred growth rate.

The simulation players needn't grapple with the details of policy implementation, however. All that is needed now is for the planning commission to recommend to council a preferred growth rate. The staff will do the rest.

At stake here are the implications for a city of a rapid rate of growth. Not only will there be a rapid escalation in the prices of land and houses, but in addition, as population growth quickens, there will be a corresponding increase in need and demand for recreation facilities, schools, utilities (water and sewage), fire and police protection, and so on. Will churches be increased in size and/or number to accommodate the growth? Will parks? Will public buildings accommodate the growth? Will the street and highway system suffice, or will it bulge and strain at the seams? Can the city administration keep abreast of rapid change, or will the supply of facilities and amenities lag behind demand? Ponder, for example, what the chart that follows reveals about a 15 percent annual increase in population in 10 years. In 20 years. Of course, such a rate is unlikely to be reached in most cities, let alone sustained. But even a 4 percent growth rate would mean that the population of your hometown would more than double between your birth and your 21st birthday.

Population Growth Implications of Varying Growth Rates

	2 Percent	5 Percent	10 Percent	15 Percent
This year	138,000	138,000	138,000	138,000
+ 5 years	152,363	167,899	222,250	277,567
+ 10 years	168,221	204,273	357,936	558,286
+ 15 years	185,729	248,529	576,460	1,122,913
+ 20 years	205,060	302,374	928,395	2,258,579

The rate of growth of a city has to be viewed from two different aspects: the impact of rapid growth on the individual, and the impact on city government. Two questions come to mind on the topic of impact of more rapid growth on the individual. What is the objective of those who favor a more rapid growth rate, as compared with those who favor a slow rate? What is the impact of each of these positions?

Some citizens believe that growth equals progress and that the forces of change bring an opportunity for economic growth and an improvement in the life of the citizenry. They also argue that a more rapid rate of growth will bring a sizable increase in the number of jobs in the city: jobs in construction, city services, and new industries. In addition there will be a growth in city revenues from income and property taxes as a result of industries enticed or encouraged to come to the area, or to expand existing plants already in the area.

Other citizens argue that all changes cause problems, and more rapid *rates* of change impose more stress on both the entire city and on the affected neighborhoods, which threatens the quality of life. Change is not just a word. One has to cope with change, and that is why change creates stress. The citizens arguing against rapid growth also believe neither they nor the city as a whole will receive much benefit from the additional population, or from the expansion of the industrial, retail, or service base.

Change disturbs those who are already comfortable and who live in the more stable sections of the city. These stable areas often include working and middle class neighborhoods, and especially ethnic neighborhoods. Thus, more rapid growth suggests to them that there will be in-migration of newcomers who may be deemed "outsiders"; that is, the many new families will seek employment opportunities and housing. These older neighborhoods often experience a decline in property values as housing is converted to rooming houses or apartments to meet the needs of the newcomers. The more affluent and mobile residents of the older areas, upset by the changes, begin to flee to the more desirable, and newer, suburbs. As the land on the fringes of the city is developed, medical services, professional offices, retail and service businesses, and other types of enterprise will relocate in the new industrial parks. Shopping centers will be built either in the suburbs or in the open spaces beyond the suburbs as retail stores try to offer the customers convenient and enticing places in which to shop and park.

Many of those who are caught by the changes resulting from growth, by the decline in property values and the loss of the stability of the old neighborhoods, will be retirees or the elderly, who cannot afford the cost of the new suburban homes, or whose personal history, churches, families, and friends are likely to be tied to the old neighborhoods. They see little to applaud when viewing the infusion of newcomers to their neighborhoods, newcomers who include transients as well as working class individuals seeking new opportunities. Change also provides increased chances for opportunistic behavior and criminal activities in these older and increasingly unstable neighborhoods.

The gain of those who benefit from more rapid growth has to be balanced against the pain of those who lose from growth. But there is also the impact of more rapid growth on the city itself, an impact quite separate from what happens to those individuals affected by growth.

Growth is expected to provide new revenues for the city as the new properties generate property tax increases and the new job opportunities generate income tax revenues. And that is true. Often unmentioned by the proponents of more rapid growth is that the demand for city services may exceed by far the amount of increase in tax revenues.

It is natural for those facing the question of what shall be the rate of growth to ask: (1) What new services must the city provide? (2) What will be the cost of those new services? (3) How much revenue will be generated by the different rates of growth? Even brief reflection will reveal that there is no way on earth to know the exact answer to any of these questions. One can guess the number of police, fire fighters, schools, and teachers needed by asking other cities that have experienced rapid growth—but one can only guess. And only a small number of needs can be identified with even approximate accuracy. Here is a single example of the many problems to be faced and of the variables to ponder:

1. Does one build sewer lines for current needs or for possible future needs? The answer will determine the size of the pipe, the locations of the plant, the sophistication of the system, construction costs now, and adequacy in twenty years.
2. Sewage treatment plants have capacity limits. If the limits are exceeded, one doesn't merely put on an added part. It isn't like adding a larger speaker to a stereo system. You have to predict the needed capacity of a proposed system by deciding how large the population will be in five years, or ten years, and build a plant to meet the estimated demand. Does one always build a plant to meet the greatest possible increase in population, the least, or something in the middle range? The same is true of schools and hospitals. If you opt for the largest increase, where does the money come from to pay for all the new staff and facilities? Do you add to the tax burden of the present population to pay for services on the possibility that they might be needed some day? The impact on the less affluent, retirees, and the elderly is immediately apparent.

Unfortunately, predicting population growth is an inexact science. There are instances, such as Petaluma, California, where growth was 25% a year for several years during the late 1960s and early 1970s! Thus how does one estimate the costs that will result from such growth?

In addition to the effects of more rapid growth on the city's governmental activities and programs, there is also the impact on societal organizations and institutions. The appropriate question here is whether they expand as rapidly as the population growth. For example, you cannot instantly double the number of places of worship or the size of recreation facilities. If they are not available, the new citizens will have to travel to former churches and recreation facilities or forego these activities. Either of these choices means that the new citizens are not being integrated into the new neighborhoods. This delay in the creation of facilities will affect every other activity people engage in: movie theaters, social clubs, restaurants, retail shopping centers. No matter how rapidly facilities are built, continuous rapid growth results in the inability of such organizations and institutions to keep up with demand.

As if that were not enough of a problem, think of the impact of rapid growth on something as essential as streets and highways. Rush hour traffic becomes an experience resembling insanity. You can't simply double the width of existing streets to meet the new crush of automobiles as people drive to and from places of work. Each city institution will be working frantically to keep up with the impact of the arrival of all the new residents, and continually failing. Just as rapid change creates stress for the older residents, it also is stressful for the newcomers. Change is a challenge for everyone.

A second major problem for rapidly growing cities (or school systems) is that revenues do not keep up with expenditures. Let us suggest that rapid growth has prompted the adoption this month of a tax increase effective next January 1 to pay for an additional school building, another police station, and an additional fire station, all to open on January 1, *next* year. Thus the city (or the school board) will have to pay for these new facilities, plus all the salaries for the new police officers, fire fighters, and teachers, plus all the maintenance costs for the buildings as of January 1, *next* year. However, the property tax bills in many states are a year late. Thus in January *next* year, the property owner will receive a bill for taxes accrued during the first six months of *this* year. The result for the city and the school board is that the additional property tax revenues resulting from the population growth will arrive at least one year after the expenses have to be paid.

Of equal importance, the city may have granted tax abatements to a particular company in order to create new jobs. As an inducement to a company to build a new plant, expand an existing plant, or move to the city, the city offered the company a full or partial exemption from property taxes on the plant (tax abatement) for a period of time, from five to twenty years. As in the previous example, the city council and the school board must meet the immediate costs created by the new or expanded company and by newcomers brought to the city by the new job opportunities, but the council and the board will not have the property taxes to help pay for these costs for five, ten, or more years.

And there you have some of the dilemmas the planning commission and the council must face. An increase in growth offers economic revitalization for the city. It holds the promise of creating new jobs and new tax revenues, and thus the means to pay for new services for the citizenry. It also will bring pain and suffering, both financial and personal, to those for whom population growth may bring the destruction of older neighborhoods without compensating benefits.

THE NOISE ORDINANCE ISSUE

The following issue will be presented to COUNCIL at the simulation session indicated by your instructor.

Camelot is not alone in its quest for quieter streets and neighborhoods. About 1,000 other U.S. cities have noise ordinances, and more are considering drafting such legislation.

An average noise ordinance has a daytime maximum of 55 decibels, and an evening level of 45 to 50 decibels. The level proposed for Camelot would be 70 decibels for the daytime and 50 for evening.

Noise ordinances differ among cities. While some stress vehicular and industrial noise, others have ordinances which focus primarily on noise in residential areas. Still others attempt to control loud radios, stereos, or boom boxes. The method of measurement differs also. For example, Akron, Ohio's, ordinance states that if a police officer standing 80 feet away from a house can hear noise from that house, it merits a citation: if a police officer standing 100 feet from a car stereo or a boom box can hear noise from that stereo or boom box, it merits a citation. No complaint is required. A North Olmstead, Ohio, ordinance restricts noise within places of entertainment. The level cannot exceed 95 decibels on a sound-level meter "at any point that is normally occupied by a customer." Richmond Heights, Ohio, sets the decibel level at 55, measured at any lot line within a residential district. Industrial or commercial districts cannot exceed noise levels beyond 60 decibels at the lot line. Trotwood, Ohio, has an ordinance restricting the noise of motor vehicles. A level of 80 decibels cannot be exceeded at any time.

The legal justification for such ordinances is twofold: excessive noise violates laws against disturbing the peace and/or violates road safety laws in that individuals driving cars whose stereos exceed the prescribed limits cannot hear horns, sirens, or other warning devices.

The effects of noise levels on humans have been estimated and reported by the U.S. Environmental Protection Agency. At 10 decibels, a noise is just audible. At 50, the noise is described as quiet. The noise becomes "intrusive" at 60 decibels, and annoying at 80. Hearing damage may result from prolonged exposure to noise at the 90-decibel level and beyond, according to the EPA.

The report also said an increase in 10 decibels doubles the perceived sound to the observer. An average clothes dryer has a reading of 50 to 55 decibels from a distance of 15 feet.

When drafting noise ordinances, cities take into account the nature of the population. A college or resort town sometimes legislates slightly higher noise levels than average residential areas. It should also be noted that when the federal Office of Noise Abatement and Control was abolished in 1982, due to federal budget cuts, its responsibilities were transferred to the states. Though Huron does not have a statewide law, cities where excessive noise has become bothersome have adopted their own ordinances.

Camelot citizens in College Town and University Park, in the area east and west of the university, are up in arms over the blasting stereos, the loud parties which often last all night long, and the impromptu parades of "fraternity" students in the middle of the night. The crux of the difficulty is that this area is undergoing changes. It contains a variety of lifestyles and socioeconomic classes. The noise problem is more acute on the streets nearer to the university. Many of the older homes are now crowded rental properties containing hordes of students, nonstudents, visiting transients, plus even some drifters no one knows. Interspersed with these buildings are extensively remodeled as well as new homes of young professionals, young faculty members, and clerical and technical workers connected with the university. On one street there are even three fraternity houses.

A delegation of citizens, including the junior high school teacher (Role 43), the director of Public Health (Role 44), and the publisher of *The Camelot Daily News* (Role 19), are going to demand that council pass a noise ordinance and enforce it. The police chief supports such legislation because it will give him a more easily enforceable standard than the "disturbing the peace" ordinance. The student newspaper has editorialized against such an ordinance, and several fraternities have hired an attorney (Role 49) to represent their interests.

Two types of noise ordinances exist, as discussed earlier in this section. One sets decibel levels and involves the use of devices that measure decibel level. The second type relies on a police officer's ability to hear sound beyond a set distance. Council thus has several decisions it may have to make. Council may, if it chooses, do the following:

1. Ignore the demands of the citizens for a noise ordinance.
2. Pass a resolution that instructs the city manager to draft an enforceable noise ordinance that will apply to noise beyond a designated level. Council should include in its instructions to the city manager such items as
   a. a recommendation concerning whether the ordinance will apply to audible sound from a residence and/or noise from a vehicle.
   b. whether enforcement will rely on a device to measure decibel levels and/or on a human ear.
   c. the decibel level permitted at specified times of day or night, or on the allowed distance beyond which sound may not be audible.

If council agrees to pass a noise ordinance, then it should also add a penalty section. Below are two approaches, each of which is in use in some locations:

A. *Offenses Committed by Individuals*
   1st offense—Warning
   2nd offense—Minor misdemeanor, maximum fine of $200
   3rd offense—If within six months of previous offense, 4th degree misdemeanor, maximum fine of $250, maximum of 10 days in jail.

   Offenses Committed by Organizations
   1st offense—Warning

2nd offense—Maximum fine of $500
3rd offense—Maximum fine of $1000

B. 1st offense—$100
2nd offense—$200 and forfeiture of stereo equipment if applicable

Council must decide:

1. whether a noise ordinance should be adopted,
2. what the penalties should be for violation of the ordinance, if one is adopted, and
3. if the noise ordinance will be enforced only if there are complaints, or if there will be routine noise patrols.

THE AIDS EXAMINATION AND DRUG TESTING ISSUE

The following issue will be presented to COUNCIL at the simulation session indicated by your instructor.

An outbreak of AIDS has occurred in the Camelot area. The director of the Department of Health (Role 44) is alarmed at the prospects for the entire population. The Department of Health has been deluged by phone calls, and the department clinics are overwhelmed with requests for appointments, examinations, and treatment.

Since there is at present neither a preventative vaccine nor a cure, the director believes that several steps must be taken to stop, or at least to slow down, the spread of the disease. The director has drafted a proposal, entitled "The Community Protection Plan," and the city manager is now presenting it to council (it has the manager's support). The proposal includes the following provisions:

1. All businesses licensed to serve liquor will be required to have condom vending machines on the premises.
2. Final applicants for all city jobs must undergo a drug test before hiring.
3. Existing employees may be asked to undergo a drug test if their supervisor has a reasonable suspicion of workplace drug abuse.
4. If a pattern of drug abuse is validated after several tests, an employee will be subject to disciplinary action or dismissal.
5. Convicted prostitutes will be required to take a test for AIDS.
6. Any person who has tested HIV-positive and then engages in unprotected sex with another person may be quarantined for a period

of at least six months during which period the individual must undergo a 60-day substance abuse program. The period of quarantine may be extended indefinitely if the program is not completed.

(Note: Each of the above provisions has been adopted or is being considered by one or more communities or states. Whether or not a quarantine, for example, is constitutional is not yet clear at this writing, therefore the Camelot city council need not be deterred from considering it or other provisions mentioned above.)

If your instructor decides to use this issue, the city manager will make sure that it is added to a council agenda. When it is considered by council, *the city manager will ask the director of the Health Department (Role 44) to explain the proposal and answer any questions which may arise.* The entire proposal will be endorsed by councillor 3, who is also very upset by the apparent epidemic of drug use in Camelot and its connection to the spread of the AIDS virus.

12

Reference Materials

CAMELOT: BASIC DATA

Population

Of 138,000 citizens:

82,000 are white and not students.
25,000 are minority and not students.
31,000 are students (all over 18 and therefore eligible to vote).

Camelot has an *unusually high percentage of middle-class minorities and whites.* There is an absence of overly depressing slums and a greater than usual degree of integration of the races.

However, there are many commuting low-skilled minority employees hired by the service and manufacturing businesses. Housing in Camelot tends to cost more than some of them believe they can afford.

Because of the nature of the city and its principal industry, Camelot State University, apartment housing is widely used. There is, however, much single-family housing, and some new housing developments are being built in neighboring and more distant suburban areas where less-expensive open land is available. There is a noticeable trend in Camelot to tear down older homes and replace them with apartments. Several luxury condominiums have been and are being built.

Although the presence of the university gives a strong middle- and upper-middle class thrust to the employment market, as with any city this size, some portion of the population will be at the margins of employment possibility and mental competence. Every university community attracts numbers of hangers-on, some former students, some attracted by the variety of lifestyles to be found in such an area. Although there is no unusual source of poverty, there are some individuals who fall into the poverty range, some elderly, some physically or mentally infirm, some unemployable, some unemployed because of a closing within Camelot's small but old industrial base—the Camelot Steel Wheel Foundry.

Economics in Camelot

The major employer in Camelot is the university. It has a reputation for excellence, both in graduate and undergraduate programs. It has a policy of selective admissions with large, prestigious professional schools and many out-of-state and foreign students.

Quite a number of small- and medium-size high-tech industries have been developed in the last 10 years as a result of the advanced research orientation of the science, medical, and engineering faculty of Camelot State University. This has been a rapidly expanding segment of the economic base of Camelot. The past decade also has witnessed the rapid growth of banking, insurance, and other service businesses. One national fast food chain began in Camelot and now has its headquarters here. The steel wheel factory has long since closed its doors.

Camelot is at a critical point in its existence. The downtown area is slowly but surely becoming run-down and dirty. Suburban developments and the Camelot Mall on the outskirts of the city have taken over the downtown's functions, the future of which will in large part be decided in the coming months through the decisions of the Camelot City Council.

CAMELOT: AREA DESCRIPTIONS

Camelot Heights

This area of Camelot was all built up after World War II. It is located east of Robert Street in the northeast corner of Camelot and is zoned R-2. The entire subdivision is basically working class to middle class. The homes vary in age from 20 to 40 years and are modest three-bedroom homes priced 20 to 25 percent below the price of the average three-bedroom homes in the newer subdivisions of Camelot. The homes in the northeast corner of this subdivision are slightly newer and more expensive but are not valued as high as homes in the northwest corner of this section.

The Central Business District (CBD)

The CBD is bounded by Woodworth Road on the north and Robert Street on the west. The east boundary of the CBD abuts Madisonville and Government Square. At the southwest corner is a finger of land which extends to the Russo River and has Robert Street to the west and Pioneer Park to the east (see "The Downtown Hotel Plaza Issue"). Except for this finger, the southern border of the CBD faces Pioneer Park and Government Square. Camelot is the state capital of the state of Huron. It is also the county seat of Madison County.

As you move north from Government Square there are numerous banks and financial service offices, and then retail stores and restaurants, many of which occupy older structures. This area is zoned C-3.

College Town

The area east of the university is zoned R-4, and while there are some houses that rent to students, especially adjacent to the campus, this area is basically inhabited by professors, clerical and professional workers connected with the university, and some government employees who commute to Government Square. The area includes many retired people. The streets are lined with trees, and the houses are fairly old but for the most part are well preserved and attractive. In some sections of College Town older houses are being renovated and extensively modernized; in other cases old houses are being replaced by architect-designed, modern homes. College Town is not the "elite" section of Camelot, but it is stylish and popular with younger individuals and couples. It is racially integrated.

Crown Knolls

The area north of Woodworth Road all the way to Patricia Road and west of Robert Street (and including the land west of the Interstate Highway) is known as Crown Knolls. In the portion immediately north of Woodworth Road there are many old homes occupied mainly by lower middle-class and low-income minorities and some low-income whites. The homes are, in many cases, run down and dilapidated, in urgent need of repair. There are also many old garages and much refuse cluttering up the lots and alleys. This section is zoned R-4. The northern portion of this bottom third of Crown Knolls contains working-class homes of similar small-frame bungalow style—the post–World War II type of home. They appear to be consistently well kept (but modest). On the periphery there are some large, well-kept old homes with large lots.

The next portion to the north, still to the west side of Robert Street, recently underwent urban renewal, and it now contains respectable apartments and condominiums, as well as several fashionable townhouses. It has been zoned R-3.

The most northern third of Crown Knolls, just south of Patricia Road, has a higher proportion of middle-class residents, mainly white-collar workers. Lots here are modest, but the houses are neat and the streets tree lined. It is zoned R-2.

Forest Acres

Forest Acres, located west of Robert Street and north of Patricia Road, is zoned R-l and is rather hilly in terrain—hence its later development. This is a wealthy area, where the upper middle class of Camelot live. The homes are big and expensive; they vary in age but are distinctive in architecture and landscaping. The lots tend to be large.

Madisonville

The area south of Woodworth Road and east of Government Square is a stable older community. There are several small office buildings and retail stores, such as drugstores, barber/beauty salons, and newsstands, but the area is predominantly residential; zoning is R-4. This is an integrated area, and middle class. There are many small apartment buildings of about four to six apartments, and the farther you are from the CBD the more single-family homes there are, intermixed with smaller apartments. It is zoned R-3. The streets are lined with shade trees and are rather old but pleasant.

North Madisonville

This area of Camelot is north of Madisonville, with Woodworth Road as the dividing line. Its western boundary is Robert Street. Its characteristics are very similar to Madisonville. Almost all of it is zoned R-3.

The only exception is the southwest corner just to the north of the CBD, which is zoned R-4. In the western part of North Madisonville, along the railroad tracks, there are some old multiple-family houses and small older apartments occupied by low-income residents, many of whom feel threatened by the possibility that they will be evicted from their homes after the absentee landlords sell out to land speculators. This small neighborhood is looked down upon by its neighbors; the area has a bad reputation (middle-class residents tend to avoid the area at night). The remainder of North Madisonville is mostly white working class, becoming mostly white middle-class as one goes north.

River Town

This entire area is zoned M-1. It used to be the traditional manufacturing and industrial area of Camelot. Some sections of it near the Interstate Highway have been cleared of the old structures, and those areas have been opened up for an industrial park. High-tech industries have been given incentives (tax abatements, cleared land, access streets) to locate here. Some have, although many have moved outside the city limits. Other new businesses include light manufacturing, a truck terminal, and a regional warehouse for a large grocery chain. There continues to be a severe parking shortage in most of this area although the program of razing of old factories is easing this problem on some streets. The Camelot Steel Wheel Foundry stands empty, a silent monument to the smokestack era.

Immediately to the west of Robert Street and south of Woodworth Road are warehouses and wholesale establishments. The general appearance is one of age and grime.

University Park

Camelot State University is located with University Park to its west and south and College Town to its east. The majority of the residents of University Park, especially the first several blocks to the west of the university, are either students or are connected in some way with the university. All of University Park is zoned R-5. The area contains many apartments and rooming houses; the homes closest to the university are old and run down. As you move farther west the buildings become newer, with those farthest away from the campus (west of the interstate) being single-family ranch houses, many of which are owned by professors or administrators.

A large portion of the southwest corner of the city is undeveloped land.

Camelot Acres

This is a new subdivision, as is South Ridge. Camelot Acres is located immediately south of University Park subdivision, and west of Robert Street, which provides the means of access. Lancelot Creek's ravine separates Camelot Acres from the more expensive South Ridge subdivision. Camelot Acres is the site of moderately priced homes, ranging in price from $125,000 to $200,000. While these are all very nice homes, the lots are small and modestly landscaped. About 75 homes have been built in this area, with space remaining for perhaps 25 to 30 more.

South Ridge

One of the newest subdivisions, it is situated west of Robert Street and south of the Camelot Acres subdivision. Lancelot Creek's ravine separates the two subdivisions. Access is available from Robert Street. The homes are upscale, ranging in price from a few at $250,00 to the upper end of the scale at $500,000. There are 25 homes already built, three more are under construction, and ten more are in the planning stage.

The smallest home has 3,000 square feet, the largest thus far has 5,000 square feet. The typical home has four bedrooms, a media room, a study, four bathrooms, and a fitness room. There are the usual public rooms, including an atrium. All the rooms are spacious. The largest lot is only an acre in size, but all the homes are beautifully landscaped. The streets are cobblestone with European-style lamps.

The foyer of the most expensive home has a two-story atrium, and a thirty- by twenty-foot living room with cathedral ceiling. The twenty-foot square master bedroom has a bathroom with glass-brick enclosed shower with multiple faucet heads, a step-in tub large enough for two people, a bidet, and a dressing room. (Note: The $450,000 price is considered by a developer to be a reasonably accurate guess for such a home built in much of the United States, except for parts of the Southwest, the West Coast, and the Eastern Corridor from Virginia to Maine. For those areas, the price would be higher by an additional $100,000 to $300,000.

THE CHARTER

The City Charter is the basic organizing document of the city. It establishes the city government in much the same way that a state constitution establishes the state government, by providing for organization, powers, and duties.

You may find more details in the Charter than you use. Our purpose is to show you what a typical charter looks like, and what you read is based on a real charter. Thus, the "Powers of Council" Section (2.11) lists all the powers a typical council might have, even though the Camelot council will not need to use all of them in this simulation.

In the simulation, as in life, knowledge of the Charter will be unevenly distributed among the citizenry. Those who wish to put it to use will become familiar with it.

The Charter of the City of Camelot

County of Madison
State of Huron

Preamble

We, the people of the City of Camelot, Madison County, State of Huron, in order to secure for ourselves the benefits of local self-government under the Constitution of the State of Huron, do ordain and establish this Charter for the government of the municipality of Camelot.

Article I

INCORPORATION, FORM OF GOVERNMENT, POWERS

SECTION 1.02 POWERS.   Except as prohibited by the Constitution of this State or restricted by this Charter, the City of Camelot shall have and may exercise all municipal powers, functions, rights, privileges and immunities of every name and nature whatsoever. The enumeration of particular powers in this Charter shall not be deemed to be exclusive, and in addition to the powers enumerated herein or implied hereby or appropriate to the exercise of such powers, it is intended that the City shall have and may exercise all powers which, under the Constitution of this State or under the laws of the State of Huron, it would be competent for this Charter specifically to enumerate.

SECTION 1.03 MANNER OF EXERCISING POWERS.   All powers of the corporation shall be vested in an elective Council which shall enact local ordinances and resolutions, adopt budgets, determine general policies and appoint a City Manager, who shall see that the policies and legislation adopted by the Council are enforced. All powers of the corporation shall be exercised in the manner prescribed by this Charter,

or if the manner be not prescribed, then in such manner as may be prescribed by ordinance or by general law.

SECTION 1.04 FORM OF GOVERNMENT.   The form of government provided under this Charter shall be known as the "Council-Manager Plan."

Article II

THE COUNCIL

SECTION 2.01 NUMBER, SELECTION, TERM.   The City Council shall consist of five members,[1] elected at large, for four-year overlapping terms. All elections of Council members shall be on a nonpartisan ballot.

SECTION 2.02 QUALIFICATIONS.   Any qualified elector shall be eligible to serve as a member of Council, when elected as hereinafter provided. No member of Council shall hold any other public office. A councillor who ceases to be a qualified elector, or who accepts and enters upon the performance of the duties of an incompatible office, or who is absent, without excuse by the other members of Council, from meetings of Council during two consecutive meetings, shall automatically vacate the office on the Council.

SECTION 2.03 VACANCIES, FILLING OF.   Vacancies in the office of Council members shall be filled at the next simulation session by vote of a majority of the remaining members of Council, by the selection of a qualified elector. If Council fails to make this selection at the next simulation session, the

---

[1]May be enlarged to seven or more members by instructor.

Mayor shall make the appointment. Such person so chosen shall serve until the next regular municipal election. At such election a successor shall be elected to serve for the unexpired term, if any; if not, for a full term.

SECTION 2.06 ORGANIZATION AND MEETINGS. Following each municipal election Council shall meet for the purpose of organizing. At such meeting the newly elected members of Council shall take the oath of office and the Council shall proceed to elect a Mayor and a Vice Mayor and may transact such other business as may come before it. Thereafter, regular meetings shall be held as prescribed in the Council rules. All meetings of Council shall be open to the public. A majority of the members elected shall constitute a quorum at all meetings.

SECTION 2.07 MAYOR AND VICE MAYOR. The Council shall select from among its own members one to serve as Mayor and one as Vice Mayor. The Mayor shall preside at Council meetings, when present, and shall have a vote on all matters which come before Council, but shall have no power to veto. He or she shall be the ceremonial head of the municipality, but shall exercise no administrative authority. The Vice Mayor shall preside over the meetings of the Council when the Mayor is absent and shall perform such other duties as may be assigned him or her by ordinance.

SECTION 2.09 CLERK OF COUNCIL. There shall be a Clerk of Council, elected by vote of a majority of the members of the Council from outside its membership, to serve until a successor is chosen and enters upon the duties of the clerk's office. The Clerk may be appointed to serve full time or part time, and the Council may assign the duties of the Clerk of Council to any employee of the municipality as an additional duty. The Clerk shall give notice of Council meetings, keep the journal, advertise public hearings, record in separate books all ordinances and resolutions enacted by Council and have the same published in the manner provided by this Charter. The Clerk shall perform such other duties as may be assigned by this Charter or by ordinance.

SECTION 2.11 POWERS OF THE COUNCIL. Among other powers the Council shall have authority to:

Adopt ordinances and resolutions on any subject within the scope of its powers, and to provide penalties for the violation thereof.

Establish the internal organization, staffing and compensation of the departments, boards and commissions created by this Charter; set up such additional departments, boards or commissions as it may deem necessary and determine their powers and duties.

Adopt and modify the master plan and official map of the municipality.

Regulate the use of private real estate in the municipality by establishing zones, limiting the uses in each zone, and limiting the height of buildings and the intensity of land use.

Adopt a subdivision platting ordinance and approve subdivision plats which conform thereto.

Enact a comprehensive building code.

Authorize the levy of taxes and the issuance of bonds as provided in this Charter.

Adopt an annual appropriation ordinance based upon the annual budget.

Appoint and remove the City Manager, establish his or her salary, and appoint an Acting City Manager when necessary.

Inquire into the conduct of any municipal officer or employee in the performance of his or her public functions.

Make investigations of any office, department or agency of the municipality.

Grant public utility franchises by vote of two thirds (2/3) of the members of Council.

Provide for the employment of engineering and other professional services on a consulting basis when deemed necessary.

Issue subpoenas for witnesses and to require the production of books and papers which may be necessary in the conduct of any hearing or investigation.

Article III
ORDINANCES AND RESOLUTIONS

SECTION 3.01 ACTION OF COUNCIL. The action of Council shall be by ordinance or resolution. On all matters of a general or permanent nature, or granting a franchise, or levying a tax, or appropriating money, or contracting an indebtedness, or issuing bonds or notes, or for the purchase, lease or transfer of property, action shall be taken formally, by ordinance in the manner hereinafter provided. Action on all other matters of a temporary or informal nature may be taken by resolution.

SECTION 3.02 ENACTMENT OF ORDINANCES. Each proposed ordinance shall be introduced in writing by a member of the Council, and in addition to the title shall contain an opening clause reading as follows, "Be it ordained by the Council of the City of Camelot, State of Huron." The action proposed to be taken shall be fully and clearly set forth in the body of the ordinance. Each ordinance shall contain one subject only, which shall be stated clearly in the title. No ordinance shall be passed without the concurrence of a majority of all members elected to Council, except that emergency ordinances, as hereinafter provided, shall require concurrence of three fourths (3/4) of all the members elected to Council for passage. Final passage of all ordinances and resolutions shall be certified by the Mayor or Vice Mayor and the Clerk of Council.

SECTION 3.03 EFFECTIVE DATE. Ordinances providing for appropriations for current expenses of the municipality, or for raising revenue, or ordinances wherein an emergency is declared to exist, shall become effective immediately upon passage or at such later date as may be provided therein, and such ordinances shall not be subject to referendum. All other ordinances shall take effect thirty minutes after passage. An emergency ordinance as referred to herein is one which must be passed and made effective at once or in less than thirty minutes to meet an emergency in the operation of the city government, or which is necessary for the immediate preservation of the public peace, health, safety, morals or welfare. Each emergency ordinance must contain therein a separate section setting forth the reason for the emergency. No ordinance granting a franchise or fixing a rate to be charged by a public utility shall be passed as an emergency measure.

Article IV
CITY MANAGER

SECTION 4.01 APPOINTMENT OF MANAGER. The Council shall appoint, by majority vote of all members elected thereto, an officer of the City who shall have the title of Manager. The Manager shall be chosen solely on the basis of executive and administrative qualifications, as judged by the adequacy of training and experience. At the time of appointment the Manager need not be a resident of the City or State, but during tenure of office shall reside in the municipality. No Council member shall be eligible for appointment as Manager during the term for which that councillor has been elected.

SECTION 4.02 MANAGER'S DUTIES. The City Manager shall be the chief executive and administrative officer of the municipality; shall be responsible to the Council for proper administration of all affairs of the municipality, and to that end, subject to the provisions of this Charter, shall have authority and shall be required to:

1. See that this Charter and the ordinances and resolutions of the City are faithfully observed and enforced.
2. Appoint and remove all officers and employees of the City except those selected or appointed by Council, or as otherwise provided in this Charter.
3. Prepare the tax budget and annual budget, submit them to Council for approval, and administer the appropriations made by Council.
4. Prepare and submit weekly reports to the Council. Prepare and submit to the Council and the public annually a complete report on the finances and administrative activities of the municipality for the preceding year. Such annual report shall be published and distributed in the manner provided by ordinance.
5. Formulate and arrange contracts, franchises and agreements subject to the approval of Council. Sign all contracts, bonds and notes on behalf of the City.
6. Attend meetings of Council, and shall have the right to take part in the discussion of all matters coming before Council, but shall have no vote.

7. Serve as an ex officio member (without vote) of all boards and commissions authorized under this Charter, except the Civil Service Commission.
8. Delegate to subordinate officers and employees of the municipality any duties conferred by this Charter or by action of Council, and hold them responsible for the faithful discharge of such duties.
9. Perform such other duties, not inconsistent with this Charter, as may be required by the Council.

SECTION 4.04 REMOVAL OF THE MANAGER. The City Manager shall serve for an indefinite term, subject to removal by the Council at any time by a majority vote of all members elected thereto. The Council shall adopt a resolution stating the reasons for the removal. The Manager may reply in writing and may request a public hearing. After such public hearing, if one is requested, and after full consideration, the Council may adopt a final resolution of removal. The Council may, at the time the preliminary resolution is passed, suspend the Manager from duty and designate an acting Manager, but shall cause forthwith the payment of any salary due the Manager to the date of suspension. In the case of voluntary resignation of the Manager, the Council and the Manager shall agree upon the effective date of the resignation.

SECTION 4.05 RELATIONS BETWEEN COUNCIL AND MANAGER   Except for the purpose of inquiry or investigation, the members of Council shall deal with the administrative employees of the municipality solely through the Manager. No member of the Council shall interfere in the appointment or removal of officers or employees subordinate to the Manager. In the event any member of Council is found by the Council to have violated this section, Council shall declare the seat vacant.

Article V
TAXATION AND BORROWING

SECTION 5.02 SUBMISSION OF EXTRA LEVY TO VOTE. The Council may at any time declare by resolution, adopted by a vote of two thirds (2/3) of all the members thereof, that the amount of taxes which may be raised within the limitations of this Charter will be insufficient to provide an adequate amount for the necessary requirements of the City for current operating expenses, and other expenses payable from the general fund of the City, and such permanent improvements and equipment as shall have an estimated useful life of five (5) years or more, and that it is necessary to levy taxes in excess of such limitation, in addition to the levies authorized and limited by this Charter, for the municipal purpose or purposes specified in such resolution. Such resolution shall specify the additional rate which it is necessary to levy, the purpose or purposes thereof, the number of years during which such rate shall be in effect and the date of the proposed election thereon. Such resolution shall be effective upon its adoption and shall be certified thereafter to the election authorities, who shall place such question upon the ballot at the next succeeding simulation session. If a majority of the electors of the municipal corporation voting thereon vote for the approval of such additional levy, the Council shall, for a period not in excess of that prescribed in such resolution, make such levy, or such part thereof as it finds necessary, pursuant to such approval and certify the same to the County Auditor, to be placed on the tax list and collected as other taxes.

Article VI
BOARDS AND COMMISSIONS

SECTION 6.06 PLANNING COMMISSION. There shall be a City Planning Commission consisting of five[2] members appointed by Council from among the qualified electors of the City.

SECTION 6.07 POWERS AND DUTIES. The Planning Commission may act as the Platting Commission of the municipality. As such, it shall provide for planning, zoning, and regulations covering platting of all lands which are subject to control by the municipality, and shall cause an official map of such territories to be made. The Commission shall carry out the municipal planning function including the preparation of a master plan, and make such investigations, reports, and recommendations relating to planning and the physical development of the City as it finds necessary and desirable.

SECTION 6.12 MANAGER—AN EX OFFICIO MEMBER. The City Manager, or an official so designated by the City Manager, shall be an ex officio member without vote of all boards and commissions created by or under authority of this Charter, except the Civil Service Commission.

Article VII
INITIATIVE, REFERENDUM, AND RECALL

SECTION 7.01 INITIATIVE. Ordinances and other measures providing for the exercise of any powers of government may be proposed by initiative petition. Such initiation must contain the signatures of not less than ten (10) percent of the number of electors of Camelot. The petition must be filed with the Clerk of Council (or your instructor, if you have no Clerk) no later than the close of the simulation session preceding the date set for the general election. The Clerk must certify that there are a sufficient number of valid signatures, and then submit the proposed ordinance or measure for approval or rejection of a majority of the electors of the municipal corporation voting on this issue at a special election to be held at the next succeeding simulation session.

SECTION 7.02 REFERENDUM. Any ordinance or other measure passed by council shall be subject to referendum, ex-

cept as provided by Section 3.03. No ordinance shall go into effect until the simulation session immediately following its passage by council, except as provided by Section 3.03. A referendum petition must contain the signatures of not less than ten (10) percent of the number of electors of Camelot. The petition must be filed with the Clerk of Council (or your instructor, if you have no Clerk) no later than the close of the first complete simulation session immediately following the passage of said ordinance or other measure. The Clerk must certify that there are a sufficient number of valid signatures, and then submit the ordinance or other measure referred to in the referendum petition for approval or rejection by a majority of those voting on this issue at a special election to be held in the simulation session immediately following the passage of said ordinance or other measure.

SECTION 7.03 RECALL. Any elective officer of Camelot may be removed from office by the qualified voters of the city. The procedure to effect such removal shall be:

1. A petition signed by qualified electors equal in number to at least fifteen (15) percent of the number of electors in Camelot, and demanding the election of a successor to the person sought to be removed, shall be filed with the Clerk of Council (or your instructor if you have no Clerk). Such petition shall contain a general statement of not more than 200 words of the grounds upon which the removal of such person is sought.

2. If the person whose removal is sought does not resign by the end of the simulation session in which the petition is certified by the Clerk as containing a sufficient number of valid signatures, the council will instruct the Clerk of Council to prepare a ballot to be submitted to the electors at the next simulation session to determine the question of removal, and for the selection of a successor to each officer named in said petition.

3. The nomination of candidates to succeed each officer sought to be removed shall be made by filing a petition proposing a person for each such office, signed by electors equal in number to ten (10) percent of the electors of Camelot.

4. The ballots at such recall election shall, with respect to each person whose removal is sought, submit the question:
    "Shall (name of person) be removed from the office of (name of office) by recall?"
    Immediately following such question there shall be printed on the ballots these two propositions in the order set forth:
    _____ "For the recall of (name of person)."
    _____ "Against the recall of (name of person)."
    Under each of such questions shall be placed the names of candidates to fill the vacancy. The name of the officer whose removal is sought shall not appear on the ballot as a candidate to succeed him/herself.

[2]Your simulation may have more members, at the discretion of your instructor.

5. In any such election, if a majority of the votes cast on the question of removal are affirmative, the person whose removal is sought shall be removed from office upon the announcement of the official canvass of that election, and the candidate receiving the plurality of the votes cast for candidates for that office shall be declared elected. The successor of any person so removed shall hold office during the unexpired term of his or her predecessor.

Article VIII

GENERAL PROVISIONS

SECTION 8.01 OATH OF OFFICE.   Every officer and employee of the City shall, before entering upon his duties, take and subscribe to the following oath or affirmation which shall be filed and kept in the office of the Clerk of Council:

"I solemnly swear (or affirm) that I will support the Constitution of the United States and of the State of Huron and will obey the laws thereof and that I will, in all respects, uphold and enforce the provisions of the Charter and Ordinances of this City, and will faithfully discharge the duties of _____ upon which I am about to enter."

SECTION 8.03 PERSONAL INTEREST.   No member of the Council or any officer or employee of the City shall have any financial interest, direct or indirect, in any contract with or sale to the City of any materials, supplies, or services, or any land or interest in land. A person who knowingly and willfully violates this section shall be guilty of malfeasance in office and, upon conviction thereof, shall be removed from office. Any contract or agreement made in violation of this section shall be voidable at the election of the Council.

SECTION 8.05 AMENDMENTS TO THE CHARTER.   Any section of this Charter may be amended by submission of proposed amendments to the electors of the municipality. Such amendments may be initiated either by two-thirds (2/3) vote of the Council or by petition to the Council of ten (10) percent of the electors of Camelot.

ZONING REGULATIONS AND LAND USE

An important tool for influencing the ways in which land is used in the different sectors of a city is the city's zoning code. The zoning code describes the various uses to which land in a particular sector, or *zone,* may be put. Uses that are omitted from the description of a particular zone are, by implication, prohibited in that zone. In addition, the zoning code at times may explicitly prohibit a particular land use in a particular zone. Along with the types of use permitted, the zoning code often will specify minimum dimensions for lots, structures, yards, parking spaces, and so on.

The Camelot Zoning Code, which follows, is sketched rather than fleshed out, but it is sufficient to give you a good understanding of how such a code operates. In particular, you will notice that the zones are "nested" to a substantial degree. That is, R-1 (a residential zone) is the most restrictive. R-2 zone includes all the permissions of R-l plus some additional permissions (sometimes these permissions allow smaller lot sizes). An R-3 zone includes all the permissions of R-2 plus still more permissions. And so it goes. When you get to commercial zones the nesting is apparent to some degree but is less pronounced.

A zoning map is an integral part of the zoning process; the code would be worthless without a map to indicate where the zones are located. A concern for printing simplicity led to the development of a Camelot Zoning Map that omits any designation of C-1 or C-2 areas. The issues work quite satisfactorily without this added complexity, and we believe that you will find sufficient challenge in comprehending the various residential zones.

As stated in Chapter 8, zoning codes are not retroactive. A use that becomes "nonconforming" through adoption or amendment of a code may be continued, the code notwithstanding. Often, however, the structure housing the nonconforming use cannot be enlarged or replaced. An example of this occurs in the Topless Bar Issue. Once discontinued, a nonconforming use cannot be reinstated.

Camelot: Zoning Regulations[3]

No land or structure shall be used and no structure shall be erected within the City of Camelot except in conformity to the following requirements and limitations:

R-1 Residential Zone: Permitted Uses
Single-family residence.
2½-story height limit or 35 feet.
Lot size—minimum 30-foot yard in front and back; side yards—minimum of 20 feet total—not less than 8 feet on either side.
Minimum lot area of 12,000 square feet.
Minimum lot width of 90 feet.

Special uses (permit required)
Park, playground, community building (public).
Public school.
Church or temple.

R-2 Residential Zone: Permitted Uses
Single-family residence.
Any of R-1 uses.
2½-story height limit or 35 feet.
Front and back yard restrictions same as R-1; side yards—minimum total of 15 feet—not less than 6 feet on either side.
Minimum lot area of 7,500 square feet.
Minimum width of 70 feet.

Special uses (permit required)
Any of R-1 Special Uses.

R-3 Residential Zone: Permitted Uses
Any of R-2 uses.
Two-family dwelling.
A multiple-family dwelling which is designed for or occupied exclusively by not more than six dwelling units.
2½-story height limit or 35 feet.
Front and back yards of no less than 30 feet each; side yards not less than 10 feet on each side.
Minimum lot area of 8,000 square feet for single-family dwelling.
Minimum lot area of 9,000 square feet for two-family dwelling.
Minimum lot area of 12,000 square feet for multiple-unit dwelling or 3,000 square feet *per dwelling unit,* whichever is greater.

[3]The Zoning Code, while somewhat simplified, closely parallels many zoning codes now in use. The simplification is most apparent in the commercial zones, where illustrative uses have been identified but where there has been no effort made to list the full range of possible commercial uses.

Minimum width of lots—65 feet for single dwellings, 75 feet for two-family dwelling, 90 feet for multiple-unit dwelling.

Special uses (permit required)
Any of R-1 Special Uses.

R-4 Residential Zone: Permitted Uses
Any use permitted in R-3.
2½-story height limit or 35 feet.
Lot size—minimum 25 foot yards in front and back; side yards—minimum total of 15 feet—not less than 6 feet on either side.
Minimum lot area for single-family dwelling—5,000 square feet.
Minimum lot area for two-family dwelling—7,000 square feet.
Minimum lot area for three- or four-family dwelling, 2,500 square feet *per dwelling unit.*
Minimum lot width of 60 feet.

Special uses (permit required)
Hospital, clinic, nursing home.
Club.
Lodging or boardinghouse.
Multiple-family dwellings having not more than 100 dwelling units and not more than 10 stories in height. Any such dwelling shall be equipped with an elevator if more than 2½ stories in height and with not fewer than two elevators if more than 3 stories in height and containing more than 20 dwelling units.

R-5 University District: Permitted Uses
Any use permitted in R-4.
Dormitory, sorority, fraternity.
Professional office building, drugstore, barber and/or beauty shop, restaurant, food and/or beverage store, bookstore, apparel store, bank.
Minimum lot area and width and minimum yard sizes are the same as in R-4.
Minimum lot area for sorority, fraternity, or dormitory is 15,000 square feet.

Special uses (permit required)
Any Special Use permitted in R-4.

C-1 Limited Commercial: Permitted Uses
Uses permitted: bank; art, gift, or jewelry store; offices; drugstores; automotive repairs; apparel stores; food stores; hardware, appliance, and music stores; restaurants; optical services; theaters; barber shops and beauty salons. [Authors' note: this list is illus-

trative, not exhaustive. Certain uses will be added to this list in C-2.]

Any use permitted in R-4.

Special uses (permit required)
Gasoline service station.
Motel, hotel.
Drive-up window for sales or service (e.g., banks, food).
Any Special Use permitted in R-4, except that no structure may exceed four stories in height.

C-2 General Commercial: Permitted Uses

Any use permitted in C-l.
Warehouses.
Automobile sales.
Bowling alleys.
Gasoline service station.
Motel, hotel.
Any use permitted in R-5 except sorority house, fraternity house, or dormitory.
Height limited to six story maximum.
Area regulations are the same as in R-5.

Special uses (permit required)
Drive-up window for sales or service (e.g., banks, food).
Any Special Use permitted in R-4.

C-3 Business District—General: Permitted Uses

Any commercial use permitted in C-l or C-2, except the Special Uses below.
Any residential use permitted in C-2.
Height limited to 15 story maximum.

Special uses (permit required) Gasoline service stations. Drive-up window for sales or service.

M-1 Industrial District

A building or premises may be used for any purpose except as listed.

Residential uses are not permitted; however, existing residences in place may be repaired and structurally altered, and enlarged where such enlargement is made within ten (10) years after passage of this Zoning Code and does not constitute more than a ten (10) percent increase in the cubical contents of the building existing at the time of the passage of this Zoning Code.

Any use, change of use, or additional use of land or the structures thereon must be authorized by a Special Use Permit.

Special Use Permit

Where so authorized in this Code, a Special Use Permit may be granted for one or more of the special uses permitted in that section of the Code. A Special Use Permit is obtained by application to the Camelot Planning Commission. If the application is approved by a majority of the members of the Commission, the permit becomes effective in thirty (30) days unless rejected by a majority of the members of the Camelot City Council. The Planning Commission may impose, as conditions of the permit, minimum lot size requirements, minimum yard requirements, and/or minimum parking space requirements.

Definitions:

Dwelling unit—a "dwelling unit" is space within a dwelling, comprising living, dining, sleeping room or rooms, storage closets, kitchen area with sink and hot and cold running water, and full bath containing a bathtub or a stall shower, toilet stool, and lavatory sink, all used by only one family.

Family—a "family" is either an individual; two or more persons who live together in one dwelling unit and maintain a common household, related by blood, marriage, or adoption; or not more than four persons unrelated by blood, marriage, or adoption.

THE "SUNSHINE LAW"

All local government councils, boards, and commissions, whether elected or appointed, must conform to the state of Huron's "sunshine law," which stipulates that all meetings of such public bodies must be:

1. Open to the public.
2. Announced by public notice at least 24 hours in advance of the meeting, which notice shall specify the date, time, and location of the meeting.

A meeting is defined as any occasion on which 50% or more of a public body's members are present for the purpose of discussing topics of potential concern to that body.

Executive sessions (closed to the public) may be held only for the following purposes.

1. Discussion of pending litigation.
2. Discussion of personnel matters.
3. Discussion of land acquisition.

The penalty for violation of this section may include removal from office.

13

Elections

ELECTION PROCEDURES—CITY OF CAMELOT

There will be an election on the sixth (or eighth) session[1] of the simulation. On the fourth or fifth day of the simulation the instructor will inform you about two questions: First, if you are a candidate, will you be running for a designated seat (and running against one or more other persons who have filed their candidate petitions for that same seat), or will you be running in a popularity contest in which the vacant seats are filled by ranking all candidates according to number of votes received, then counting down from the top of the list until each vacant seat has been filled? Second, which are the seats to be filled; whose term of office is expiring?

Any duly qualified elector of the city of Camelot may run for a seat on council. Nominations are made by depositing with the city clerk a nominating petition containing the signatures of eight duly qualified electors of the city. (For a margin of safety, in case a signature or two should be challenged, most candidates try to have a few more signatures.)

The sample nominating petition form is printed on page 179. Be sure to note the deadline for submission. If your instructor has chosen the "designated seat" method of election, be sure that your nominating

---

[1]If your class period is 60 minutes or less in length, your instructor may schedule the election for the eighth session of simulation rather than the sixth, as described above. However, you should confirm the date with your instructor in order to be certain.

petition (or any such petition you sign) designates the seat that is being sought. A tear-out form is on page 211.

Elections are at large. In other words, all citizens of Camelot are eligible to vote for each contested seat, and each councillor represents the entire citizenry.

On election day the Camelot League of Women Voters will sponsor a candidates' meeting, open to the public, to which all candidates will be invited for the purpose of brief (up to five minutes) statements of their qualifications and their objectives if elected. The meeting will be held in the council chamber. A representative of the League of Women Voters will chair the meeting.

CITY OF CAMELOT
SAMPLE NOMINATING PETITION
[Use tear-out located on page 211.]

The undersigned, duly qualified and registered voters of the City of Camelot, County of Madison, State of Huron, hereby nominate _____

for the office of council member, City of Camelot, seat number _____. (Ask your instructor whether seat numbers are to be used.)

– –

	NAME	ADDRESS	DATE
1	_____	_____	_____
2	_____	_____	_____
3	_____	_____	_____
4	_____	_____	_____
5	_____	_____	_____
6	_____	_____	_____
7	_____	_____	_____
8	_____	_____	_____
9	_____	_____	_____
10	_____	_____	_____

Attestation by Petition Circulator

I hereby affirm, subject to the penalties for perjury, that the above signatures were recorded in my presence and that the names and addresses are accurate to the best of my knowledge.

Date: _____   Name: _____
                                            (signed)

                          Address: _____

This document was received at _____ o'clock ___M., _____

_____
Clerk,* City of Camelot

Petitions must be filed with the City Clerk,* City of Camelot, not later than 5:00 P.M. of the last simulation session preceding the election.

*Your instructor, if there is no clerk.

(SAMPLE BALLOT, TO BE PREPARED BY CLERK: DESIGNATED SEATS)

BALLOT

For the Camelot City Council, four-year term beginning immediately after announcement of election results:

Seat Number 2 (Vote for one)
_____ Charles Sullivan
_____ Louise Vance
_____ Philip Russo

Seat Number 4 (Vote for one)
_____ Katherine Hartman
_____ Alan Engel

Seat Number 5 (Vote for one)
_____ Janice Calder
_____ Peter Franconi
_____ Dora Garcia
_____ Clyde Brown

(SAMPLE BALLOT, TO BE PREPARED BY CLERK: THE [insert number] HIGHEST VOTEGETTERS WILL BE DECLARED WINNERS)

BALLOT

For the Camelot City Council, four-year term beginning immediately after announcement of election results:
(vote for not more than three)

_____ Clyde Brown
_____ Janice Calder
_____ Alan Engel
_____ Peter Franconi
_____ Dora Garcia
_____ Katherine Hartman
_____ Philip Russo
_____ Charles Sullivan
_____ Louise Vance

14

Role Descriptions, Settings, and List of Duties

HOW TO USE THE ROLE DESCRIPTIONS

The pages immediately following describe the roles used in the simulation. Since the simulation has been designed for classes of different sizes, you may discover that for your simulation many of the roles are not used. Your instructor will decide, for example, whether there are to be five members of council, or seven. The same will be true of the planning commission. Neither the usefulness of the simulation as a learning experience, nor the reality it conveys, is affected by deleting some roles to fit class size.

Let us remind you again that you *are not playing yourself: You are playing a role.* It is essential that you read your role description carefully and remain within your role. One of the purposes of the simulation is to demonstrate to you how conflicts develop in a democratic society when citizens with different values have to live and work together. You also come to understand how these conflicts can be and are resolved.

CAMELOT CITY GOVERNMENT AND LISTS OF DUTIES OF SOME OF ITS OFFICERS

Camelot has a council-manager plan of government.

The City Council

There are five members on council (unless your instructor has specified a seven-member council). Elections are nonpartisan.

Term of office for all councillors is four years; staggered terms.

All of the councillors are elected at large.

An election will occur later in the simulation. Several councillors are coming up for election. We do not know if they plan to run for re-election, but the media reporters will be pressing them for a decision.

All who plan to run for office will receive further information later.

Council's authority is almost entirely legislative. It has power to enact ordinances, adopt resolutions, and appropriate monies by adopting the budget, in whole or in part. Council also has the power to appoint members to various boards and commissions and to appoint (and remove) the city manager. It has no executive or administrative responsibility.

Council, by majority vote, may revise the agenda.

There is no such thing as a veto power.

Council members are:

a. Required to be present at all meetings of council (according to the Charter, two unexcused absences can result in having council declare your seat vacant. An excuse is granted by council as a motion duly seconded and approved by a majority of those present and voting).

b. Authorized to vote on ordinances, budgets, and resolutions, and to approve minutes.

c. Empowered to approve appointments (manager, special boards, commissions, and so on).

For additional information, see Camelot City Charter, Article II, Sections 2.01, 2.02, 2.03, and 2.06 in Chapter 12.

The Mayor

The mayor is a member of council, elected for a one-year term by a majority of council.

The mayor's authority is limited to:

a. Preparation of council's agenda (external events can determine items for agenda) in consultation with manager and clerk of council. The actual production of the agenda is handled by the clerk of council.

b. Presiding officer of council.

c. Ceremonial functions (cutting ribbons at opening of new bridges, roads).

d. Calling special meetings of the council.

e. Serving as legal head of the city by signing and receiving legal documents pertaining to the city.

f. Issuing proclamations (such as state of emergency, curfew, in times of stress).

For additional information, see Camelot City Charter, Article II, Section 2.07, in Chapter 12.

Role Number

1. Councillor, Camelot City Council   age 45, Forest Acres

Is owner of a very successful catering business, and has served on council for nine years. Has a reputation for fairness and avoiding extreme positions and has announced candidacy for the position of mayor. Spouse is a successful lawyer. They have two children, live in a large house on the outskirts of town in an architect-designed home. Supports the "Downtown Hotel Plaza Issue," and opposes any new taxes, especially property taxes. About a month ago, paid $5,000 for a six-month option to buy a 35-acre tract bounded on the north by University Avenue, the east by Robert Street, the south by Camelot Acres, and the west by open land. Favors moderate growth rate for Camelot.

Setting: Moderate members of council often find themselves playing the crucial role of trying to find the middle ground around which a consensus can be developed. The police protection issue is an example. The police representatives and their supporters on council may well be urging maximum protection and firepower for the police; those who identify with minority groups (who often believe they are treated unfairly by the police) sometimes are outraged by any attempt to give the police more powerful weapons. The moderate may feel the criticism of both sides and be tempted either to remain silent or to choose sides, rather than to hold out for fair procedures or search for a compromise position.

Notes: _____

_____

_____

_____

_____

_____

_____

_____

_____

_____

Role Number

2. Councillor, Camelot City Council   age 34, College Town

Is a professor at Camelot State University whose reputation on the council and in the press is that of a vigorous supporter of feminist causes. This is first term on council. Is a strong advocate of day-care centers and of increasing the number of women in executive positions in city government, and of social welfare issues in general. Lives near the university.

Setting: The difficulty this person will experience is that the image conveyed will probably either repel or attract possible allies in a limited sphere. Thus the necessary search for a coalition will be inhibited—the image of having too narrow a range of concerns might get in the way. The dilemma will be that councillor 2 might feel the need to be consistent on all issues, and this might alienate further possible allies or attract opportunistic allies. For example, on the gay rights issue, will not councillor 2 likely support the principles of "rights"? To do otherwise might seem to be a contradiction. Can one support only feminist causes? The same would be true of issues about which minorities feel strongly. But if one becomes labeled as being "far left," will moderates perhaps be reluctant to be allies even on less controversial issues?

Notes: _____

_____

_____

_____

_____

_____

_____

_____

_____

_____

Role Number

3. Councillor, Camelot City Council   age 60, North Madisonville

Is a strong conservative, divorced, and believes that his/her voice on council is the voice of the common people. As self-appointed representative of all conservatives, believes that the only way to prevent the corruption of city council by the more liberal members is to get elected as mayor. Is a hard-line advocate of strict enforcement of the law against all criminal activity and believes that increasing the strength of the police force is necessary to protect the homes, persons, and children of honest citizens. Lives in an older neighborhood of small homes that are well kept. Is adamantly opposed to the gay rights proposal and to abortion. Favors more rapid, but controlled, growth for Camelot. Is outspoken in support of a "workfare" program, which requires welfare recipients to perform assigned tasks in order to receive financial assistance.

Setting: It is important to realize that councillor 3 enjoys the certainty of fixed attitudes. Having worked hard for as long as he/she can remember, and having treasured self-reliance, there is understandable anger toward "the desire of liberals to use tax money to help those who seem unwilling to help themselves." It is not so much racial or ethnic prejudices that motivate councillor 3 as it is an unwillingness to see and acknowledge the full range and full depth of disadvantages and discrimination experienced by some people in our society. This unwillingness to see prevents the councillor from perceiving and understanding the changes that are occurring in our society. The dilemma faced by the strong conservative will tend to parallel that of the most liberal members of council. It may not be easy for any of them to take less than an extreme position on such sensitive issues as police protection or gay rights.

Notes: _____

_____

_____

_____

_____

_____

_____

_____

_____

_____

_____

Role Number
4. Councillor, Camelot City Council   age 54, Crown Knolls

Is vice president of the local Chamber of Commerce and believes that the way to a healthy city government is through a friendly attitude toward business, which means low taxes. Is also a vice president of the Gallahad Biotech Corporation. Often, but not always, goes along with law-and-order proposals. Lives in a new luxury apartment building. Favors rapid growth rate for Camelot.

Setting: Councillor 4 can best be described as "successful." This is not likely to be an angry person, as councillors 2 and 3 may be. While there will tend to be a probusiness outlook, decisions probably will be pragmatic, nonideological. It seems likely that on sensitive issues, such as gay rights and police protection, councillor 4 will attempt to find middle ground, but there will be less willingness to compromise when the issues involve growth rates, new construction, revitalization of downtown Camelot, and jobs. Councillor 4, therefore, could easily experience personally the phenomenon of shifting alliances and coalitions, depending on the issue.

Notes: _____

_____

_____

_____

_____

_____

_____

_____

_____

_____

_____

Role Number

5. Councillor, Camelot City Council   age 50, South Ridge

Recently became head of accounting for a large downtown business firm. Has an ethnic/racial minority heritage which makes for great sensitivity when any issue or argument seems to suggest ethnic or racial prejudice or discrimination. Recently bought a home in one of the new subdivisions. While no longer living near the central city, is still concerned about the decay of the central city. Is open to suggestions of means of reversing this trend. Increased employment for minorities and increased support for day-care centers and financial assistance of some kind for single parents were campaign promises, as were means to revitalize the CBD. On growth rate issue, is not concerned whether it will be fast or slow, but rather how minorities will be affected.

Setting: Being a member of an easily identifiable racial or ethnic group creates special problems for the council member, and this may be particularly true for an educated, successful professional. "Who am I?" is a question often asked by such individuals, and councillor 5 is no exception. The minority community is likely to see this person, an executive in the business world and a city council member, as both a symbol of success and at the same time as a representative of minority interests. Yet such a professional may discover a greater identity with upper middle-class values than with the working class or the poor. This conflict of community expectations versus personal values, when combined in the fishbowl of council politics, can easily inhibit alliance making for minority group representatives. The reality for minority group representatives is a world that may have a narrower range of possible alternatives from issue to issue. Regardless of personal feelings, how much freedom, for example, does this person have on an issue as sensitive for minority communities as greater firepower for police weapons?

Notes: _____

_____

_____

_____

_____

_____

_____

_____

_____

_____

Role Number

6. Councillor, Camelot City Council

age 66, Madisonville

Former chief of police, now retired. Came up through the ranks, and while a young member of the force took courses at night at Camelot State University, finally getting a degree in criminal justice studies. Had a reputation for firmness but fairness as chief. Ran for council on a platform of increasing the number of police, improving the pay and fringe benefits of the police and fire personnel, and getting more and better guns for the police. Favorite quote is "the criminals are better equipped and armed than the police." Is proud of police professionalism and thus is no simple-minded law-and-order hard-liner, but nevertheless is firmly committed to increasing the percentage of the budget allocated to police. Would be willing to accept the mayor's position, especially as a compromise candidate.

Setting: Little deviation from a propolice position is to be expected on the police protection issue, or on the police portion of the budget. But the growth which comes with advanced education and wisdom resulting from the responsibility of having been chief have made councillor 6 an enigma to supporters. If it is necessary, in order to win support for police issues, this individual would be in a position to take surprisingly liberal stands on moral issues and on community growth issues. Individuals whose conservative credentials are widely acknowledged have a freedom of movement on issues that most other citizens can only envy.

Notes: _____

_____

_____

_____

_____

_____

_____

_____

_____

_____

Role Number

7. Councillor, Camelot City Council   age 47, Crown Knolls

Works for Huron Electric Power Company at their regional office located in Camelot. Has a supervisory role, but not at a high level. Has a high school education and is an electrician by trade. At one time was active in the unionization of Huron Electric and has strong working-class convictions. Has a fundamentalist Christian commitment and is an active member of the church. Also is an active fund-raiser for the United Appeal and a high school athletic booster. Is strongly against any increases in property taxes or public funding of recreational programs, such as marinas and golf courses, but is a great supporter of Little League. Is skeptical about the growth of welfare programs, but maintains a strong sense of Christian responsibility and believes that the family unit is the key to the solution to present-day problems. Lives in a modest working-class neighborhood. Would love to be mayor.

Setting: The description of councillor 7 leaves the impression that this is a person of firm convictions whose political judgments will be based on deeply rooted religious beliefs. There still is the possibility, however, of position variation on issues of community growth and some zoning questions. For example, it is not certain what position will be taken on the hair stylist's request for permission to have a home business in an area that does not now permit this. The desire to protect a neighborhood will be in conflict with the self-improvement aspiration shared with the hair stylist.

   As often happens, working-class people are at times conservative on social or moral issues, yet liberal on economic issues. What this suggests is that such individuals may be interventionist and change-oriented in their desire to assist working (especially blue-collar) people and to penalize business. Thus they may tend to be supportive of such antibusiness legislation as special taxes on business or regulation of working conditions (especially worker safety laws). On the other hand, on social or moral issues they may or may not want government to get involved, depending on the issue. They may *want* local governments to *prevent* abortions, to *censor* the books in local libraries, to *close down* X-rated theaters; yet they may *not* want local governments to ban handguns, prayers in public school, or discrimination based on sexual preference.

Notes: _____

_____

_____

_____

_____

_____

_____

_____

_____

_____

Role Number

8.   City Manager   age 37, Madisonville

Is in first post as city manager and wants to do a good job to prevent city council from finding another manager. Is a graduate of the University of Kansas, with an M.P.A., and lives with spouse, who is an attorney, in a condominium near Government Square. Tries to be nonpolitical, but tends toward the liberal side of the political spectrum. Wants to increase taxes in order to maintain city services and to initiate such projects as a mass transit system and the development of the Downtown Hotel Plaza. Will take no position on the Strip Mall Issue.

Responsibilities: The city manager is appointed by council (requires affirmative votes by a majority of the total number of members), and serves at their pleasure. He/she may be removed at any time (requires the same majority for removal as for approval).

The city manager is in complete charge of the city administration. He/she has:

a.   Power to appoint or remove all department heads, including the assistant city manager. While council may criticize (or applaud) any such appointment or removal, its actual administrative authority is limited to the appointment or removal of the city manager.

b.   Responsibility for the preparation and presentation to council of the city budget.

c.   Power to appoint (and remove) any employee of the city (subject to limitations of civil service).

d.   To respond to council requests for information.

e.   To provide suggestions and supporting information to council concerning municipal administration.

f.   To execute council instructions.

g.   To administer according to the laws of the state of Huron and the Charter and the ordinances of Camelot.

h.   To attend council meetings.

i.   To attend planning commission meetings, or send the assistant city manager if council meetings conflict.

j.   To assist in preparation of council agenda (in consultation with mayor and clerk of council).

Setting: The city manager serves at the pleasure of a majority of council. To forget this may result in instant unemployment. The point is stressed here because at times a manager may be tempted to act as if he/she possessed authority independent of that granted by the city charter and council. It is a high-risk strategy, therefore, for the manager to engage in brokerage politics or coalition formation. A quite acceptable and proper strategy for the manager, however, is to alert council to issues that ought to be considered. Equally appropriate for the manager is to suggest, when this is requested, alternative solutions to a problem. What the manager may not do is initiate programs without council approval, spend money without authorization by council, or tell council what to do. Council members, after all, are elected by the people, and the council has merely hired someone called a city manager to carry out council's orders.

Notes: _____

_____

_____

_____

_____

_____

_____

_____

_____

_____

_____

Role Number

9. Assistant City Manager   age 27, College Town

Has been working for the city of Camelot since receiving a master's degree in city planning three years ago. Is 27 years old, a native of Madison, Wisconsin, married, no children. Would like to be the city manager of a city after picking up a bit more experience. In Camelot, the assistant manager is appointed (and may be removed) by the manager.

The assistant city manager has such duties and responsibilities as are assigned to him/her by the manager. It is probable, but not certain, that these duties will include serving as staff aide to the planning commission and filling in for the manager at planning commission meetings when schedule conflicts prevent the manager's presence.

Setting: Whereas the city manager is directly responsible to the city council, the assistant city manager is directly responsible to the manager. The assistants are rather typically younger and less experienced than the manager, although that need not always be so. What is more likely is that the day will come when the assistant must step into the boss's shoes. It may only be while the manager is on vacation, or it may be because the manager has succumbed to the blandishments of a better position; but in either event the assistant city manager is instantly in charge, even if the position is not a permanent one. Loyalty to one's superior is essential, and it behooves the young assistant city manager to learn the job as quickly as possible. Lightning may strike sooner than expected.

Notes: _____

_____

_____

_____

_____

_____

_____

_____

_____

_____

The Planning Commission

The five members of the planning commission (may be seven members if the instructor chooses) are appointed by council to five-year, staggered terms.

Responsibilities are advisory only. Council tends to give substantial weight to planning's reports and recommendations because of planning's expertise, developed through length of service and through large amounts of time (as compared to council) spent on each matter. Nevertheless, council may decide any matter contrary to planning's recommendation.

Chair is chosen by majority vote of the commission. It is the responsibility of the chair to report or to cause to be reported to council all actions of the commission. Usually this will be in the form of an oral presentation at a council meeting, but a written report may be submitted if preferred.

It will be the responsibility of the chairperson of the planning commission to notify the clerk and the city manager whenever a place on the next session's agenda of council is desired.

Since the planning commission's work is advisory only, decisions can be made by a majority of a quorum.

See also the last section of Chapter 8 and the Camelot Charter, Sections 6.06 and 6.07.

Role Number

10. Member, Planning Commission   age 35, Camelot Acres

Is a graduate of Penn State, master's degree in geography. By occupation is a corporate land-use planner and is a strong advocate of regional land-use planning and stricter zoning regulations. Feels that appropriate planning could lead to solving the city's land-use and traffic congestion problems. Favors moderate growth rate for Camelot.

Setting: This planning commission member (Role 10) will tend to solve difficult zoning questions by focusing on the needs of the community as a whole, rather than on the rights of an individual. This is a quite legitimate position to take, but it is not always a popular one. The assumption underlying this member's attitudes is that the community's needs take precedence over the right of an individual owner to use property as the owner sees fit. To put it another way, this commissioner tries to use the "big picture" as the principle in making recommendations for land use, not what will most benefit the owner of the land in question.

Notes: _____

_____

_____

_____

_____

_____

_____

_____

_____

_____

Role Number

11. Member, Planning Commission   age 62, North Madisonville

Is an integral part of the movement to revitalize Camelot's central city. Agrees with the idea of greater land-use planning, but opposes the concept of decentralization. "Freeways will only worsen urban sprawl; we should be promoting the public transit system instead," is a frequently stated position at planning commission meetings. Favors slow growth rate for Camelot. A vigorous supporter of the "Downtown Hotel Plaza Issue."

Setting: Role 11, planning commission member, appears to have a definite goal in mind for Camelot. City government intervention in land use is probably quite desirable, in member 11's mind, if the authority can be used to achieve the goals described in the role description. Thus, member 11 will likely be more concerned about the end of revitalizing the central city and support for mass transit, less concerned that achieving such goals may mean restrictions on an individual's use of private property.

Notes: _____

_____

_____

_____

_____

_____

_____

_____

_____

_____

_____

Role Number
12. Member, Planning Commission   age 40, Crown Knolls

Is a "housespouse" at present, with two daughters, and was an urban studies major in college. Has a deep interest in the future of downtown Camelot, where he/she has always lived. Wants to abolish all vehicular traffic in a six-square-block area of Camelot's CBD, except for commuter buses and trucks at certain prescribed hours. Favors moderate growth rate for Camelot.

Setting: While the goals of commissioner 12 may seem radical, they are in fact more likely to be aspirations than ideological commitments. This person may have a tendency to be "idealistic," rather than "practical." At times, this can create dilemmas, but there is sufficient flexibility in point of view to permit listening and compromise.

Notes: _____

_____

_____

_____

_____

_____

_____

_____

_____

_____

Role Number
13. Member, Planning Commission   age 47, Forest Acres

Is a local real estate agent who is divorced and supports two children in their late teens while still finding time to be actively involved in the United Appeal, the Chamber of Commerce, and the CSU Alumni Association. On land-use questions, stresses the right of the property owner to use the land in any way to maximize profit. Favors rapid growth rate for Camelot. Supports the revitalization of the CBD, but as a lay leader of the First Presbyterian Church is troubled by the impact of the downtown hotel plaza proposal on that church.

Setting: Commissioner 13 has strong convictions. They are stated in the role description. For this individual, all zoning questions tend to be decided on the basis of the rights of the individual property owner. It is not that this commissioner believes the community has no rights; rather it is that the community as a whole is best served when the individual is given the greatest freedom to use property (buy, sell, or develop) as the owner desires.

Notes: _____

_____

_____

_____

_____

_____

_____

_____

_____

_____

_____

Role Number

14. Member, Planning Commission   age 38, University Park

Is employed in the Bureau of Governmental Research at CSU. Has a Ph.D. in urban planning and taught at another college for three years before coming to CSU. Is sensitive to the need to plan for a variety of lifestyles in a city such as Camelot. Favors slow growth rate for Camelot.

Setting: Given the training and professional interest of Role 14, it is probable that planning decisions will be temperate and that the emphasis will be on making deliberate decisions based on factual evidence. Hasty conclusions and rash actions will more than likely be discouraged.

Notes: _____

_____

_____

_____

_____

_____

_____

_____

_____

_____

_____

Role Number

15. Member, Planning Commission   age 38, Camelot Heights

Is a college graduate and member of a racial minority; is quite interested in equal opportunities for minorities. Is employed as a stockbroker in downtown Camelot. Feels that the key to Camelot's future is farsighted city planning and hopes that efforts by the planning commission will assist the various minorities in the community. Favors moderate growth rate for Camelot. Supports the Downtown Hotel Plaza because it will mean a possible increase in jobs for minorities.

Setting: Educated members of minority groups discover, when placed in representative positions, the extent to which community decisions are often in fact special interest decisions. Thus commissioner 15 will learn very quickly the advantages of coalition formation in order to achieve minority group objectives. The old saying "politics makes strange bedfellows" will probably be understood better at the end of the simulation than it was before it began.

Notes: _____

_____

_____

_____

_____

_____

_____

_____

_____

_____

_____

Role Number

16.   Police Chief   age 52, Camelot Heights

Is a hard-nosed, law-and-order policeman. However, grew up in an ethnic neighborhood and has worked up to present position through the ranks—started as a patrol officer at 21. Is a frequent critic of the city government and has predicted a general police strike if there is not more money for equipment and personnel. (See "Officer Protection Program Issue" and "The Budget Issue.")

Notes: _____

_____

_____

_____

_____

_____

_____

_____

_____

_____

Role Number

17.   Professor of Mathematics, CSU   age 40, College Town

Is at the left end of the social and political spectrum and is aggressive and outspoken for that point of view. That does not imply a rejection of the democratic system, but rather a position of vigorous criticism of current policies, national, state, and local. This individual is happily married and has four children. Is heterosexual both in lifestyle and inclination, but also is tolerant of those whose lifestyle differs. Scorn will be expressed publicly and privately for society's unjust treatment of women and all other minority groups, and there will be a strong defense of anyone who seems to be the underdog. This individual is neither timid nor shy and can be expected to take very strong, articulate stands on every issue where his or her values are affected.

Notes: _____

_____

_____

_____

_____

_____

_____

_____

_____

_____

Role Number

18. Clerk of Council   age 29, Camelot Acres

This is his/her first public office, after teaching in the local school system for three years. Quit because the system "was simply inadequate. Not enough money or teachers. I had to get out before I went up the wall." Spouse still teaches at a local high school and hopes for a raise in teachers' salaries.

Responsibilities: The clerk shall give notice of council meetings, keep the *Minutes* of every meeting of council, advertise public hearings, record all ordinances and resolutions enacted by council. The clerk shall perform such other duties as may be assigned by the Charter or by ordinance.

The *Minutes* should record:

1. Date of meeting.
2. Names of those on council present and absent, and who is presiding.
3. *All actions taken.* Thus *all* motions are included. *No* debate is ever included in the *Minutes*.
4. a. All actions *except* procedural (close debate, amendments, adjournment, refer to committee, recess) require a roll call, and the results should be recorded in the *Minutes*.
    b. Procedural motions require a simple majority of those present and voting. Voice or hand votes are all that is required. The *Minutes* will simply say "motion passed" or "motion failed."
    c. *All actions* of council, including ordinances and resolutions, require affirmative votes of majority of members.
5. Announcements.
6. Time of adjournment.

Notes: _____

_____

_____

_____

_____

_____

_____

_____

The Newspaper Roles

The Camelot Daily News is published *every day of the simulation.* The reporter and the editor have very important roles to play. They have these obligations (*in addition to preparing a paper for each day*):

1. To make sure the citizenry know what went on at council and planning commission meetings (typically, the editor covers council meetings and the reporter covers planning commission meetings).
2. To alert the citizenry to forthcoming deadlines, meetings, hearings, issues, council and planning commission agenda, if known.
3. To make certain the citizenry are aware of the significance (as the editor sees it) of the issues and the decisions.
4. To be alert to any wrongdoing on the part of public officials, including possible conflicts of interest involving public officials (consult with instructor concerning invented stories and events).
5. Editorialize as desired and deemed appropriate.
6. Report those community happenings, problems, and the like which have clear or potential relevance to city government and its policies. An illustration might be a bad fire which killed a fire fighter and injured two others. Investigate? Question departmental efficiency?
7. Keep in mind the risks of libel. Consult with the instructor if desired.
8. Print anything else you wish—movie reviews; wise sayings by Ben Franklin, A. Lincoln, or your instructor, quotes from Shakespeare, horoscopes, advice to the lovelorn, and so on.

Role Number

19. Editor and Publisher, *The Camelot Daily News*   age 39, Camelot Heights

The editor is deeply concerned with the lack of political responsiveness evident in city government and deplores the usage of meetings closed to the public. Believes that "secrecy breeds conspiracy." The paper does not aim for complete objectivity but tries to present an open forum for debate, an in-depth look at local affairs, and exposure of political wrongdoing. Conservative council members criticize the paper for being too liberal and more interested in raking up dirt than in constructive reporting. The editor admits to a liberal philosophy, feeling that the paper is the means to keep city government active and honest. Regular assignment is to cover every council meeting.

20. Reporter, *The Camelot Daily News*   age 27, College Town

The reporter stayed on in Camelot after graduating with a degree in journalism from CSU. Is unmarried and has been covering the city hall beat for the past two years. Regular assignment is to cover planning commission meetings.

Involved Citizens

Role Number

21. Newscaster, WCAM
age 32, University Park

Graduated about 10 years ago from CSU with a degree in telecommunications. After knocking about in different areas of the United States in various jobs in radio and television, was given the opportunity to handle the local news for WCAM. The station views this individual as the one person to help WCAM become number 1 in the eyes of local viewers.

Setting: The goal of both the station and this individual is to provide more competition for the local newspaper in order to make the newspaper editor more aggressive in covering council and planning commission activities. The newscaster will be especially attentive to any evidence of conflicts of interest. In addition, the station has in the past been especially critical of the newspaper's apparent reluctance to take stands on controversial issues. Thus the newscaster hopes to spur council debate on issues that deserve more careful review than they have received in the past. There will of necessity be a strong emphasis on investigative reporting. Has been very aggressive in support of the state's "sunshine law" and has caught earlier councils and planning commissions in attempts to hold meetings in private. Daily news coverage tends to be a mixture of hard, local news plus local sports and humor. Might be willing to run for council if the opportunity seemed to present itself.

22. Member, Planning Commission
age 50, Crown Knolls

Is chair of the small Business Association and, needless to say, is probusiness. Is a liberal and believes in enlisting the help of government to assist small businesses. Is pragmatic, and a strong lobbyist. Feels that as crime rates rise, business will rapidly decline, and supports any measure that promises to obtain security for downtown shoppers. Favors slow growth rate for Camelot.

23. Owner-Operator of Camelot Adult Bookstore and Massage Parlor
age 31, Madisonville

Lives in an old loft apartment near the central city, south of Woodworth Road. Distrusts government (of any kind), but voted in the last election for individuals who would be most likely to leave small businesses alone. Opposes increase in funds for police (see police issues, Chapter 9). "All they do is try to hassle people in business."

24. President, Camelot State University
age 43, University Park

Defines the job as fundamentally being a PR person for CSU; it is his/her job to influence the government and the people to enact laws favorable to the university. Graduated from Camelot University and is a strong advocate of the status quo.

25. Owner, Large Business
age 60, Forest Acres

Owns the now closed Merchandise Mart, Camelot's largest downtown retail establishment. Inherited the business. Plans to build a huge discount outlet in the proposed Strip Mall. Favors moderate growth rate for Camelot. Very supportive of police.

26. Owner, Small Business
age 69, Camelot Acres

Has operated a delicatessen in the same place for the last 30 years, but is now encountering financial difficulties. Many of the customers in the past lived in buildings that have been torn down to make parking lots. This small business owner's fate lies with the central city. If Camelot's downtown continues to deteriorate there will not be enough customers, and the delicatessen will go bankrupt. Is very supportive of police.

27.   President, Police Benevolent Association, Local 402   age 57, Crown Knolls

Is a former Camelot police officer, who was elected PBA president 10 years ago. Has been a very successful, very aggressive spokesperson for the police. In bargaining sessions has a reputation for bluntness, and has insisted on getting better salaries and more fringe benefits for the police. Has been neutral (at best) on the NAACP demand for more black police officers. (See "The Officer Protection Program Issue," "The Budget Issue," and "The Affirmative Action Issue.")

28.   President of League of Women Voters   age 39, Camelot Heights

Has a Ph.D. from a prestigious university and is a tenured member of the English department faculty. Uses position to try to elect council members who advocate increased city services. As parent of three children, the quality of the Camelot school system is of great concern. In the last election the LWV succeeded in defeating an initiative petition to cut the school budget; is pledged to continue League action to achieve "a quality environment." Lives in a nice home on Patricia Road, east of Robert Street.

Although this individual is not part of the official city administration, it is his/her responsibility to chair the candidates' meeting that is held the day before the election.

29.   Retired Professional Football Player   age 34, South Ridge

After a successful and lucrative career as a quarterback for one of the NFL teams, he retired last year. Since then he has not been employed full time but has engaged in some television work, appearing as a guest commentator when one of the major networks telecasts football games. This has not been completely satisfying, and now his goal is to get into politics, using the name identification that has come to him us a result of his many years as a football star and now his current exposure in television. He has begun to attend regularly the meetings of council in order to understand local politics and to find his own set of political values. He has a strong desire to run for local office as a means of gaining experience in getting elected and in holding office. His political inexperience will force him to choose carefully the issues on which he will take a public stand. However, it is very important that he should be seen and heard, for it will not serve his ambitions at all to be viewed as merely a quiet observer.

30.   Hair Stylist   age 30, North Madisonville

Is divorced and has four children. Is learning to be a hair stylist, recently received cosmetologist license, and now wishes to open a beauty salon in her living room. In this way, will be able to remain off welfare, yet be closer to children.

31.   Affirmative Action Officer, City of Camelot   age 36, University Park

Has been in the present post for 18 months and is the first affirmative action officer the city has had. Came to Camelot after college in another state, obtained a job as caseworker in the welfare department, became a supervisor there, transferred to the Department of Public Housing when it was established in Camelot, went from there to the personnel office of the city, and now has responsibility for implementing federal and state prohibitions against discrimination on the basis of race or sex in hiring, compensation, promotions, and terminations.

32.   Minister, A.M.E. Church   age 59, Madisonville

The reverend is a man of moderate views. He reminds people of Martin Luther King, Jr.—sensitive to racial injustices and working for their elimination, but always doing so in a reasonable way and in a spirit of Christian charity. He tries to inspire others by his example of dignified civility;

he is not a table thumper. Some of his younger parishioners criticize him for not doing enough for the cause of racial equality. Has some political ambitions, and has contemplated running for council. Will be upset by "Officer Protection Program Issue," because of allegations it is an antiminority program.

33. Director, Planning Department, City of Camelot   age 41, University Park

Was appointed to the planning department 12 years ago and became its director just recently. Is a professionally trained planner with a master's degree from the University of Virginia. Is more than a "bricks and mortar" physical planner and thus is interested in preservation—of green space; of graceful, old buildings; of neighborhoods—and land use for people, as well as being concerned (as must be all planning directors) with maintaining the city's economic base.

34. Student Body President, CSU   age 20, College Town

Takes pride in being independent, sometimes makes considerable effort to remind others of those traits. Won office by a wide margin, and sometimes toys with the question of whether the student body has the potential to be welded into a strong political force in Camelot. Very much in favor of gay rights as a matter of principle.

35. Insurance Agent   age 55, Forest Acres

Served a term on council and then declined to run for reelection because of illness in the family. Since the graduation of the youngest son from college, friends have urged consideration of running again. Appears not to have decided the question, but maintains a lively interest in local affairs. As an occupant of a downtown office, is especially sensitive to the quality of the CBD. Self-view is that of a moderate Republican, rather than a conservative type. Favors rapid growth rate for Camelot, supportive of police on all such issues.

36. Director, CSU Institute for Applied Gerontological Studies   age 47, Camelot Acres

While primarily an academic, also regards Camelot us a prime setting for the application of gerontological information and ideas. In practice, this means concern with such matters as transportation for the elderly, the relation of housing to shopping, to part-time employment opportunities, and to amenities. Problems of crime, which especially victimize the elderly, are of special concern. Believes that academics have a duty to intervene in civic affairs and to offer their advice and expertise on current problems.

37. Director of Urban Welfare Programs   age 34, Madisonville

This is the second job as a professional since graduating from college. Worked as a retail clerk after high school, then later entered evening classes at CSU, but after graduation could not find employment other than a sales position for quite some time. Has considerable empathy with Camelot's poor. While believing in the central city, believes also that housing for the poor must be near employment opportunities. If Camelot's industry moves to the suburbs, is committed to locating low-cost housing there, too. Supportive of health department proposals (see "The Budget Issue").

38. Real Estate Developer   age 52, Forest Acres

Is one of three partners in Crown Real Estate Development Corporation. Believes that the trend toward suburbanization is the way to make money. Has a large interest in the Downtown Hotel

Plaza that he/she proposes to build, and frequently attends planning commission and city council meetings to push views. Is a very smooth representative for this successful firm, Crown Developers. Very much favors rapid growth for Camelot (see "The Growth Rate Issue" and "The Downtown Hotel Plaza Issue").

39. Real Estate Developer   age 32, Forest Acres

Is the young, ambitious partner in the very successful development firm, Crown Real Estate Development Corporation. Is active in planning many new projects. Politically is conservative, wants council to stay out of private affairs and to play a supportive role in improving the city's tax base. Very much favors rapid growth for Camelot (see "The Growth Rate Issue" and "The Downtown Hotel Plaza Issue").

40. Real Estate Developer   age 50, Forest Acres

Took over spouse's interest in Crown Real Estate Development Corporation after his/her untimely death three years ago. Spouse was one of the three founders of the firm. He/she had begun as an accountant with the firm, thus is very familiar with every aspect of the business. With death of the spouse, is now a one-third owner of the company. Very much favors rapid growth for Camelot (see "The Growth Rate Issue" and "The Downtown Hotel Plaza Issue").

41. Attorney   age 32, Camelot Heights

This young attorney, only two years out of law school, decided to hang up a shingle to see if it is possible to find enough clients to keep food on the table. He/she is willing sometimes to offer services at little or no charge to deserving groups (and perhaps individuals) in order to become better known and to build a law practice. Has been retained by those opposing the proposed strip mall developments.

42. Lancelot PTA Vice President   age 40, North Madisonville

Is a graduate of CSU, an art designer for a local publishing company. Now divorced and is raising two daughters, age eight and six. Is concerned about the quality of education in Camelot, thus has been deeply involved in the PTA. While city council has no control over the school system, Role 42 is concerned about taxes, crime, and any issue that involves the future of Camelot.

43. Junior High Teacher   age 43, Crown Knolls

Is a math teacher in a junior high school, unmarried, and an active member (born again) of an evangelical Protestant church. Has become disturbed by the opening of a massage parlor west of the CBD and has been searching for allies so that an effective complaint might be made to the council, the manager, perhaps the planning commission, or anyone else who might be able to help close what is suspected to be a front for prostitution. Favors slow growth for Camelot (see "The Growth Rate Issue").

44. Director, Public Health Department   age 39, College Town

Is an M.D. and very "middle class" in attitudes. Frequently one finds that the scientific or technical training of persons whose profession is an "applied" endeavor (as, for example, a doctor) produces training experiences that tend to create an intolerance for mistakes and errors. This intolerance also can form the foundation for an exaggerated confidence in their own analyses. Persons accustomed to working in a black and white world, even a complex one, do not always adjust easily to the rich coloration and vibrant diversity of matters outside their field of expertise. The director is, of course, a vigorous supporter of "The Home for the Mentally Ill Issue." One also may expect this individual to support such legislation as compulsory AIDS examinations (proposed by the Public Health Department).

45.   Copywriter   age 29, College Town

She is employed as a copywriter in a local advertising firm. Several times has felt the sting of discrimination because she is a female, and has been quite active in the ERA movement and other feminist causes. She views with contempt such exploitively sexist events as beauty pageants, and she is at least equally hostile to prostitution and other aspects of "the skin trade." Will support gay rights in principle.

This young woman has become more angry each year as she views what to her are examples of the exploitation of women, such as the failure of the passage of ERA, and the apparent double standards used to justify the lack of equal pay between men and women for comparable work. She will, of course, take strong stands against the topless bar and restrictions on abortion clinics. In addition, she is an outspoken supporter of "save Pioneer Park" and a persistent and staunch conservationist. She will have to decide as each issue comes before the planning commission and council how she feels about them.

46.   Police Officer   age 32, Madisonville

Presently is a five-year veteran of the Camelot Police Force after serving in the U.S. Marines for four years, has been going to the CSU evening program and working toward a two-year certificate in the criminal justice program. Is married, has a child. Ranks third on the civil service examination, and strongly believes that if a vacancy occurs or if an increase in the strength of the force is authorized, will be promoted to sergeant. Will support all police-related issues.

47.   President, Data Tech Corporation   age 35, Forest Acres

A product of Camelot State's computer programming department and an inventive genius. Has successfully developed and marketed new software programs and is already a multimillionaire. Is a solid Republican of a conservative sort, but is quite practical. Has little use for ideologues, whether conservative or liberal, but does favor keeping government out of business. Believes that what this country (and this community) needs is more people who think that government should be run on sound business principles. Favors moderate growth rate for Camelot (see "The Growth Rate Issue"). Supportive of police on all such issues.

48.   Minister, First Presbyterian Church   age 44, Camelot Heights

The reverend's church probably is the most fashionable church in town, drawing heavily from Forest Acres for its congregation. He is concerned to avoid becoming insulated from the larger problems of the times: he recognizes the risks of insularity as one ministers to an affluent congregation. Consequently, he has established close ties with the United Campus Ministry at CSU, and his church extends a friendly welcome to students each Sunday. He is concerned with social questions, but he is practical enough to believe that he must appeal to the more traditional views among his communicants as well as to the more liberal views of some. As a result, his desire for racial equality and for urban renewal coexists with a strong opposition to vice and organized crime. He is especially embarrassed by the continuing presence of the massage parlor, which, it is alleged, occasionally has been visited by CSU students. Favors slow growth for Camelot (see "The Growth Rate Issue"). His church and neighboring cemetery are threatened by the Downtown Hotel Plaza.

49. Attorney
age 43, Forest Acres

Is a very successful attorney with a lucrative private practice. As a result, has become increasingly able to pursue an interest in "causes." Often acts as representative for groups such as Welfare Mothers and environmental groups. Often represents neighborhood groups on zoning change issues. Was hired by the neighbors fighting the Beauty Salon Zone Variance. Is a member of the First Presbyterian Church, and has ancestors buried in the cemetery there. Especially interested in causes involving women. Thus can be counted on to be a willing representative for women's groups on the issues described in Role 45.

50. Head of Local Chapter, NAACP
age 42, College Town

Feels that the way for a black community to advance is to secure governmental positions. Has a reputation for being a powerful orator, an effective organizer. Has stated publicly that if any more black homes are torn down for highways or parking lots, the city of Camelot is in for the hassle of all times. Is very supportive of the Downtown Hotel Plaza, and bitterly opposed the officer protection program issue (the more powerful revolvers, not the body armor).

51. Attorney
age 60, Forest Acres

Is very likely the highest paid attorney in Camelot. Lives in Forest Acres in the most exclusive section. Is on retainer from the Excalibur Restaurant Corporation, (which owns a chain of fast food restaurants), a subsidiary of a conglomerate known as Associated Industries, Inc. Represents The Professional Indoor Recreation and Tactile Ecstasy Services Union. There is some suggestion that the union has organized crime connections. This union represents the female employees of the topless bar and grill, and their attorney will be supportive of gaining council's approval of the activity. Has been hired by a group of residents to resist the locating of the Home for the Mentally Ill in their neighborhood.

52. President, Camelot Chapter of Business and Professional Women's Organization
age 46, College Town

An energetic, successful, female executive. She is a vice president in charge of research and development for one of the largest home products manufacturers in the nation. The research center is located in a lovely wooded section of Madison County, approximately 10 miles out of town. She has a Ph.D. in chemistry from an Ivy League university, but her academic passion is concern about protection of the environment, including preservation of our architectural heritage. She is single and lives in one of the restored older homes in the trendy area of College Town. She is self-confident and assertive, but her experience as a successful administrator has made her a skillful mediator of conflicting interests and personalities. She takes frequent stands on public issues, and her independent attitudes make it difficult to predict her positions in advance.

53. President, Right to Life Society of Greater Camelot
age 40, Camelot Acres

A well-educated professional who in the past was not interested or involved in political activities. However, as a result of a profound religious experience five years ago, he/she suddenly felt compelled to take strong stands on moral issues, in particular those involving children and human life. Especially on the issue of abortion there is a strongly felt obligation to resist all governmental attempts to legitimize what is viewed as a violation of the most basic of Christian principles, protection of the unborn.

54. Head, Camelot Chapter of National Organization of Women   age 38, Camelot Heights

A very successful executive of an advertising agency. Is bright, articulate, and aggressive. She is supportive of NOW's political agenda and committed to confrontational tactics. Will take a strong stand on any issue where she senses women have a stake. Is not known for her willingness to compromise.

55. Student Body Vice President, CSU   age 19, Camelot State U.

Lives in a university residence hall. Is a born-again Christian and opposed to almost all the liberal causes of the day. Will oppose gay rights, massage parlors, and any similar issues that come before council.

56. Vice President, Christian Revival Movement   age 22, Camelot State U.

Lives in a university residence hall and is a history major at CSU. Views are similar to those described in Role 55.

57. Director, Camelot Public Library   age 49, University Park

Has built the library into one of the best in the state by aggressive advocacy of its importance. Is proud of the advanced information retrieval system adopted by the library and the high level of professionalism of its staff. Is concerned about the implications for the library of the attack on pornography and the call by some elements of the community for book banning. Will defend the First Amendment with great vigor.

58. High School Teacher   age 42, Camelot Acres

A social studies teacher, married, politically active on social issues—but careful not to get too controversial. Is very concerned that minorities, especially Hispanics, get fair treatment in terms of access to housing and employment. Wants the council to put more teeth into its present anti-discrimination laws so that violators, especially real estate agents, will be subject to severe fines and imprisonment for "steering" clients into segregated areas. Has been known to urge friends that what Camelot needs is a strong rent control law.

59. Owner, Topless Bar and Grill   age 50, River Town

Is very angry that the press seems to be against what is personally seen as a legitimate business. Started as the bartender, and as a result of very hard work and a shrewd business sense was able to buy the bar at a good price and build it into a successful enterprise. Has stated publicly that he/she sees nothing wrong with a public display of the human body, although is firm in opposition to anything beyond toplessness at the bar.

60. Owner, Firehouse Bookstore   age 58, CBD

After graduating from CSU as a philosophy and English major, used a modest inheritance to buy an abandoned fire station in the Central Business District close to the university and converted it into a bookstore. The bookstore has become a legend in its time, for the owner has accumulated a vast collection of new and used books. Yet this is no recluse from life, hiding from the issues of the day in a dust-covered corner stocked with books. Will take vigorous positions on any issue of interest. Often is allied with councillor 2. Writes angry letters to the editor and can be counted on to testify before council. Although on most issues is a staunch supporter of liberal causes, takes exception to the liberal agenda on the issue of handgun control legislation. Is a gun collector and an active member of the NRA, the National Rifle Association.

61. Director, Camelot Art Museum   age 55, University Park

Lives in an expensive condominium near the university. Last member of Camelot's founding family. His/her great-great grandfather was first preacher of First Presbyterian Church; family plot is in that cemetery. Educated in eastern schools; travels yearly to Europe. Believes no one should censor art. Collects art prints.

62. Executive Director, Camelot Chamber of Commerce   age 52, Camelot Acres

Married, three children in college, two at CSU. Began business career in real estate development with first cousin, Role 38. Was one of the founders of the Chamber of Commerce ten years ago; owns several pieces of rental property; is a part owner of two retail businesses in Camelot, a restaurant and a wine shop.

63. Single Parent on Welfare   age 18, Rivertown

Was married, spouse deserted, parents are divorced and unable to provide much help. Was a bright science student but could not finish high school. Began job training, but was forced to stop when the child became ill. Wants new opportunity for job training; needs a job.

64. Unemployed Accountant   age 45, Madisonville

Spouse inherited the family restaurant located in Rivertown, which spouse and Role 64 ran together until it closed because of decline of neighborhood and the proliferation of fast food restaurant outlets in Camelot. Spouse ran the restaurant, Role 64 handled the restaurant books, having gone to business school to study accounting. Cannot find an accounting job, and spouse's income as assistant manager of a fast food restaurant is not sufficient to pay the family's bills. Lost their home in Crown Knolls, now they and their teenage children have moved back into parents' home.

65. Homeless Person   age 45, CBD

A Vietnam veteran, unskilled laborer, factory worker before he was drafted. Came home from Vietnam needing psychological counseling, but worked at the steel wheel factory until it closed in the 1970s. Has history of drug and alcohol abuse; is currently free of the abuse and has been for ten years or so. Sleeps sometimes in basement of First Presbyterian Church, or in the church cemetery, or on a park bench.

66. Part-time Worker   age 70, North Madisonville

Owns a trailer in the Celestial Trailer Park. When Social Security proved to be inadequate, to survive took a part-time job at a fast food restaurant, serving coffee seconds, mopping up spills, picking up trash left by customers, doing whatever needed to be done. Has a bright, positive, flippant sense of reality. A no-nonsense person that others like immediately.

67. Maker of Toy Soldiers   age 35, North Madisonville

Business set up in garage. Molds from molten metal, paints the soldiers, and ships to customers contacted through catalogues. Customers rarely come to the house. No sign on premises. Technically, a violation of zoning, but no neighbor has complained.

68. Pizza Deliverer   age 21, College Town

Rents a room in one of the old homes near CSU. Working through college, political science major. Diet includes considerable quantities of pizza.

69. Social Worker   age 37, Madisonville

Married, spouse works as parole officer; child attends private boarding school. Owns small cottage on resort lake. Income barely covers monthly bills.

70. Bartender, Mike's Bar and Grill   age 42, Rivertown

Mike's is a neighborhood bar, clientele mainly working class, but has lately been discovered by college students. House specialty is a steak sandwich. Role 70 lives in apartment above the bar; does all the ordering, and so on, except for kitchen supplies.

71. Public Nurse   age 60, Crown Knolls

Divorced, has raised two daughters and seen them married. Owns a home in the northern section of the bottom third portion of Crown Knolls, in an area of transition; is concerned about whether retirement income will cover city taxes and rising expenses. Often allied with police officers in dealing with health emergencies.

72. Chairman of Camelot Hispanic Coalition   age 29, Crown Knolls

An aggressive, outspoken individual. The Hispanic community of Camelot is divided by ethnicity, age, years of residence in the United States, and attitude toward authority. Thus there is no single Hispanic point of view, although there is a shared distrust of government and politicians. Role 72's goal is to focus on issues that are important to all, or at least to many, Latinos. Like other spokespersons for minority groups, the emphasis will be on issues that may bring jobs to Camelot, and on policies that will assure equal opportunity for Hispanics to be hired and equal treatment by the police and the judicial system.

73. ACLU Director   age 41, Forest Acres

He/she is a forty-one-year-old attorney who earns about three-fourths of his/her income by serving as Executive Director of the American Civil Liberties Union for the state of Huron. The law practice has variety, but as you might expect, some of the cases reflect the strong concerns of the director for justice and equality under the law. In addition to the ever-present problem of assuring that due process of law is accorded defendants in criminal prosecutions, issues of freedom of speech, press, assembly, and worship, as well as issues of separation of church and state, have a potential for involving both the ACLU and its director. The ACLU also has come to the defense of persons accused of crime where the accusation seems to be a politically motivated effort to stifle dissent or unpopular opinion. Is responsible for administering the state office operations (membership lists, dues collections and contributions, publicity, public relations, newsletter, and so on) and for providing information to the membership as issues and cases arise .

ROLE REQUEST

NAME_____

In the simulation, I prefer:

1. *An active role.*   I understand that this role may well involve some time out-side of class as well as public activity in class. I also realize that if I accept an active role, it is necessary that I attend class regularly on simulation days. (Examples are city manager, mayor, member of council, clerk of council, the newspaper roles, the newscaster.)

2. *A semiactive role.*   I understand that these roles could also involve some time outside of class, but less than that of an active role. My activities in class will not be so public, except when I am involved in a particular issue. These roles also require my presence during days of simulation. (Examples are chief of police, city planning commission, the ministers, the attorneys, the developers.)

3. *A more modest role.*   I understand that these roles will not require much out-of-class time, unless I choose to be involved. There is generally much less public involvement, but I will not be anonymous. My presence is essen-tial when there is a particular issue that involves me, but otherwise my pres-ence is desirable but not essential to the simulation.

4. *A small role.*   I understand that these are roles that will make me part of a group of which someone else may be leader and spokesperson. My pres-ence will be useful, but not essential. However, if I find a particular issue important to me, there is no reason why I cannot feel free to participate to any extent I wish.

If any of the above-mentioned roles sound interesting to you, please list below as many of them as you wish:

_____

_____

_____

_____

_____

_____

_____

CITY OF CAMELOT
NOMINATING PETITION

The undersigned, duly qualified and registered voters of the City of Camelot, County of Madison, State of Huron, hereby nominate _____
for the office of council member, City of Camelot, seat number _____. (Ask your instructor whether seat numbers are to be used.)

	NAME	ADDRESS	DATE
1	_____	_____	_____
2	_____	_____	_____
3	_____	_____	_____
4	_____	_____	_____
5	_____	_____	_____
6	_____	_____	_____
7	_____	_____	_____
8	_____	_____	_____
9	_____	_____	_____
10	_____	_____	_____

Attestation by Petition Circulator

I hereby affirm, subject to the penalties for perjury, that the above signatures were recorded in my presence and that the names and addresses are accurate to the best of my knowledge.

Date: _____   Name: _____
                                                        (signed)

                          Address: _____

This document was received at _____ o'clock ___M., _____

                                      _____
                                      Clerk,* City of Camelot

Petitions must be filed with the City Clerk,* City of Camelot, not later than 5:00 P.M. of the last simulation session preceding the election.

*Your instructor, if there is no clerk.

Your Evaluation of *Camelot*

Your instructor will indicate when this form should be filled out.

1. In comparison with other courses, or portions of courses, that you have taken, how would you rate the Camelot simulation?

2. What do you consider to be the most important thing (or things) you learned from the simulation?

3. Was there anything about the simulation that you found disappointing?

4. Do you have any suggestion as to how the simulation might be improved?

5. Suppose that a friend had a choice of different sections of the Urban Politics course, or the American Government course, and one of the sections of each of those courses used Camelot. The friend asks you whether he or she should choose the section offering Camelot. What would be your advice?

6. Please indicate whether your role was:

    _____ a. An active role, such as council member, clerk, editor, city manager.
    _____ b. A semiactive role, such as planning commissioner, developer, and so on.
    _____ c. A more modest role, such as president of the LWV, the owner of the Firehouse Bookstore, and so forth.
    _____ d. A small role—just one of the interested citizens.

Topical Bibliographies

Overview Perspectives

Boulding, Kenneth. 1990. *Three faces of power*. Newbury Park, CA: Sage.

Greer, Scott. 1962. *The emerging city*. New York: Free Press of Glencoe.

Hall, Edward T. 1966. *The hidden dimension*. Garden City, NY: Doubleday.

Wilson, James Q. 1970. Review. *American Political Science Review 64* (March):198.

Participants: People and Organizations

Dahl, Robert A. 1961. *Who governs? Democracy and power in an American city*. New Haven, CT: Yale University Press.

Eisinger, Peter K. 1983. Black mayors and the politics of racial advancement. In W. C. McReady (Ed.), *Culture, ethnicity, and identity*. New York: Academic Press.

Green, Roy E., and B. J. Reed. 1988. Occupational stress and mobility among professional local government managers: A decade of change. In *The municipal yearbook*. Washington, DC: ICMA.

Jennings, M. Kent. 1964. *Community influentials: The elites of Atlanta*. New York: The Free Press of Glencoe.

Kelly, Rita Mae, Michelle A. Saint-Germain, and Judy A. Horn. 1991. Female public officials: A different voice? *The Annals of the American Academy of Political and Social Science 515* (May):77–87.

MacManus, Susan, and Charles S. Bulloch, III. 1989. Women on southern city councils: A decade of change. *Journal of Political Science 17* (Spring): 32–49.

Murphy, Russell D. 1986. The mayoralty and the democratic creed. *Urban Affairs Quarterly 22,* No. 1 (Sept.):3–23.

Potter, John K., and Paul R. Lawrence. 1974. *Mayors in action.* New York: Wiley.

Rakove, Milton. 1975. *Don't make no waves, don't back no losers.* Bloomington: Indiana University Press.

Schattschneider, E. E. 1980. *The semi-sovereign people.* New York: Holt, Rinehart & Winston.

Stillman, Richard J., II. 1982. Local public management in transition. In *The Municipal Yearbook* (pp. 161–173). Washington, DC: ICMA.

Waste, Robert J. (Ed.). 1986. *Community power: Directions for future research.* Newbury Park, CA: Sage.

Zimmerman, Joseph. 1986. *Participatory democracy: Populism revisited.* New York: Praeger.

Processes

Browning, Rufus, Dale Rogers Marshall, and David H. Tabb. 1984. *Protest is not enough: The struggle of Blacks and Hispanics for equality in urban politics.* Berkeley: University of California Press.

Browning, Rufus, Dale Rogers Marshall, and David H. Tabb (Eds.). 1990. *Racial politics in American cities.* New York: Longman.

Cobb, Roger W., and Charles Elder. 1983. *Participation in American politics: The dynamics of agenda building* (2nd ed.). Baltimore: The Johns Hopkins University Press.

Fisher, Roger, William Ury, and Bruce Patton. 1991. *Getting to yes: Negotiating agreement without giving in* (2nd ed.). New York: Penguin Books.

Jones, Charles O. 1977. *An introduction to the study of public policy* (2nd ed.). North Scituate, MA: Duxbury Press.

Levy, John M. 1991. *Contemporary urban planning* (2nd ed.). Englewood Cliffs, NJ: Prentice-Hall.

Lyon, William E., and Malcolm E. Jewell. 1986. Redrawing council districts in American cities. *State and Local Government Review 18,* No. 2 (Spring):71–81.

Stone, Clarence. 1980. Systemic power in community decision making: A restatement of stratification theory. *American Political Science Review 74* (Dec.):978–990.

Stone, Clarence. 1989. *Regime politics: Governing Atlanta 1946–1988.* Lawrence: University of Kansas Press.

Svara, James H. 1985. Dichotomy and duality: Reconceptualizing the relationship in council-manager cities. *Public Administration Review 45,* No. 1 (Jan.–Feb.):221–232.

Svara, James H. 1987. Mayoral leadership in council-manager cities: Preconditions versus preconceptions. *Journal of Politics 49,* No. 1 (Feb.):207–227.

Wates, Nick. 1976. *The battle of Tolmers Square.* London: Routledge and Kegan Paul.

Welch, Susan, and Timothy Bledsoe. 1988. *Urban reform and its consequences: A study in representation.* Chicago: University of Chicago Press.

Wright, Deil S. 1988. *Understanding intergovernmental relations* (3rd ed.). Pacific Grove, CA: Brooks/Cole.

Policies

Babcock, Richard F. 1966. *The zoning game.* Madison: University of Wisconsin Press.

Clark, Cal, and B. Oliver Walter. 1991. Urban political culture, financial stress, and city fiscal austerity strategies. *Western Political Quarterly 44* (Spring):676–697.

Jencks, Christopher, and Paul E. Peterson (Eds.). 1991. *The urban underclass.* Washington, DC: Brookings Institution.

Nelson, Robert H. 1980. *Zoning and property rights.* Cambridge, MA: MIT Press.

Reid, Gary J. 1988. How cities in California have responded to fiscal pressure since Proposition 13. *Public Budgeting and Finance 8* (Spring):20–37.

Sharp, Elaine B. 1990. *Urban politics and administration: From service delivery to economic development.* New York: Longman.

Sharp, Elaine B., and David Elkins. 1987. The impact of fiscal limitations: A tale of seven cities. *Public Administration Review 47* (Sept./Oct.):385–392.

Wilson, William Julius. 1987. *The truly disadvantaged: The inner city, the underclass, and public policy.* Chicago: University of Chicago Press.

Index

ABOUT THE AUTHORS

James R. Woodworth has been a member of the Department of Political Science at Miami University (Ohio) since 1948. He received a Ph.D. in Political Science from Harvard University and had a Postdoctoral Fellowship at the University of Minnesota. He has served in several administrative positions at Miami University, including the chair of the Department of Political Science.

Dr. Woodworth has been a member of the Oxford City Council, chaired the Oxford Charter Commission, and served as a trustee for a local hospital and as a consultant to the Fairfield (Ohio) Charter Commission. His publications include *Atlantis: Role Playing Simulations for the Study of American Politics* (with W. R. Gump), *Parliamentary Procedure,* plus articles.

W. Robert Gump has been a member of the Department of Political Science at Miami University (Ohio) since 1962. He received a Ph.D. in Political Science from The Ohio State University and a J.D. from the University of Michigan. He was admitted to practice at the Ohio Bar in 1952.

Dr. Gump has served as chairman of the Oxford City Planning Commission, as a trustee for a local hospital, and as a consultant to the Charles F. Kettering Foundation, the City of Dayton Charter Review Committee, the City of Middletown Charter Review Committee, and the City of Hamilton Charter Review Committee. His publications include *Atlantis: Role Playing Simulations for the Study of American Politics* (with J. R. Woodworth), plus articles.

QUICK REFERENCE PAGE

I. Constraints on Simulation Participants

1. You cannot violate the laws of the state and nation.
2. You are constrained by the city charter and city ordinances, especially the budget and zoning regulations.
3. You must remain within the bounds of realism.
4. You must remain within your role.

II. Abbreviated Index

III. Issues

Don't forget—there will be a debriefing and critique session at the close of the simulation, and you will be involved in it. You may want to read pages 93–96 in order to be prepared for it.